Advance Praise for *Killer Facebook Ads*: *Master Cutting-Edge Facebook Advertising Techniques*

With humor and incredible intelligence, Marty and his team of Facebook Ads experts take you from Kindergarten to Grad school in this incredibly comprehensive review. The aimClear® team twist and bend Facebook ads, making the average search marketer scream for mercy. This is a book my team has been waiting for. You can be sure we'll have many a dog-eared copy floating around our office.

    —WILLIAM W. SCOTT, Search Influence

Marty's skills and knowledge of Facebook are only matched by his creativity and ability to think outside of the box. Marty's "no fear" approach to marketing and trail campaigns is what has set him apart from any other marketer who deals with Facebook PPC; he is a true genius. Marty is a burst of energy, and this book is Marty on paper. His personality and passion for what he does jump out at you in each information-packed page. After reading this book, if you have never met Marty, you will feel like he is an old buddy that you have known for years.

    —MICHAEL STREKO, Co-Founder/Owner, KnowEm.com, LLC

OMG—Marty Rocks! He's the Facebook ad master! You need this book.

    —BRUCE CLAY, Founder and President, Bruce Clay Incorporated

Marty Weintraub of aimClear is one of the industry's shining stars. His research, clients, and results speak for themselves. No one has ever seen Marty speak and not come away in awe of the passion, dedication and deep expertise he shines.

    —RAND FISHKIN, CEO and Co-Founder, SEOmoz

Marty blew me away the first time I heard him speak. His energy, passion, and unique view on how to harness the power of social media to drive tangible results for customers was music to my ears. It was social media marketing love, and now you can get his wisdom in this book!

    —BRAD ROBERTSON, President, GannettLocal

For years, Marty's obsession with innovation has inspired me to be a better marketer, and his dedication to Facebook Ads and the potential they hold is no exception. His depth of knowledge in Facebook Ads is unparalleled, and his ability to distill it down into actionable steps that anyone can maneuver is nothing short of genius. If you have something to sell online, Facebook advertising simply cannot be overlooked, and subsequently I would argue neither can this book. It will surely be the first great guidebook written for anyone looking to make money online with Facebook Ads.
—JOANNA LORD, Director of Customer Acquisition, SEOmoz

Marty Weintraub wows conference crowds, writes a digital marketing blog that's chock-full of tangible tips, and teaches Facebook training sessions that are more useful than any others I've attended (I've been to many). Specific, how-to details are Marty's stock-in-trade, so it's no surprise his first book is filled with them. There's no fluff or platitudes here. He offers well-researched insights and step-by-step guidelines for setting and meeting goals, creating ads, branding, targeting, community building, conversion tracking and a lot more. I'll be adding Killer Facebook Ads *to the reading list for my Social Media Marketing class at Portland State University.*
—CARRI BUGBEE, Adjunct professor, Portland State University,
President, Big Deal PR

Killer Facebook® Ads

Killer Facebook® Ads

Master Cutting-Edge Facebook Advertising Techniques

Marty Weintraub

John Wiley & Sons, Inc.

Senior Acquisitions Editor: Willem Knibbe
Development Editor: Alexa Murphy
Technical Editors: Chris Treadaway, Merry Morud
Production Editor: Liz Britten
Copy Editor: Judy Flynn
Editorial Manager: Pete Gaughan
Production Manager: Tim Tate
Vice President and Executive Group Publisher: Richard Swadley
Vice President and Publisher: Neil Edde
Book Designer: Franz Baumhackl
Compositor: Maureen Forys, Happenstance Type-O-Rama
Proofreader: Paul Sagan, Word One, New York
Indexer: Ted Laux
Project Coordinator, Cover: Katherine Crocker
Cover Designer: Ryan Sneed

Cover Images:
Ninja: © mh-werbedesign/Fotolia
Girl with Slingshot: © clearviewstock/Fotolia
Happy Woman Shouting: © Maridav/Fotolia
Boy with Globe Face: © Perrush/Fotolia
Red Target: © JJAVA/Fotolia
Icon Set 1: © Fredy Sujono/Fotolia
Icon Set 2: © Cristian Laza/Fotolia
Icon Set 3: © arrow / Fotolia
Question Mark with Glove: © pytagus/Fotolia
Calendar: © pytagus/Mikhail Mishchenko

Dear Reader,

Thank you for choosing *Killer Facebook Ads: Master Cutting-Edge Facebook Advertising Techniques*. This book is part of a family of premium-quality Sybex books, all of which are written by outstanding authors who combine practical experience with a gift for teaching.

Sybex was founded in 1976. More than 30 years later, we're still committed to producing consistently exceptional books. With each of our titles, we're working hard to set a new standard for the industry. From the paper we print on to the authors we work with, our goal is to bring you the best books available.

I hope you see all that reflected in these pages. I'd be very interested to hear your comments and get your feedback on how we're doing. Feel free to let me know what you think about this or any other Sybex book by sending me an email at nedde@wiley.com. If you think you've found a technical error in this book, please visit http://sybex.custhelp.com. Customer feedback is critical to our efforts at Sybex.

Best regards,

Neil Edde
Vice President and Publisher
Sybex, an imprint of Wiley

This book is lovingly dedicated to my parents, David and Jane. Thanks for all of your sacrifice and love and for being such empowering allies.

Acknowledgments

First, I could not have written this book without incredible support and encouragement from my family, Sybex, our aimClear team, and dear friends.

Thank you so much to Laura, for holding our family and business together while I devoted over 1,000 hours (of time we didn't have) to the project across nearly eight months. Thanks to my awesome kids, Lee and Sylvie, for somehow understanding why Dad had to speak in Sydney, Seattle, London, New York, San Francisco, or wherever in the world I was during soccer matches, proms, and awards ceremonies at school. I love you guys. This is your book too, and you're everything to me.

I owe extraordinary thanks to my Wiley/Sybex acquisitions editor, Willem Knibbe, for conceiving this book, choosing me to write it, teaching so much about being a better author, and being completely unconditional in his belief and support. Trust this: Willem talked me down from the ledge a couple of times and deserves credit as an artist, mentor, and reliable friend. I also want to express gratitude to my technical editor, Chris Treadaway, author of *Facebook Marketing: An Hour A Day* (Sybex, 2010). Chris's dedicated feedback was imperative, deep, technically impeccable, empowering, and absolutely unflinching—regardless of my reaction. That's exactly what this book needed. Thanks to development editor, Alexa Murphy, for her steady hand, editorial prowess, and hard work, especially at crunch time. Additionally, I'm grateful to Pete Gaughan, production editor Liz Britten, copy editor Judy Flynn, proofreader Paul Sagan, and the whole Wiley/Sybex crew. You guys are the very best in the business.

I could never have written this book without my aimClear team. First, make no mistake, Merry Morud is a freaky-targeting-genius. After we trained her on Facebook Ads a few years ago, she proceeded to develop inferred targeting theories that I believe to be best in the world. Her techniques are well represented in this book and she was the second technical editor. Likewise, Matt Peterson, our most senior online marketing account manager, is one of the purest talents I've ever known in any arena and one heck of a marketer. Lauren Litwinka, aimClear's publication manager, made countless contributions to the substance and form of this book and was involved in the process every step of the way. Her encouragement, unadulterated journalistic instincts, and depth of Facebook marketing knowledge were instrumental to completion of the project. Thank you to Manny Rivas III for his inspirational contextual targeting guile and marketing acumen; Manny's research is all over this book. Lindsay Childs, in our Saint Paul office, added fabulous professionalism to the editing and formatting processes. I'd like to thank Alyssa Engleson for contributing crucial research, additional technical editing, and hundreds of hours of proofing at crunch time. I'd like to acknowledge Kathy, Joe W, Molly, Joe D, and Erica for their dedication and important contributions to our company.

Here's a huge tip of the hat to my brilliant friend Michael Streko, cofounder of the reputation monitoring service KnowEm, for introducing me to Facebook Ads in 2007 and teaching me so much, so often. Thanks to Danny Sullivan, Barry Schwartz, and Rand Fishkin for all they give away and writing so eloquently as ambassadors of industry. Finally, many thanks to Chris Sherman (my futurist hero), Marilyn Crafts, Mike Grehan, Bret Tabke, Todd Mintz, Stewart Quealy, John Goldfine, Lance Sabin, Pete Gaughan, and Tim Ash for giving me a shot.

About the Author

Marty Weintraub is CEO of aimClear, an online marketing agency that has managed Facebook ad campaigns generating over 10 billion impressions internationally for clients including MarthaStewart.com, Siemens, Second Life, BudgetDirect.au, and other global brands. He's written extensively for *SearchEngineWatch*, *SearchEngineLand*, *SearchEngineRoundTable*, and others. Marty's aimClear Blog (aimclearblog.com) has been cited as among the Technorati Top 10 Small Business Blogs, Cison Top Ten Social Media Blogs, and PRWeb's 25 Essential Public Relations Blogs You Should Be Reading, and has been listed in the AdAge Power150.

A fixture on the international conference circuit, he speaks regularly at Search Engine Strategies (SES), Search Marketing Expo (SMX), PubCon, SEMpdx, International Search Summit, All Facebook Summit, Socialize, OMMA, Search Insider Summit, universities, and others. Marty founded and produces the aimClear® Full Day Facebook Marketing Intensive Workshop.

aimClear is known for its radical social media demographic targeting and sits among the best-known Facebook Ads marketers in the world. Having trained in-house and agency teams for years, aimClear's system for mapping real-world topical hubs, search data, and userclusters to social PPC has proven revolutionary.

Marty has been a professional search marketer since 1993. Having lived through every generation of Internet marketing, he brings a depth of online experience rare among today's marketers. Marty lives in Duluth, Minnesota, along the scenic shores of Lake Superior, with his family and sweet black Abyssinian cat, Rita. He loves fine wine, international travel, college hockey, and James Beard Award–winning restaurants.

Contents

Introduction   *xix*

Chapter 1   Marketing and the Facebook Revolution   1

Facebook's Reach 2

Understanding the Social Graph 7

What Marketers Can and Can't Do With Facebook Ads 10
Facebook Ads Terms of Services   10

The Ethical Marketer's Rules of Engagement 14
Follow the Law   14

Chapter 2   Key Performance Indicators (KPIs)   19

Setting Expectations 20

Defining KPIs 21
Branding KPIs: Seeding Tomorrow's Conversions Today   22
Direct Response KPIs: Need Conversion Now?   23
Friending KPIs: One Is Silver and the Other's Gold   25
Customer Service KPIs: The Holy Grail   26
Crisis Management KPIs   27
Community Relations KPIs   28
Internal Relations KPIs   29
Investor Relations KPIs   30
Media Relations KPIs   31
Research and Message-Testing KPIs   32

Facebook Ads and Attribution 33

Chapter 3   The Facebook Ad Creation UI   35

Web UI and Power Editor 36

Module 1: Design Your Ad 36

Module 2: Facebook's Powerful Targeting 37
Estimated Reach   38
Targeting Attributes   39
And Operator   40
Or Operator   41
And and *Or* Together   41
Typing Patterns Reveal Related Segments   42
Location   44
Demographics: Age and Sex   48
World-Famous Interests Bucket   49
Advanced Demographics   56
Education & Work   59

Connections on Facebook   61
Ad Targeting Options Help Center   62

Module 3: Campaigns, Pricing, and Scheduling 63
CPC vs. CPM   63
Pricing   64

Chapter 4   Facebook Ads Production Workflow   65

Power Editor 66

Understanding Account Structure 66

First Step: Wireframe Demographic Research 69

Second Step: Create Your First Ads 69

Structural Best Practices 72
Creating Alternate Ad Variations   74
Naming Conventions   75

Chapter 5   Guerilla User Targeting Checklist   77

Literal, Competitive, and Inferred Targeting 78
Literal Targeting   78
Competitive Targeting   79
Inferred Targeting   83

Occupations and Employment 86
Interests Bucket Occupations   87
Places of Employment: Education & Work   89

Real-Life Groups and Affiliations 90

Real-World Publications 93
Magazines   94
Books: Subjects and Authors   98

Online, Off Facebook 99
Applications   101

Product Categories 102
Product Usage Examples   103
Software   104

Classic Mainstream Interests 104
Leisure Activities   104
Political Orientation and Pundits   105
Figureheads   106
Family Roles   106
Ideas, Ideals, and Beliefs   108

Chapter 6   Mastering Compound Targeting   111

Age, Interest, and Gender Mashups 112

Workplace and Precise Interest Amalgamations 115
Targeting Politicians   115
Targeting Media Influencers   115

Occupation Targeting (Facebook's Hidden Jewels)   116

Education and Interest Amalgamations. 119
High School Students   119
College Students   120
Alumni   121

Sexuality, Relationship Status, and Interests   121
Interested In (Sexual Orientation)   122
Relationship Status   122

Country + Language + Interest Combinations. 123

Chapter 7   Creating Killer Facebook Ads   127

The Five Levels of Brand Clarity 128

Headlines. 130
Literal Headlines   131
Sideways Headlines   133
Classic Headline Approaches   135
Be a Headline Ninja   138
Additional Tips   139

Ad Images 140
Image Size and File Type   142
Colors and Color Hacks   142
Zoom and Cropping   144
Image Sources   145

Putting It All Together with Body Copy 147
Body Copy Best Practices   147
Body Copy Length   152

Chapter 8   Deploying Your Facebook Ads Campaign   155

Facebook Ads Finances 156
Payment Options   156
Budgeting and Spend Limits   156

Landing Page Considerations 163
Dynamic Landing Pages, Tagging, and Conversion Tracking   167
Socializing External Landing Pages   169
"Buying Fans" with Ads and Social Landing Pages   170

Final Prelaunch Checklist 172

Chapter 9   Field Guide to Optimization and Reporting   173

Introducing Ads Manager 174

Navigating Facebook Ads Manager. 174
All Campaigns Screen   175
(Individual) Campaign Screen's List of Ads   177
Inline Ad Preview, Targeting, and Performance   181
All Ads Screen's List of Ads   182

Optimization 184
Optimizing for CTR   185
Optimizing for CPC   188
Optimizing for CPM   189
Optimizing for Conversion   189
Ad Fatigue, Rotation, and Variants   193

Facebook Reports 194
Advertiser Performance Reports   194
Responder Demographics   199
Responder Profiles   200
Conversions by Impression Time   201

Wrapping Up and Looking Forward 201

Appendix A Facebook Ads Preflight Pocket Checklist   205

Appendix B The Great Big Search & Social Media Marketing Twitter Follow List   209

Appendix C Facebook Targeting Segments   219

Fortune 500 Companies 220

Job Titles 222

Weapons 225

Tech and Gaming 226

Interests Bucket Family Roles 228

Health 229

Outdoor Activities 231

Winter Sports and Activities 234

Sports 236

Green Living 238

Wine 239

Home/Garden 239

Discount 240

Tough Times 240

Music 241

Hobbies 242

Business 242

Chatting/RPG 243

Media with Cult Followings 244

Index   249

Introduction

Facebook represents the largest online sampling of human beings on the planet, with around 700 million users worldwide. Among social media communities, this channel is an epic crucible for advertisers, nearly anthropological in nature. This book is all about tapping Facebook's potential for branding, sales, public relations, and other classic key performance indicators (KPIs).

Cradle to grave, *Killer Facebook Ads* is the marketing mavens' unofficial Facebook Ads handbook, the missing manual that includes dozens of never-revealed insider tips and tricks as practiced by some of the most creative social pay-per-click (PPC) professionals in the world.

The book you are holding embodies four years of total immersion in deploying advertisements to users via the Facebook Ads platform. If you want to learn Facebook advertising, from fundamental techniques to advanced tactics, you've come to the right place. Never before have so many insider tips been packaged in one volume, to the benefit of readers.

Facebook Ads demographic targeting is nothing short of revolutionary, and the implications for marketers are staggering. Now, advertisers can reach out and serve ads to real people based on their most personal interests, predilections, proclivities, and even perversions. This book lays it all on the line for advertisers at all levels, from newbies to hard-core display ad professionals.

Who Should Buy This Book

This book is for anyone interested in Facebook advertising (multinational corporate types, small businesses, educators, and everyone in between):

- Marketers who already use Facebook Ads and want greater success
- New Facebook marketers looking for an overview and kick start
- Entrepreneurs seeking to promote their products and/or services in Facebook space
- In-house pros and agencies
- Professors who wish to augment curriculum with cutting-edge social demographic targeting theories for marketing and real-world anthropological analysis globally
- Advanced Facebook marketers seeking a serious edge
- Online marketing managers who want to grow the capabilities of their team

- Advertising agency and public relations professionals seeking an edge in social media marketing
- Small business owners who want more friends, business, and prominence for their brand
- Pay-per-click (PPC) practitioners who want a piece of the Facebook Ads gold rush
- Social media community a (managers) seeking greater insight as to the distribution of Facebook users and demographic segments.

There's something in *Killer Facebook Ads* for everyone. Facebook/FB Ads newbies to advanced power users will find nuggets of information, many of which are potentially transformational to your thinking about FB as a marketing channel.

What's Inside

Here is a glance at what's in each chapter:

Chapter 1, "Marketing and the Facebook Revolution," serves up a high-level overview of Facebook and the enormous implications for marketers. From its unassuming creation in a Harvard dorm room to fundamental dos and don'ts for social marketers, we scrutinize Facebook's historic ride, understanding the social graph, terms of service, and why privacy advocates hate (but marketers love) Facebook.

Chapter 2, "Key Performance Indicators (KPIs)," focuses on defining various goal types in a classic marketing sense. Learn how to realistically apply branding, direct response, sales, lead generation, public relations, and advertising objectives to Facebook Ads and achieve buy-in from your team.

Chapter 3, "The Facebook Ad Creation UI," provides an overview of the Facebook Ads creation process, including ad design, demographic targeting, and campaign pricing and scheduling.

Chapter 4, "Facebook Ads Production Workflow," reveals productivity hacks to streamline assembly. Discover how to optimize account structure and learn about sane campaign and ads layout, the importance of up-front demographic research.

Chapter 5, "Guerilla User Targeting Checklist," is the crux of the book. You will discover how to find your audience by leveraging extremely personal combinations of Facebook users' traits. We'll put you on the road to mastering highly focused targeting on Facebook's social graph, from holistic treatment of professional characteristics to exploiting radically private predilections.

Chapter 6, "Mastering Compound Targeting," discloses more complex combinations of attributes to achieve an even higher level of demographic focus. This chapter is meant to spark creativity by adding deep layers of mashed-up targeting, which include age, interest and gender mashups, workplace and like amalgamations, education attributes, sexuality, relationship, geo', and languages.

Chapter 7, "Creating Killer Facebook Ads," shows you how to build ads that resonate once you've set KPIs and targeted users. Though writing ad copy and choosing images for Facebook involve processes similar to those used for other advertising channels, Facebook ads are a special animal unto themselves. This chapter focuses on creating ads that get the job done by rising above the noise and clutter to push emotional buttons.

Chapter 8, "Deploying Your Facebook Ads Campaign," deals with payment options, budgeting, bidding, landing pages, tracking, and dialing in optimization tweaks—in other words, making sure things are set up, copacetic, and ready to rumble.

Chapter 9, "Field Guide to Optimization and Reporting," details essential Facebook Ads metrics, including how to glean actionable insights, take action to optimize the account, and report progress to team members. The main topics we discuss are navigating Facebook Ads Manager, optimization, and Facebook Reports.

Appendix A, "Facebook Ads Preflight Pocket Checklist," is a cradle-to-grave worksheet of suggested steps and things to remember. Grab the file online, print it off, and modify it as you see fit for your own process. The suggestions are just that, but we use a similar document internally at aimClear. If you modify it, send it along and we'll consider posting, with attribution, for our readers. Hey, you'll get a link out of it.

Appendix B, "The Great Big Search and Social Media Marketing Twitter Follow List," lists blogs, bloggers, conference speakers, and Twitter profiles of Facebook Ads jockeys that we recommend. I've also noted straight-up marketers focused on analytics, KPIs, and other contextual marketing channels. Follow these smart folks and it will be of great benefit.

Appendix C, "Facebook Targeting Segments," is chock-full of incredibly useful pre-researched targeting presets, from major media outlets, Fortune 500 firms, to earth mamas. Don't eat it all at once. Hop online at www.KillerFBAds.com for copy-and-paste versions.

> **Note:** Things change quickly in Facebookland. Visit the *Killer Facebook Ads* companion website at www.KillerFBAds.com for valuable, free resources updating information in this book. You will be asked to register one time and confirm, using your email address. The password is the ISBN of this book, 978-1-118-02251-1. You can change the password once your account is set up.

How to Contact the Author

I welcome feedback from you about this book or about articles and books you'd like to see from me in the future. You can reach me by writing to martyw@aimclear.com. For more information about aimClear, consulting services, upcoming speaking engagements, and other fun stuff, please visit our website at www.aimclear.com. This book has an accompanying website, www.KillerFBAds.com, which contains additional resources and free tools. To log in, simply use your email address as the user name, with the password **022511**, which is this book's ISBN.

Sybex strives to keep you supplied with the latest tools and information you need for your work. Please check www.sybex.com/go/killerfacebookads, where we'll post additional content and updates that supplement this book should the need arise.

Killer Facebook® Ads

Marketing and the Facebook Revolution

1

Since its inception nearly seven years ago, Facebook has culled a following of, unofficially, more than 700 million users around the world. The largest social networking website has infiltrated pop culture with citations in sitcoms and even its own feature-length film. "Like us on Facebook" has almost become common vernacular for local and enterprise brands alike. This first chapter will take you through a high-level look at Facebook, from its unassuming creation in a Harvard dorm room to fundamental dos and don'ts for social marketers.

Chapter Contents

Facebook's Reach

Understanding the Social Graph

Why Privacy Advocates Hate (and Marketers Love) Facebook

Facebook Ads Terms of Service

The Ethical Marketer's Rules of Engagement

Facebook's Reach

Facebook's rapid rise, utter dominance, user-base girth, global reach, and raw marketing power are staggering—a total contextual marketing paradigm-buster. According to Facebook's published statistics as of this writing, more than half of Facebook's officially revealed 500 million users log in every day, engaging for an aggregate 700 billion minutes per month. That's right, 700 *billion*. With a *b*.

According to Experian Hitwise, "Facebook" was the top search term in 2010 for the second straight year. Measured by Google's own tool, Insights for Search, search interest for Facebook is fanatical, obliterating search buzz for Google around the world. The graph in Figure 1.1 represents the search interest in Google, Facebook, Twitter, and President Obama as indicated by Insights for Search.

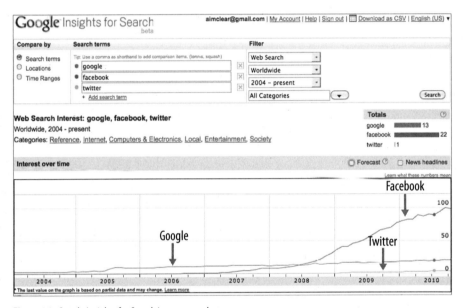

Figure 1.1 Google Insights for Search interest graph

The social networking site has amassed over 900 million pages, groups, events, and community pages. Users generate upwards of 30 billion monthly web links, news stories, blog posts, notes, photo albums, and other shared content blocks. Because approximately 70 percent of users hail from outside the United States, a virtual army of 300,000 volunteers translates content using the Translations app.

Two hundred fifty million on-the-go mobile users currently access Facebook through their cell phones, iPads, and other devices. More than a million entrepreneurs and developers from 190 countries have created more than half a billion applications. Since social plugins launched in April, 2010, an average of 10,000 new websites integrate with Facebook every day. More than 2.5 million websites have integrated with Facebook, including over 80 of comScore's U.S. Top 100 websites and over half of comScore's Global Top 100.

Facebook's rise to power was as frighteningly fast and, in a way, as prodigal as its eccentric, youthful brain trust. The social network was founded by a group of four now-infamous Harvard students led by Mark Zuckerberg, a computer science student and brilliant hacker with a gift for black hat website scraping and deep intuition about human social motivations. Zuckerberg and cofounders Dustin Moskovitz, Chris Hughes, and Eduardo Saverin launched Facebook (known then as "The Facebook") in February 2004 from their Harvard dorm room. By March that year, the site, which had formerly been an exclusive Harvard-only online network, expanded to include students from Columbia, Stanford, and Yale. In June, the Facebook crew migrated to Palo Alto, California, where Facebook Groups and the distinguishing *Wall* were added as staple profile features. The upstart social network celebrated reaching the one-million active-user mark in December—incredibly, less than one year after launch. It was clear that the Facebook revolution was now seriously underway.

In May 2005, the relocated Bay Area startup raised $12.7 million in venture capital from Accel Partners, and by August grew to envelop more than 800 colleges and universities. Students fell in love with Facebook's heady mix of community, dating, college play, and friendships. For a guy with a serious nerd rap, Zuckerberg was proving himself a freakishly genius wizard of the new online virtual pheromones crucible.

In September, things really started to heat up when Facebook began allowing high school students around the country to create accounts. The Photos core application was deployed in October, at which point the site also began the assimilation of international school networks. By December 2005, the user base had expanded by an astonishing 500 percent to comprise more than 5.5 million active users. It was clear that Zuckerberg had his finger on the beating pulse of emergent Internet social media. Though far from mainstream, Facebook raised plenty of eyebrows, chiefly from marketers wondering where this was going to lead. By then, clever marketers were finding ways to gain access to college accounts to test word-of-mouth marketing, among other things. Facebook was especially fertile at this time because college kids had no idea whatsoever that marketers were in the mix.

In 2006, another year of astronomical growth, Facebook opened the once ivy-clad walled garden even more, providing free registration to anyone who wanted to join. No longer strictly for students, the future king of social networks was poised to explode into international mind share. The $27.5 million from Greylock Partners and Meritech Capital Partners helped keep things scaling. More features were launched, including the Notes app, the now ubiquitous News Feed, Mini-Feed, the Development Platform, additional privacy controls, and *Share* functionality. Facebook and Microsoft entered into a strategic alliance to serve syndicated banner ads. By December, the user base had expanded internationally to 12 million people. The volume and diversity of the user base had marketers salivating. Many of us wondered what the FB crew had up their sleeves to make community members accessible to advertisers.

By April 2007, there were 20 million active users, connecting more than 2 million Canadian and 1 million active UK users of all ages and stripes to the main Facebook community. Yet to come that year were developments of seismic proportions that would ultimately rock the known Internet universe straight to the end of the millennium's first decade. Facebook was poised to move past "website" status all the way to becoming an "operating system," and ultimately set the stage for Facebook Ads.

On May 24, 2007, the new Facebook Platform was unveiled during the f8 Event in San Francisco. An official press release read, "Facebook, the Internet's leading social utility, today announced that more than 65 developer partners have built applications on Facebook Platform, a new development platform that enables companies and engineers to integrate with the Facebook website and gain access to millions of users." The ability of third-party developers to create social applications brought a level of wit to Facebook, instrumental to hooking users. Though marketers were still wondering what was in Facebook for them, the platform approach was a huge factor in attracting users who make up the Facebook Ads targeting pool today.

In short order, Microsoft took a $240 million equity stake in Facebook and cut an international advertising partnership deal. Marketers wondered what that meant. Would there be a do-it-yourself (DIY) ad platform or would media buys on Facebook be forever restricted to buying banners from Microsoft? Google's Content Network allowed us some access to certain pages in Facebook, but marketers wanted more. We wondered what was coming next. Facebook then launched its fledgling mobile platform and the community mushroomed in size to an impressive 50 million active users. Marketers thought, "All these users are good. When are we going to get some *real* access?"

Then, the marketing tsunami hit with a vengeance when, in November, Facebook Ads was born. To a relatively small sect of attentive online marketers, this was a mind-bending development—Facebook's speedily expanding user base was now straightforwardly accessible to any advertiser in a sleek DIY interface. It was incredible—instead of marketing to *searches* for the keyword "audio recording college Minnesota," marketers were able to target high school guys who were interested in playing guitar, were single, or maybe played in a band. The rest, as they say, is history. The gold standard of online contextual marketing was born.

It was important for early adopting Facebook Ads marketers to understand the evolving demographics. Failure to do so meant that many search marketers had early failures. At the time, Facebook was still somewhat skewed toward college students, naturally, as they were there from the beginning. Speaking at Search Engine Strategies New York 2008, I preached to a crowd that barely cared about the "impending social PPC revolution." aimClear, previously adept at segmenting landing pages based on inbound search queries, started creating landing page variations marketing to inbound gender, age, interests, relationship status, and other highly personal attributes.

Facebook took a radically mainstream turn in January 2008, cosponsoring the presidential debates in partnership with ABC News. On the heels of launching in Spanish, French, and German, friend list privacy controls were put in place along with a 21-language translation application. *Chat* was released and the next milestone was reached: Facebook blew across the 100-million-user mark without looking back.

As of Christmas Eve 2009, Facebook garnered 7.56 percent of the United States Internet traffic market share versus Google's 7.56 percent (Figure 1.2).

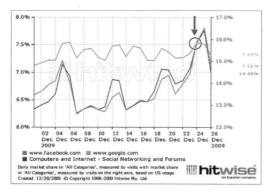

Figure 1.2 Hitwise graph of Internet traffic – 12/29/09

Several key developments in 2009 wove Facebook into the fabric of human media and culture. First, CNN Live integrated Facebook into its online product, and at the same time, there was a significant promotional push on live cable newscasts. The *Like* element was added, and after Digital Sky Technologies invested $200 million for preferred stock, Facebook was then valued at an impressive $10 billion. Facebook *Usernames* launched, which directly (and perhaps deliberately) messed with Google, Yahoo!, and Bing; usernames meant that pages and individual profiles had a greater propensity to index in organic search engine results for keywords and names in the Facebook titles. The feature also permitted "vanity" URLs, such as Facebook.com/mashable or Facebook.com/MartyWeintraub. After the acquisition of FriendFeed, Facebook boasted a cool 350 million users.

In 2010, we witnessed the launch of two internal applications: *Questions* and *Places*. Things are still growing at an incredible pace; Facebook is the most visited website in the United States, blowing the nearest social media contender, YouTube, out of the water by more than a 3:1 ratio and with more than 3 percent greater traffic share than the second contender, Google.

Hitwise generates reports on a variety of traffic metrics. Figure 1.3 illustrates sites for All Categories ranked by visits for the week ending 5/28/2011.

Top 10 visited US websites

The following report shows **websites** for the industry '**All Categories**', ranked by **Visits** for the **week** ending **05/28/2011**.

Rank	Website	Visits Share
1.	Facebook	10.54%
2.	Google	8.73%
3.	YouTube	3.57%
4.	Yahoo!	2.71%
5.	Yahoo! Mail	2.59%
6.	Bing	1.78%
7.	Yahoo! Search	1.26%
8.	Windows Live Mail	1.09%
9.	msn	1.08%
10.	Gmail	0.97%

Figure 1.3 Hitwise site traffic reports: All Categories – 5/28/2011

Figure 1.4 shows top websites in the category Computers and Internet – Social Networking and Forums, ranked by visits for the week ending 5/28/2011.

Top 10 Social Networking sites

The following report shows **websites** for the industry '**Computers and Internet - Social Networking and Forums**', ranked by **Visits** for the **week** ending 05/28/2011.

Rank	Website	Visits Share
1.	Facebook	62.52%
2.	YouTube	21.16%
3.	Twitter	1.19%
4.	Meebo	1.10%
5.	MySpace	1.04%
6.	Yahoo! Answers	1.01%
7.	Tagged	0.73%
8.	myYearbook	0.41%
9.	CafeMom	0.40%
10.	Linkedin	0.38%

Figure 1.4 Hitwise site traffic reports: Computer and Internet—
Social Networking and Forums, ranked by Visits for the week ending 05/28/2011

This much is clear: In the six and a half years since its inception, Facebook has grown from the playfully mischievous activities of a data-scraping dorm-room IT prankster to become the global social media gold standard. Mark Zuckerberg is both revered and reviled and, according to his July 2010 profile in *Forbes* magazine, has a net worth of about $6.9 billion—not bad for a 26-year-old hacker from White Plains, New York. Facebook itself is reportedly valued at around $70 billion, of which "Zuck" reportedly owns 24 percent. His hard-driven vision for social product, design, service, core technology development, human nature, and open-source infrastructure has proven both prescient and remarkable.

Understanding the Social Graph

The concept of tracking an individual's defining characteristics is nothing new. French sociologist David Émile Durkheim (1858–1917) wrote of a "mechanical solidarity," which wins out when personality differences are bridged, and "organic solidarity," which occurs when differentiated individuals cooperate, taking autonomous roles.

In their 1921 book, *Personality Traits: Their Classification and Measurement*, Floyd Henry Allport and Gordon Willard Allport methodically rendered their hand-sketched "social graphs" to undertake colorful analysis on 11 nodes of human behavior, shown in Figure 1.5.

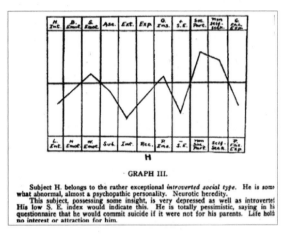

Figure 1.5 Allports' social graphs

Mark Zuckerberg is widely credited with applying this concept, in name, to online social media. The designation seems appropriate. Certainly, in today's data-driven world, people can be reduced, at least to a great extent, to a grid of personal affinities.

These days, the term *social graph* refers to Facebook's matrix of interests and personal proclivities that make each person unique in their meanderings. Every Facebook user's inimitable footprint is "graphed" and subsequently stored in the site's clustered database. These captured personality traits make up the targeting grid—the "inventory" Facebook sells to advertisers.

Facebook tracks both known and unrevealed variables of users' participation, to form its social graph. Like Google's storied organic search results ranking algorithm, there are any number of "black box" graph variables marketers can only guess at. This tuned combination of data points on the social graph is the secret sauce behind Facebook Ads. In all likelihood, the algorithmic lattice evolves often in subtle ways without announcement or fanfare from Facebook corporate.

> **Note:** *Social graph* refers to an identifying grid of interests and personal proclivities that make individuals unique.

The easiest social graph data points to understand are those in the Facebook ads targeting UI. The base targeting attributes, essentially data points on the social graph, are revolutionary in terms of advertisers' ability to target users for advertisements. Gender, geographic location, age, sexual preference, relationship status, workplace, and education attributes are very powerful in combination. As an example of targeting depth, Figure 1.6 shows the social graph attributes for 24- to 55-year-old married male Criminal Justice and Criminology college graduates, who work at various police departments around the United States.

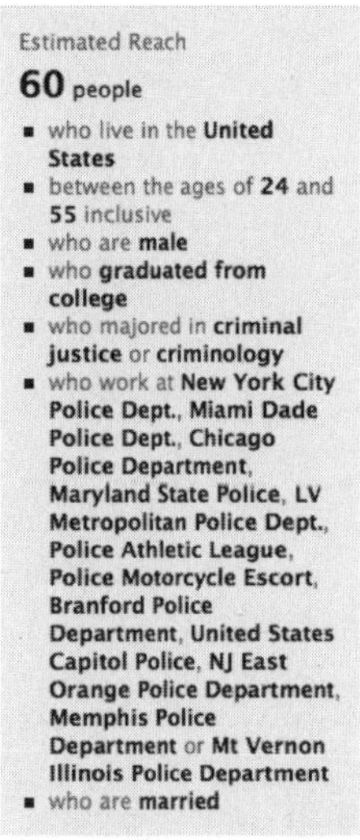
Estimated Reach
60 people
who live in the United States
between the ages of 24 and 55 inclusive
who are male
who graduated from college
who majored in criminal justice or criminology
who work at New York City Police Dept., Miami Dade Police Dept., Chicago Police Department, Maryland State Police, LV Metropolitan Police Dept., Police Athletic League, Police Motorcycle Escort, Branford Police Department, United States Capitol Police, NJ East Orange Police Department, Memphis Police Department or Mt Vernon Illinois Police Department
who are married

Figure 1.6 Facebook Ads targeting to attributes on the social graph

Facebook Ads targeting includes an attribute called, "Precise Interests," which is only sparsely documented, considering its pervasive depth. The inline help in the ad creation tool (Figure 1.7) offers only a limited explanation of what "Precise Interest" targeting entails.

You have to dig a bit through the FB help pages to really get a feel for what areas of users' profiles are culled to comprise the Precise Interests and available to target on the social graph. Here's how Facebook explains Precise Interests to advertisers in the "Likes & Interests Targeting" section of Facebook Ads Help. (The bold text is mine for emphasis.) "Likes & Interests targeting allows you to refine your ad's target audience based on the **content they've included in their profiles**, as well as the **Pages, Groups and other onsite content they've chosen to connect with**. This includes sections like **Interests, Activities, Favorite Music, Movies** and **TV Shows**." Great, cool! This gives us a better idea of what aspects of a person's persona we can access via the Precise Interests.

Let's poke around a bit more. In the, "Why do I see the particular ads I see on Facebook?" help offered users curious about the ads they're seeing, here's how FB explains ad targeting: "Facebook ads may be targeted by your location, sex, age, relationship status, professional or educational history, or to interests you've listed in your profile and the Pages and groups you're connected to... (OK, we know all that, but here's the big black-box-kicker) ...**Including more content on your profile that relates to your interests may improve the relevance or focus of the Facebook Ads you're seeing.** "More content that *relates* to interests?" "May improve relevance?" What does *that* mean? Basically FB is telling users that any aspect of their day-to-day meanderings, information in profiles, or whatever, might be included in the big black box. What does this mean to marketers? Chapters 5 and 6 are all about intensive social graph targeting. For now just keep in mind that FB does not tell us everything having to do with users that might impact targeting, and there are amazing user insights to be mined and exploited.

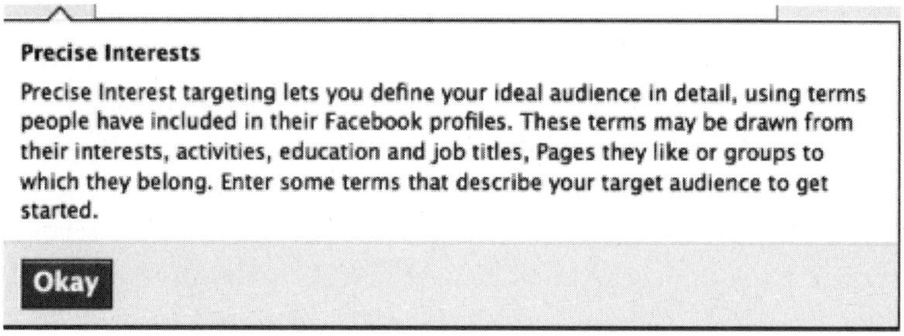

Precise Interests

Precise Interest targeting lets you define your ideal audience in detail, using terms people have included in their Facebook profiles. These terms may be drawn from their interests, activities, education and job titles, Pages they like or groups to which they belong. Enter some terms that describe your target audience to get started.

Okay

Figure 1.7 Inline help explanation of the Facebook Ads "Precise Interests" attribute

The genius of Facebook is that core features mirror types of social activities humans commonly share among themselves. The word *viral* is often applied to the phenomenon of social media. Facebook is the epitome of online virility in that the applications facilitate and amplify compelling behaviors in which humans partake in physical life. People love to send pictures to their families, reach out to make new friends, contribute to important daily discussions, explore mutual interests, and share content that matters to individuals and social groups. We listen to music, pursue professions, watch television, and read books. The social graph keeps track, silently noting our personal predilections as we express them and serving up pieces of us to the highest bidders.

Think about it: in those seemingly forever-ago pre-Internet days, sharing pictures with your mom meant getting extra prints, stuffing them in an envelope, which you'd need to address, stamp, mail, and wait for her to receive. Making friends meant going to physical events and seeing someone across the room, followed by first overtures and getting to know each other. Facebook provides awesome tools to make these, and many other universal activities and indulgences, much simpler. (The fact that it's socially acceptable for users to dabble in voyeurism and various levels of anonymity seems to make the experience all the more alluring.) Facebook pushes human buttons surrounding connection, relationships, news, events, group congregation, etc. to appeal to deeply primal aspects of being a person, making it easier to connect than in the physical world. No wonder it's such a powerful marketing medium. People love Facebook because of how it streamlines so much of what is important to social humans.

The "price" Facebook charges users in exchange for "free" use of these millennial tools comes with the revealing data yielded by our behavior. Users blindly give up their data for free. There are no privacy settings to shut off Facebook's internal data mining for Facebook ads. Facebook's social graph, the heart of Facebook demographic targeting, is perhaps the greatest development in marketing since search.

What Marketers Can and Can't Do With Facebook Ads

Users can't turn off Facebook Ads and FB does not document how privacy settings affect targeting, if at all. Our testing indicates that locking down privacy settings to the maximum protection allowed does not prevent users' attributes from being targeted. This is exciting news for marketers. Even in light of the ongoing privacy debate and "Do not track" initiatives, I sleep just fine at night knowing that users we target sign off on Facebook's privacy policies in exchange for using Facebook's free tools. One thing's for sure: The less privacy users have, the more money Facebook can make from advertisers and the more advertisers can leverage user information to sell things! The power of Facebook's core features is that they *ooze* tons of information about users. Ultimately, only Facebook knows all the aspects of users' Facebook activities that show up in corners of the FB Ads targeting algorhthm. If users don't want to be targeted by Facebook advertisers, the best answer is to close thier accounts.

Facebook Ads Terms of Services

At the end of the day, what matters most to marketers is getting ads approved, up, and running. The easiest way to know if you've violated the terms of service (TOS) is when an ad comes back disapproved. Facebook's terms of service are an interesting potpourri of rules that limit marketers from selling certain items, impose stipulations surrounding others, and ban various technical and promotional tactics outright. Some rules are common sense. Others have been added over the years in response to various spammer ploys.

It's important to note that because the system relies on humans applying editorial discretion, application of the rules is not always even. There have been many times we've run ads successfully for weeks and cloned them to change the pictures only to have the nearly duplicate ad rejected. If an ad you submit does not seem to violate any identifiable item in the terms of service list, then simply submit it again.

Here is a partial list of what's not allowed; when in doubt, always refer to the most recent FB Advertising Guidelines, found in the help section:

- Automated ads without permission.
- Ads showing URLs that don't link to the same domain as the destination URL.
- Landing pages with fake close behaviors, pop-ups, overs, or unders.

- Mouse trapping (i.e., disabled back button).
- Ads requiring personal information submission (Social Security number, email, phone, etc.), except for e-commerce, where it's made clear that a product is for sale.
- Landing pages with Facebook references (though limited references to Facebook in title body or image to clarify a destination *are* allowed).
- Facebook brand, logos, graphics, or product names.
- Implying that Facebook endorses your product, services, or ad.
- Emulating Facebook features.
- Ads that don't relate to landing page content.
- Ads that don't represent company, product, or brand of advertiser.
- Unsubstantiated claims, "including but not limited to prices, discounts, or product availability," to quote the Facebook Ads terms of service.
- Ads that threaten users.
- Any "false, misleading, fraudulent, or deceptive" ads.
- Ads that play audio automatically.
- This one's a beauty: Ads will not be permitted in cases where a business model or practice is deemed unacceptable or contrary to Facebook's overall advertising philosophy (whatever that means).
- Ads that users complain about or that violate "community standards."
- Swearing, obscenity, or "inappropriate language."
- "Obscene, defamatory, libelous, slanderous, and/or unlawful content."
- Restricted products, including tobacco products, ammunition, firearms, paintball guns, BB guns, or weapons of any kind.
- Ads promoting gambling, including online casinos, sports bets, bingo, or poker, without authorization from Facebook.
- "Scams, illegal activity, or chain letters."
- Get-rich-quick schemes, work-from-home offers, full- and part-time employment alternatives, offers of NSA money, or profit for no or little investment.
- Ads for adult or dating sites that focus on sex.
- Ads for sex toys, videos, or other products.
- Ads for uncertified pharmaceuticals.
- Ads for spy cams or other surveillance gear.
- Online nonaccredited college degrees.
- "Inflammatory religious content."
- Terrorist agendas or speech.
- Commercial use of hot button political items, with or without a political agenda.

- "Hate speech, whether directed at an individual or a group, and whether based upon the race, sex, creed, national origin, religious affiliation, marital status, sexual orientation, gender identity, or language of such individual or group."
- Negative political campaign ads.
- Derogatory or false depiction of health conditions.
- Distributing data culled from campaigns to any third party.
- Displaying user data in ads, such as names or profile pictures.
- Using data for any reason other than Facebook Ads.
- Irrelevant personal targeting; age, location, interest, and gender targeting must be relevant to the product.
- Targeting adult themes "including contraception, sex education, and health conditions" to any user under age 18.
- Ads pointing to dating sites unless the relationship settings are set to "single." Must choose single value for male or female and target individuals over age 18, interest targeting parameter must be set to "single."
- Fraudulent offers.
- Ads that include a price, discount, or "free" offer if the destination page is not the same as in the offer and to the same deal offered in the ad. The ad must say what actions are required.
- Subscription services that don't comply with tight restrictions. If you sell "ringtones, games, or other entertainment services or any site that induces a user to sign up for recurring billing of a product or service," review FB Ads TOS.
- Ads about alcohol are also tightly restricted in FB. From antisocial behavior, glorifying drinking, or even advertisers glorifying the percentage of alcohol by volume, it's very picky stuff. If you sell booze, head over to Facebook Ads TOS and study the rules.
- Infringement on any third party's rights, "including copyright, trademark, privacy, publicity, or other personal or proprietary rights."
- Spam, as defined by laws, regulations, or industry standards.
- Incentives for clicking on ads or giving personal information.
- Links in ads or landing pages that propagate spyware/malware downloads, including redirection.
- Links in ads or landing pages that mine data from users' computers without consent.
- Collecting Facebook usernames and passwords.
- Proxying Facebook usernames and passwords to automate Facebook logins.
- Sneaky software that results in an unexpected user experience, including hidden downloads of various types (see TOS for details).

- Ads with bad grammar, incomplete sentences, repeated words ("buy, buy, buy," for example), misspelled words, incorrect spacing, or capitalization schemes.
- Acronyms that are not capitalized.
- Incorrect or unnecessary punctuation or exclamation points.
- Symbols in ads that don't correlate to the correct usage of the symbol ("$ave" instead of "save," for example) or replace entire words ("&" instead of "and" or "$" instead of "cash/dollars/money," for example) except if the symbol is part of the product or brand name.

Famous Facebook Lawsuits

Facebook has been sued by a number of people. They've also sued spammers and won. Here are a few cases for and against the big *F*.

November 2008: *Facebook v. Adam Guerbuez and Atlantis Blue Capital* In 2008, Facebook was awarded $873 million in damages against defendants Adam Guerbuez and Atlantis Blue Capital for spamming users via personal Facebook messages. This case represented the largest judgment on record for action under CAN-SPAM. (The full name of the CAN-SPAM Act is Controlling the Assault of Non-Solicited Pornography And Marketing Act of 2003.)

June 2009: *Facebook v. Sanford Wallace* In a case against Sanford Wallace, self-described "spam king," Facebook was awarded $711 million in a court judgment. Wallace was accused of obtaining access to Facebook accounts through fraudulent methods and subsequently using the accounts to execute phishing scams.

February 2010: *Nine Facebookers v. Facebook* Nine Facebook users have filed two class-action lawsuits as a result of misappropriated personal information in regard to then-recent revisions in privacy settings. Those filing the suits claimed the settings were misleading and they resulted in the unintentional sharing of personal data that was then leveraged for commercial use.

August 2010: *Cohen and Orland v. Facebook* Robin Cohen and Marcia J. Orland of the Los Angeles area are suing Facebook in response to the seemingly ubiquitous "Like" button that appears on the social network's advertisements. Cohen and Orland claim their children, who are both under the age of 18, are being exploited for profit-making purposes when they "Like" ads they see mutual friends have also "Liked." The parents argue that before Facebook.com leverages minors' "Like" data for commercial purposes, parental consent should be required.

October 2010: *Facebook v. Spammers* The social networking website filed three lawsuits in U.S. federal court in San Jose, California, against persons allegedly attempting to dupe Facebook members into registering for spam mobile subscriptions, thereby violating its terms and applicable law. The defendants, Steven Richter, Jason Swan, and Max Bounty, Inc., are accused of running more than 27 fake profiles, 13 fake pages, and at least 7 applications in association with an affiliate marketing advertising scam.

> **Famous Facebook Lawsuits** *(Continued)*
>
> **October 2010:** *Nancy Walther Graf v. Facebook* Nancy Walther Graf of Minnesota is suing game developer Zynga for allegedly distributing Facebook users' personal information for money. The plaintiff alleges that in violation of Zynga's agreement with Facebook, Inc., and privacy laws, the company has deliberately transmitted personal data including users' real names to third-party advertisers and marketers without consent from users. Walther Graf is seeking class-action status from the U.S. District Court in the Northern District of California.

The Ethical Marketer's Rules of Engagement

Facebook Ads is a prodigal channel, a tactical road for marketers to take en route to attaining carefully thought-out objectives, perhaps in tandem with other channels. When targeting users to receive ad impressions, take care to understand the community you're dealing with and how your messages jive.

Because the advertisements are contextually targeted, users' acquiescence to advertisers is more tacit than search, where users query for specific results. As a result, the psychological dynamic is a lot different. It's almost as if marketers are invited into closely knit virtual municipalities where community members are connected by the essence of who they are rather than physical borders. Users *do* click those little Xs, which make specific ads go away. If enough users take the trouble to indicate that your ad annoys them, Facebook supposedly banishes the ad from showing. Here's what we think are best practices when serving socially targeted ads.

Follow the Law

In nearly every part of the world, there is at least some form of protection for intellectual property, including text, images, catchphrases, logos, product names, and other assets. At the end of the day, following laws for the jurisdiction in which marketing is deployed is the single most important consideration.

In the world of search, there have been a number of cases where litigants slugged out how laws are applied to triggering ads with keywords, displaying trademarks or service marks in ad copy, and use of copyrighted materials. Throughout legal history, concepts of slander and libel have been litigated, adjudicated, and appealed, and tons of law has been made. Scams are scams, whether perpetuated in the back alley or on Facebook. Fraud is fraud and negligence is negligence.

These types of lawsuits and the outcomes are old news in traditional channels. Also, many industries have regulations that govern where and how advertising can be done. There are certain restrictions (or not) on tobacco, booze, sex, drugs, and gambling in certain areas of the world.

Gross and subtle distinctions between applicable laws in the United States, England, China, Australia, and everywhere else in the world Facebook penetrates would easily be a book in itself. However, there are fundamental rules that, if followed, will help keep you out of trouble.

> **Note:** I'm not a lawyer so do *not* construe this as legal advice. Please visit with your friendly internationally qualified law firm for input as to your specific situation.

Don't assume that because your ad is still running, you've not violated the law somewhere. TOS violations can get you kicked off of Facebook. Violating the law can gut your business and ruin your life.

Don't say anything that's not true. Assertions of any kind should be rooted in documented and indisputable facts. That said, always telling the truth doesn't protect you from being sued. Especially when dealing with big companies, it can cost a crazy amount of money to respond to even a frivolous action brought against you.

Read and understand the license for any creative materials you purchase. If you're working with an independent contractor to create intellectual property to be used in your ads and landing pages, make sure that the contractor vouches that the intellectual property is clear of restrictions. The last thing any business needs is to get sued for ripping off somebody else's intellectual property.

Be wary of highly aggressive competitive practices. If in doubt, don't do it. We can't find any case law defining what's legal or not about triggering Facebook Ads by targeting other companies' brand-name fans who have expressed the brand proclivity in their interests. It is reasonable to expect that such case law will exist in the near future because it's a serious hot button. Always consider and explain to clients and/or your boss that such practices may result in legal exposure.

Advertising on Facebook, as mainstream as it is, still amounts to gun slinging in the old Wild West. They're more than happy to sell you the ability to target people who "like" Martha Stewart or Malt-O-Meal, regardless of the future legality thereof or where the data comes from on the social graph with respect to privacy settings.

Don't pretend you're someone you're not. In some parts of the world, it's literally against the law to run a sock puppet avatar. The legal noose is beginning to close in on those who post fake reviews in the United States. More American states are passing laws which criminalize online impersonation.

Follow terms of service. When it comes to what we can and cannot sell on Facebook, the restrictions evolved largely out of (a) the terrible advertisements Facebook accepted when the site was young, and (b) ruthless affiliate marketers spamming the tar out of Facebook users. While most marketers fudge a little here and there, finding sneaky ways to market restricted products such as lotteries or pharmaceuticals won't work out for anybody.

Only market things that have real value. It is said that the only real way to attain wealth is by the creation of value. The best Facebook Ads campaign is for a product that doesn't suck. An age-old adage in the marketing business is that "you can't wrap a turd up in a pretty bow" and expect happy customers, good reviews, and repeat business. Don't be in denial about "value" and what it really means to a targeted user. Again, if it feels wrong, don't do it. If testing shows users don't care, stop. We've seen community backlash starting with the committed and outspoken angst of a single user that mushroomed virally into reputation problems for businesses.

Facebook Ads is a double-edged sword. While we may reap the benefits of serving ads into an environment where users can easily share something good they've discovered with their peeps, it's just as easy to propagate disdain. Trust me, one bent Facebook user can cause stress, legal bills, and lost sales. Don't market products having little or no value. It can come back to bite you or your client. Trust your instincts and don't delude yourself or others.

Keep promises. Think of ad copy as making a promise, lined up with a landing page that *keeps* the promises. Strive to make landing pages validate the users' clicks with an "Atta boy (or girl), way to click on the most appropriate ad. Now you're at the perfect place."

Don't be *too* creepy. I was contacted last February by an advertiser who was selling outpatient psychological services, targeting 50- to 60-year-old women in a very small community in rural Minnesota. He wanted to target those interested in Alcoholics Anonymous with messages like, "When Going to AA is Not Enough to Get Over Your Horrible Divorce," and "Being Drunk Didn't Help, Going to AA Didn't Help," and so on. We didn't take the job. Coming from a recovery background, I knew that such messaging transcended the creep-factor I was comfortable with.

Facebook ads are insidious and lovely all at once. There's a deep psychological tug that seems to occur in tightly targeted demographics. Our agency helps to market a well-known online marketing conference series. The product, and therefore, the ads were all about SEO, PPC, social media—all things I personally love and express in my social graph. Our team deployed a number of ads, which ended up being targeted to my Facebook page. I clicked those ads over and over, only to discover that I'd been taken in by my own shop's targeting prowess! The targeting and ads are just that deep, resonating on a level beyond visceral. Watch your step. Be gentle. Don't be egregious in manipulating people's feelings and perceptions.

Manipulate only to serve. On the other hand, we're in the channel to make money, friends, or both. Guile and ingenuity that lead users to a conclusion serving mutual needs are totally in order. Reasonable manipulation might include ads that end up being served to a competitor's fans, say for a new, better, and cheaper product and without disclosing the competitive nature of the ad until the landing page.

It's not wrong to make chocolate lovers drool over a fantastic truffle picture on the way to a landing page that's about a fabulous candy recipe book. Nor is it out-of-bounds to brand orthopedic surgery targeted at high-school-age athletes and their parents. When it gets to clever-time, ask whether the desired outcome of the ad and landing page truly serves the user.

We often ask clients, "If the bionic fireman saves that cat from the burning tree, is the cat any less dead?" Sure, there was manipulation going on: The fireman wasn't real, but the cat isn't dead, right? Ergo, manipulate only to serve.

Set realistic KPIs. We'll get into this in much greater detail later on, but for now, consider this: Many marketers get poor results with their Facebook ad campaigns. People have come to us saying, "What gives? We served 80 million impressions but the CTR (click-through ratio) was only .02 percent. The visitors stayed on the landing page for 50 seconds on average, drilled into the main site, but did not buy."

OK, let's have a look. First, .02 percent is a fine CTR for many Facebook Ads campaigns. Facebook won't shut the ad down for that. Second, that's 80 *million* impressions, branding the product to pretty much everybody who sees the ads. The other side of a low CTR for CPC (cost per click) ad with massive impression volume is the incredibly low CPM (cost per thousand impressions). Google can cost upwards of five times the CPM. The campaign may be justified as an incredibly low-cost and highly targeted branding play. If the appropriate expectations had been set, the perception of success might have changed.

Sure, Facebook ads can be terrific direct response, first-touch-sales mechanisms. However, we all know that many conversions require more than one interaction with a customer. Plan what your ads are for. Set realistic goals. Don't put too much pressure on the channel with unrealistic expectations.

Key Performance Indicators (KPIs)

2

There are many ways to say goal. Objective, aspiration, purpose, aim, hope, desire. . . *In marketing, our expression for* goal, KPI, *means* key performance indicator. *I love this term when referring to marketing objectives because inclusion of the word* indicator *means that somebody, somewhere, actually plans on measuring something to prove results! Sounds simple, However, we know multinational corporations that don't set KPIs.*

The marketing universe is replete with missing, badly set, and unrealistic KPIs. That's mind-blowing because the technology to track most KPIs has been in existence for years. On the other hand, defining and tracking conversions can be a lot of work—a significant challenge, especially in the social media world. This chapter focuses on defining KPIs as applied to Facebook Ads.

Chapter Contents
Setting Expectations
Defining KPIs
Facebook Ads and Attribution

Setting Expectations

Because Facebook ads reach such a massive sampling of people, targeted with incredibly personal focus, the channel can be extremely robust in the hands of savvy marketers. Reciprocally, setting out to use Facebook ads with unrealistic expectations about what can be accomplished could be the kiss of marketing death. I can't tell you how many industry peers I've encountered since the platform was released in 2007 who acted like Facebook ads were a waste of time, money, and effort. Their disdain is easily explained. They were trying to use Facebook Ads for the wrong KPIs.

I was lucky because when I first rolled up my sleeves, my job was working for a small audio-recording-career college. Now that I understand Facebook's history and timing, I understand that the FB community was transitioning from only including college students to also encompassing high school students. Still in early 2008, there were over 21,000 people in the United States who liked "Las Vegas Vacation." The targeting capabilities blew my mind; they were obviously revolutionary. Instead of targeting searches for "audio recording college, Minneapolis," now the marketing was to "single high school senior males" that liked to "play guitar in a band" or "sing in a band."

Setting attainable KPIs in Facebook has much to do with not putting undue pressure on campaigns to perform past Facebook Ads' natural place in the marketing mix. Be aggressive: Make your marketing object a household name in the right 30,600 people's browsers.

Test direct response sales with compelling action calls. A segment of fanatical gardeners living in New York City just might be susceptible to a reasonable sales pitch for an "organic garden in a barrel." In setting expectations for Facebook Ads, match the demographic with the ad's intent. Two hundred eighty 60-plus-year-old men interested in prostate-online.com may not be available to volunteer for the mountain rescue team. You get the picture.

On the basis of cost per thousand impressions (CPM), Facebook can cost roughly 10 percent to 50 percent less than Google's Display Network. I've heard it said that "Facebook ads are sort of like what would happen if the Display Network worked really well." Don't compare Facebook Ads' click-through ratio (CTR) to search; you won't be happy. Instead, compare it to Google and Bing contextual products. Compare CTR to AOL or Yahoo! display properties. In girth and a raw targeting might, Facebook is incinerating the competition. Expect CTR between .15 percent and upwards of 1.0 percent, with clicks costing between $.02 and upwards of $1.00. Expect prodigal volume and conversion that has been known to rival or exceed search.

Lead your marketing team's expectations as to the strengths and weaknesses of Facebook Ads. Challenge everyone's thinking. Ask, "Will this headline really mean something to our customers, as defined by the demographic segment at hand?" Manage your boss's expectations by defining Facebook's role in the conversion funnel. Test enough to know the answer to the greatest extent your team is technically able.

Defining KPIs

The real value of Internet marketing is that it's technologically easy to set up analytics by channel, then roll them all up for insights necessary to direct/redirect marketing spend. Therefore, setting clear and discernable marketing KPIs is crucial.

Executing marketing campaigns in any channel is a tactic, perhaps one of several tactics that a marketing manager might include. Other online and offline channel tactics might include Google PPC, Bing SEO, newspaper ads, radio commercials, and small aircraft pulling long banner signs across Miami Beach during spring break.

It's essential to understand that Facebook Ads is a channel in which we undertake tactics to sell things. Hence, think about the perfect KPI as *what* we want to accomplish and channel tactics as the *where* and *how* we undertake marketing to achieve the KPIs.

Best practices means to state what we want to accomplish in plain language, committing to exact numbers, and defining a method of measuring. Our shop states KPIs at the project level in writing, in advance, and in simple plain-language sentences. Here are some KPI statement examples. Note that each states what we want to accomplish and what to measure:

- Sell 1,256 snarly widgets in one month, at an average cost per action (CPA) of $17.75.
- Get 65,000 video views, at an average cost per view of $.08, and drive 2.5 percent of the viewers to a page on our company website to download a white paper.
- Serve 50 million ad impressions over two weeks, at an average cost of $.43 and 6 percent conversion on the landing page to a product purchase.
- Make 22,000 new fans for our company page for us to engage with and remarket to later.
- Mine 345,000 email addresses from Canada, United States, UK, and Australia, all for females under the age of 27.
- Serve 200 million branding impressions so that our stockholders are not spooked by the oil spill in the Gulf.

Notice that the example KPIs don't address *how* we're going to get things done, only what we *want* to get done and what metric indicates success. There's nothing about what the ads will say or what the landing page will be. It's the account manager's role to work with stakeholders to determine what needs to be done and how to measure success—the KPIs. Then, it's the channel tactician's job to figure out how to best achieve the KPIs and what channels to use.

Throughout the evolution of marketing channels, common KPIs have not changed much. We marketers still pretty much do what marketers do. We sell things.

We brand things. We set out to reach goals by somehow swaying perceptions or somehow targeting audiences at some scalable level, using channel tactics and appealing to human nature. Don't be put off by modern paradigms like downloadable applications or other digital products. A sale is still a sale. Branding is still branding. While products and delivery methods have evolved and there are new product classes, core marketing tasks have not really changed much at all.

This is a fortunate reality, especially for old guys like me, because almost everything I knew about tactical marketing before the Internet is germane applied to new models. Therefore, as we evaluate Facebook Ads' rightful place in any marketing mix, remembering the "classic" mix of KPIs is a valuable exercise. Figure 2.1 illustrates the diverse KPIs and benefits associated with FB advertising, spanning a spectrum from branding to sales.

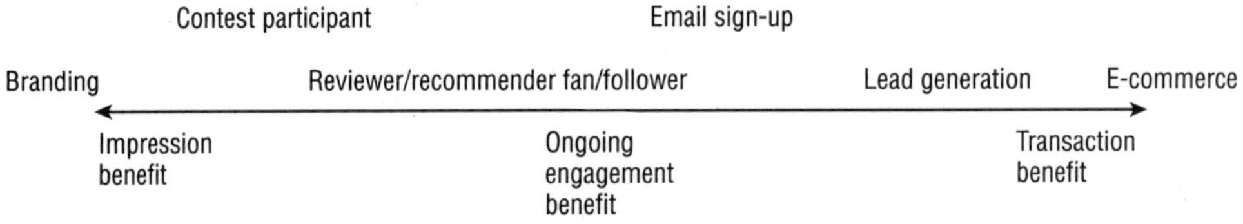

Figure 2.1 Facebook campaign KPIs and benefits

Traditionally, KPIs were spread across a subdivision of old-school disciplines and roughly divided by marketing, advertising, and public relations. Let's examine key performance indicators from a classic marketer's perspective and consider how Facebook Ads can perform when applied.

Remember, each KPI should state what the goal is specifically and how it will be measured. Some KPIs' channel tactics do estimate ad performance in terms of cost per click (CPC), cost per action (CPA), click through ratio (CTR), cost per thousand impressions (CPM), or impression count. That said, it's sometimes not possible to estimate accurately in advance, but in many cases, we are willing to give ballpark numbers. You should always assume that running test ads, in the beginning of any campaign, is a prerequisite to determine the ongoing budget. If that's the case, say so in the channel tactics portion of the KPI statement. We've focused on inclusion of campaign ad performance metrics in the first examples and creative in later ones. In later examples, we make sure to state the budget.

Also, in all likelihood, each of the example KPIs would be deployed in tandem with other channels. For the purpose of this chapter, we're focusing solely on the Facebook Ads portion of the marketing mix.

Branding KPIs: Seeding Tomorrow's Conversions Today

Branding is when the KPI is not necessarily about making an immediate sale, with full understanding that many sales require multiple interactions with a customer to close.

Here are a couple of examples and the correlating Facebook Ads tactics to help achieve the KPIs.

KPI Raise the level of awareness of our fashion eyewear among Europeans, as measured by Google's Insights for Search Tool for our brand term keyword.

Facebook Ads channel tactic Five hundred million global impressions at $.24 CPM throughout the year in a three-day rotation, displaying our positioning statement, logo, and beautiful customers wearing our glasses.

KPI Lift Google AdWords direct response search sales for our Chicago luxury hotel as measured by CTR and associated quality score after making our brand a household name to folks who love Chicago and don't live within two states of Illinois.

Facebook Ads channel tactic Sixty million impressions at $.21 CPM, in rotation and at a .06 percent Facebook CTR, showing pictures of iconic Chicago festivals, four to six weeks prior, in the same marketplaces we serve. Amplify AdWords direct response search PPC for festival names, touting discounts for festival attendees who stay at our hotel.

The time for an orthopedic surgeon to market her regional practice and hospital affiliations is not when the high school soccer captain team blows out his knee. Branding, in this case, might mean Facebook ads offering to share results of a new study about nutrition for athletes and avoiding injury. Target the campaign to high-school-age soccer players and their parents. In conjunction, the good doctor might offer free nutrition clinics for varsity athletes, mom, and dad, year after year. Obviously, when little Willem wrecks his knee at the state championship tournament, his mom and dad are more likely to request the vested orthopedic doctor who's become a trusted advisor. Such is the essence of branding.

Branding can also be an opportunistic endeavor, sort of like crisis management in reverse. When your restaurant gets a glowing review in the Sunday *Times*, a plugged-in blogger raves about your new product, or you make the Inc. 500, these are terrific times to brand, in opportunistic response.

Today's branding is tomorrow's conversion. Facebook ads are super-cool for branding because they're targeted at users' deep-seated interests. The concept of branding regionally, which is extremely inexpensive, has already become the new wave of local marketing in the hands of sharp marketers. The same is true for international marketplaces on a truly massive global scale. Branding is a classic KPI marketing goal and Facebook Ads can be a monstrous channel tactic to achieve branding KPIs.

Direct Response KPIs: Need Conversion Now?

Direct response (DR) means calling users to act now, to consummate a conversion action. While often used to describe an immediate sale, DR can mean any desired conversion result, including lead generation, event signups, free application download, and many other actions. The delimiting factor that makes a pitch direct response is the marketer's intention to close the deal now. By nature, ads tend to be more aggressive, espousing benefits such as price, quality, service, and limited-time offers.

Facebook Ads can work well for DR conversions, but as a general rule of thumb, it is not as strong a DR conversion channel as search. There are exceptions, however. For years, we've been converting Facebook users interested in "apprentice electrician," between the ages of 35 to 45, to sign up for free Yellow Pages–type products with ads that read, "Market Your Electrician Contractor Business Online For Free." We've seen success selling concert tickets to aficionados of specific artists as well as with college and university lead generation, sale of beauty products, downloadable applications, and many other "convert 'em now" sales plays. We've hawked $2.00-off coupons for sugary breakfast cereal to pot smokers and converted like gangbusters. Here are some great DR KPI examples:

KPI Get 10,000 single-touch (one-visit conversion) downloads of our Facebook urban pollution calculator. Measure conversion by demographic segment to the greatest extent possible.

Facebook Ads channel tactic Ten million impressions, in rotation and at a .03 percent Facebook CTR, showing pictures of oil-spill-tainted birds and urban blight targeted to employees of government environmental protection agencies and users interested in sustainability, recycling, biodiversity, the world's rainforests, and other related interests. Market directly to Facebook application page after using FB's internal "Connections" metric for conversion segmentation. Establish costs, evaluate, and maintain.

KPI Expand our international English-speaking customer base into Canada, the UK, Australia, New Zealand, Spain, and Portugal by new monthly sales of 350 medium duty treadmills over and above units currently sold in these countries combined.

Facebook Ads channel tactic In two-per-weekday rotation, test hard-core call-to-action ads rotating offers of free international shipping, weekly specials, celebrity endorsements, and other truly valuable inducements to purchase now. The budget is $9,500.

So, even though some will tell you that Facebook Ads is a terribly weak channel for DR, make up your own mind with clever targeting and calls to action. Just use your head. DR conversion that surrounds digital media like YouTube video plays or free white papers tends to be easy because there is little commitment required of the user. However, there are plenty of rocking ninja marketers who are adept at separating users from their hard-earned cash with one landing page touch. Such is the Zen of the direct-response marketer.

Friending KPIs: One Is Silver and the Other's Gold

Since Facebook is a place that's all about friendship, setting KPIs that are about making new friendships is natural. These days, sharp-shooting marketers generate reports showing cost-per-friend and cost-per-click Facebook ads and new fan count.

This practice has become supercompetitive, featuring open warfare as fanged marketers pursue each other's fans. There's been litigation and case law in the search space, but the concept of targeting other's brand-themed friends by way of targeting Precise Interests has yet to be fully defined legally as of this writing. Expect American and international law to evolve regarding this type of targeting. That said, few could question the benefit of targeting folks who love to cook organic food, inviting them to friend our recipe-and-wine-pairing blog's community.

Facebook Apps can be considered a "friending" channel as well. Consider defining *friend* as someone who accepts your gracious offer to provide special tools for friends. Make the CAD drawings currently offered in a list of 7,690 files with numbers for filenames available through a tag search by way of a "seek, select, preview, and download" Facebook application. Trust me, with a service application such as this, it will be easy to get the CAD-file consumer to become your friend. Here are some Facebook friending KPIs.

KPI Get 15,000 of our competitors' engaged Facebook community members to like our Facebook page. Leverage the "Connections" metric and proper campaign segmentation to know data-certain that new fans are absolutely mined from competitive segments.

Facebook Ads channel tactic Target Facebook users interested in the top six of our closest competitors' brand terms, including specific products. Rotate two million impressions with a .02 percent CTR, establish costs, evaluate, and maintain. Drive traffic directly to our Facebook page. Test ads that reveal our brand in the ads versus ads that are "blind" (meaning that users discover who our brand is after landing on the fan page).

KPI Get 16,000 Facebook users to like our blog post interview with President Jimmy Carter. Generate 120,000 additional visits in three days. Earn 1,000 "Likes" from related viral activity.

Facebook Ads channel tactic Target Facebook users directly interested in President Carter and others who are politically engaged. Serve ads that excerpt potentially inflammatory or endearing quotes from the interview, which may light up various political factions of assorted persuasions and compel them to read more. Show pictures of Carter in both flattering and subtly derogatory visual light, as appropriate for the segment targeted, to reinforce their bias and incent the click. The budget is $12,500, one-time.

Facebook is a community of friends and future friends. It only makes sense to use Facebook ads to get to know like-minded users. Measure the approach and step lightly. Make sure paid overtures of friendship offer sincere value so the friendship will last as long as possible and be mutually beneficial for both users and your business.

Customer Service KPIs: The Holy Grail

Taking clear aim at improving customer service by social media tools is, to many, the perfect intersection of commerce and viral potential. There's very little more powerful than instant and publicly visible response to users' needs. What's cool about Facebook ads is that they can be used to drive traffic to any customer support channel by targeting the users interested in the supported products. Drive customers to support pages, ranging from lists of phone numbers to YouTube video FAQs and/or live Twitter community manager support specialists. Using ads served in viral environments with destination URLs in other social media environments can be a beautiful thing because the success is public, for all to see and appreciate. Check out these case-study KPIs.

KPI Grow usage of Twitter customer support channel for our industry-standard big-brand professional image editing software suite. Measure by 6 percent increase in followers, in/outbound tweets per day, and reduction in traditional phone support by .5 percent as measured by call center volume, month over month for one quarter.

Facebook Ads channel tactic Target Facebook users under 28 who are interested in permutations of our software suite's brand terms along with college students studying graphic design and digital photography and their professors who most likely use our software. The ads will promise faster response time, individual attention, and a more personal relationship with technical support help. The landing page is the help Twitter profile via a redirect script to measure. The budget is $55,000 per month.

KPI Increase usage of our YouTube recipe videos to serve customers with special low-sodium dietary needs.

Facebook Ads channel tactic Target those interested in health issues that feature bloating, water retention, healthy eating, heart health, and low-sodium diets specifically. Offer messages of hope and health, and provide links to free video resources.

Unfortunately, poor performance in responding to customers in public can amplify a bad experience and make you look pretty bad. During PubCon 2010 in Las Vegas, a venerable and beloved online marketing conference, session organizers used Twitter really well to handle specific inquiries and interact with attendees. As is becoming common, the conference displayed the live Tweet stream on large monitors throughout the convention center. Day one lunch logistics went down in flames—a total disaster. There it was, front and center, page after page of horrible comments tweeted by hungry users at the end of their ropes.

Still, customers, be they pleased or pissed off, sure do hang out on Facebook. They can be easily targeted and told where to get help. Facebook Ads is an awesome tool to get the word out about all the ways you serve customers.

Crisis Management KPIs

In some sense, classic crisis management is a stressful permutation of branding in reverse, to prevent damage control. Facebook Ads' amazing targeting specificity can be a fast track right to the heart of reputation risk territory. Speak directly to those who might be affected, such as software users, employees of a certain company, doctors, psychologists, or nuclear engineers. Single out young parents concerned about tainted baby food that just got recalled. Here are some examples of KPIs and associated Facebook channel tactics to support them.

KPI Ensure that the entire community has the most recent safety information surrounding our chemical spill from the train derailment. Success will be measured by driving 1,500 return visitors, who spend more than 45 seconds on the page before leaving, to our blog each hour for the duration of the crisis.

Facebook Ads channel tactic Serve ads, targeted to everyone within 10 miles of the spill, in the following sequence:

- Announce the informational service with headlines such as "Worried about the chemical spill? Get critical information here."
- Every time there is a new update, post ads that note the update time.
- When the crisis is over, let citizens know the threat has passed.

The budget is flexible, depending on interest, crisis length, etc.

KPI Offset negative publicity garnered from several high-profile sexual harassment claims in our 1,500-person workplace. This example is actually a permutation of a branding KPI. Measuring branding KPIs can be a tricky deal. In this case, we'd start measuring success by counting impressions targeted to potentially concerned parties. An impression—that is, how often the ad is displayed—is the first level of branding KPIs. Next, we'd key in on the click-through ratio, as an indication of how well our message resonates with the target market. From there, engagement metrics, as in time on page and page views per session, could be indications of meeting goals—especially if the landing page herds users toward an action, such as requesting more information, making a phone call, or signing up for SMS alerts.

Facebook Ads channel tactic Run ads celebrating our pride at contributing to low unemployment in the community. Feature individual employees' testimonials as to how working for us is awesome and has changed their lives. Drive users to landing pages that feature these individual employees and statistics regarding the importance of our company to the local economy.

When a crisis hits, target those who may be affected using Facebook Ads. That's an incredible "in" to provide information, settle feelings, and otherwise interact with customers you know are stakeholders in the crisis. Be aware that user backlash is not unheard of, so make sure to take a very high road.

Don't gush, candy-coat, spin, or otherwise try to massage outcomes to be anything other than real. Stake out a humble position, operate to truly serve, and there's a great chance things will work out better. Keep in mind that common public relations axioms still apply. Not all crises require a response. When a public response is called for, however, reaching for Facebook Ads can make a difference to the outcome.

Community Relations KPIs

Community relations are all about how folks perceive your business in the place where you live. For companies with multiple locations, there are multiple communities to work with. On the negative end of things, a poor relationship with the hometown can mean dealing with roadblocks ranging from zoning ordinances to angry locals outside the main gate. It's obvious that supportive investment in the 'hood can pay dividends and help avoid misunderstanding or even acrimony.

Pretty much every city, small or large, has civic organizations like Rotary, Salvation Army, Junior League, Pop Warner Football, and high school soccer. There are a variety of local issues anywhere people live in even small concentrations. There are groups that feed the less fortunate, volunteer attorneys, pet shelters, and United Way fund drives. Building vital relationships at home is a strong focus for businesses in most cases.

In terms of classic public relations practices, keeping things cool on the home front is best accomplished by giving unconditionally and good old-fashioned communication. Facebook Ads can be a solid channel for both. In Duluth, where I live, we volunteer a few times a year to speak at the University of Minnesota's marketing department and take pride in regional economic development. Before we speak, we purchase Facebook ads targeted to students and teachers in the program that we believe would be interested. Our company's St. Paul office doubles as an art gallery and displays incredible paintings by up-and-coming local artists. We don't care what the return is. Supporting neighbors is just the right thing to do.

Serve benevolent ads that raise awareness for the Kids Voting program, enlist volunteers to clean the beach, raise money for breast cancer prevention, honor a beloved outgoing university chancellor, congratulate your UMD Bulldogs NCAA Division 1 women's hockey national champions, or publicize a matching grant for public radio. In my job, assignments like this are one of the greatest pleasures.

KPI Grow our hometown involvement and visibility by holistic engagement at the grassroots local level. Success will be measured by getting 500 Facebook event RSVPs and 300 people in physical attendance at our annual United Way Chili Cook-off charity event.

Facebook Ads channel tactic Organize the annual event using Facebook Events this year. Send out 2,000 invitations using the Facebook Events engine. Use Facebook Ads to codify the invitation. Copy will read, "Have you RSVP'd to your Annual Chili Cook-off invitation yet?" and drive users to RSVPs. Offer free cheddar-cheese topping for using Facebook to RSVP.

KPI Increase flood relief donations by $23,000 in May for Grand Forks, North Dakota, by appealing to regional users who have demonstrated a proclivity in supporting these types of campaigns. Mobilize a 50-person contingent of volunteers to load four semitrucks with donated bottled water and go to Grand Forks to distribute.

Facebook Ads channel tactic Appeal to the community's sense of family by serving ads that draw attention to the tragedy of families losing homes, senior citizens at risk, and health issues. Offer the solutions to get involved and help. Target individuals between college age and 30 years old who demonstrate interest in the Peace Corps, Salvation Army, Good Will, Red Cross, United Way, and other charitable organizations. The budget is $9,000 one-time.

Advertising has a definite place in community relations. Facebook Ads rocks the house because it's so easy to target individuals who are fanatically passionate about pretty much anything. Later on in this book, we'll look at targeting sentiment surrounding charitable organizations.

Internal Relations KPIs

Internal relations, meaning those involving employees, vendors, board members, and other inside stakeholders, can be delicate. Public relations pros will tell you that many companies forget to spin and market to their own. Attorneys have told us that Facebook targeting can be a sticky wicket. For instance, we have the ability to easily target regional Facebook users that work at a certain company with a self-reported affinity for a given union. There's a cool everyday side to internal relations as well, especially in the age of social media.

Again, advertising can have its place, given Facebook's education and workplace targeting attribute. Even where Facebook does not officially recognize smaller companies as targetable employers, much of the time, employees self-identify their workplace; occupation targeting in Facebook is often overlooked and extremely powerful. We'll talk about that more in Chapter 6. Suffice it to say that your employees are on Facebook, it's possible to reach them there, and should be a prudent course.

Promote an employee every month to the entire staff as exemplary, advertise on snowy days to remind the team about parking outside the factory, or thank everyone for exceptional work during the merger. Run a corporate cute-baby contest or enroll employees for volunteer work at the homeless shelter. The ability to target your own employees with Facebook Ads can be a valuable human resources tool.

KPI Leverage employees' personal relationships and convert 200 of those friends and family into brand advocates who patronize our deli restaurant. Success will be measured by a 45 percent redemption rate on our friends-and-family free-meal coupon.

Facebook Ads channel tactic Market friends-and-family coupon for free Reuben or Rachael sandwich "in gratitude for our employees and their families" and in exchange for liking our deli page on Facebook. The landing page will promise an ongoing program of friends-and-family discounts in the future. The budget is $6,600 per month.

KPI Reassure employees that cutbacks in seven cities don't destabilize the company and things are still going strong.

Facebook Ads channel tactic Target our own employees, with special emphasis on unions and their officers. Consult with our public relations firm and attorney to determine ad copy and to traverse the delicate balance surrounding such sensitive issues. The budget is $4,000 or less, as demand dictates.

Internal relations advertising can be as simple as announcing the location of the annual picnic or as subtle as instilling pride company-wide for a job well done and contract attained. Consider the effectiveness of Facebook as a channel as compared to more traditional means such as posters in the lunch room, email, table tents in company cafeterias, and endless meetings. To begin, Facebook distribution of messaging to internal stakeholders is measurable, in that we can confirm how many times the ad was shown, which targeting segments saw and clicked on the ads, and behavior on the landing page. While dealing with employees is sometimes a Rubik's Cube, immediate access to your team with targeted Facebook ads is certainly an arrow in the quiver.

Investor Relations KPIs

Nearly every company has some financial objective. Customers and investors look for signals as to any firm's solvency. Facebook ads can easily be targeted to the city council members weighing the potential award of a government contract or bankers considering a loan to finance your next growth phase. Angel investors are especially fertile ground for financial branding. Does this sound insidious? I think it sounds creative.

Don't doubt for one second that serving subtle messages to existing investors can instill trust and inspire patience as things grow slightly slower than was expected. Don't discount the possibility that an angel investor can be moved over the course of months with your branding messages. Though there are serious laws and regulations in America surrounding even the appearance of impropriety in influencing stock prices, certainly companies are allowed to brand, advertise their products, and spin things the way they want. Let's not be Pollyanna. Serving ads to your financial stakeholders can be terrific business!

While discretion is usually prudent, in some cases, presenting a public financial face is meritorious. Announcing major contracts, introducing a new executive hire, and touting a fabulously successful product launch or the grand opening of a new factory can instill confidence among creditors and investors.

KPI Soften the pre-IPO marketplace for our new market-defining smartphone product to create more buzz around the upcoming process. Since we'll be targeting journalists and feeding them messages laying out the product's revolutionary strengths, we'll measure this KPI by blog posts, trade pub buzz, and major media mentions.

Note: Look for the intersection of investor relations and media relations by targeting branding messages to financial writers who cover the marketplace for influential publications. In Chapter 6 we'll detail workplace targeting, matriculated with interests.

Facebook Ads channel tactic Feature ads to those interested in the stock market, bankers, entrepreneurs, stockbrokers, and those who work for wealth management firms. Announce new products, milestones recently attained, and awards won, and thank union members for the recent mutually supportive and amicable three-year labor contract. The budget is not to exceed $35,000 per month for four months preceding the IPO announcement.

KPI Use social media to increase distribution of the annual report for the regional electric utility to 8,600 (a 20 percent gain). Reduce paper and printing costs in second year. Achieve paperless distribution within four years. Nurture the community's perception that our company is green and environmentally responsible.

Facebook Ads channel tactic Ads offer the annual report by free download to anyone. Target the ads to those who should care but are not usually part of distribution. This includes politicians, economics professors, and captains of large industry.

Talk to an attorney first if you have any doubts as to the legality of marketplace advertising with an objective of influencing public perception surrounding financials.

Media Relations KPIs

When respected reporters, bloggers, television journalists, publishers, and radio disc jockeys love you, the whole world often follows. It's also true that it's not good when reporters dislike your company. Clearly, developing mutually nourishing relationships with media types can pay wonderful dividends. Since Facebook ads are targetable to a matrix of users' workplaces and interests, the best marketers proffer carefully crafted messages aimed squarely at journalists.

Remember though, Facebook has over 500 million users. It's easy to market to 300 writers who work for a single newspaper, or even a handful. It would be naive to think that great Facebook marketers would choose not to take advantage of this astonishing opportunity to delicately influence the most important influencers.

KPI Support the effort of a Minnesota Twins baseball player to get into the Hall of Fame. Influence important baseball writers who vote each year for which players should receive the honor.

Facebook Ads channel tactic Target those who work for AP, Gannett, McClatchy, *USA Today*, ESPN, television stations in every market, and specific newspapers in every market and are interested in "sports writing," "sports writers," and famous current and past baseball stars. Focus on messages that thank fans for years of support and lobby for the new baseball stadium in Minneapolis. The budget is $7,000 per month for three months.

KPI A politician targets influential bloggers, radio jocks, and local morning show hosts to garner interview requests.

Facebook Ads channel tactic Target using the work and education bucket, aimed clearly at the very media employees we want to react. Measure success by phone calls and form submissions requesting interviews.

We like to say, "Now he's got us right where we want him," when a powerful blogger contacts us for an interview or feature story. Little does our new friend know that we've been working his perception of our company for months, slowly and subtly weaving his awareness. It's important to say that marketing messages targeted to media types can't be a bunch of bunk or be gratuitous. Marketers know that you can't wrap a turd up in a bow and expect customers to enjoy the smell. Likewise, when marketing to the media, tread lightly and don't carry a stick at all.

Research and Message-Testing KPIs

In the old days, we used to test marketing messages in focus groups. It was common to herd a supposedly representative cross section of our customers into a hotel room, feed them croissants, and gauge their reactions to our beta campaign themes. Online marketing has revolutionized message-testing methodology and has turned the process into an exciting math problem.

First practiced by search marketers in the mid to late '90s, multivariate message testing is the norm in professional advertising. Marketers regularly rotate dozens, hundreds, or even thousands of permutations of headlines and body copy to prove which magical combination solves the sales puzzle.

The days of basing large campaigns on small samplings of opinion are long gone. Now, we determine which messages work in the massive crucible of serving hundreds of millions of impressions targeted head-on to our most important audiences. Each of the major search engines' ad platforms have some sort of built-in algorithm-driven tool for multivariate message testing.

KPI Prove which public relations positioning statement is more compelling to our "average" mobile phone customer as evidenced by its ability to compel clicks. We're looking for messages that result in over 8 percent CTR on a consistent basis for non-sales messaging.

Facebook Ads channel tactic Rotate to four messaging statements and logo concepts, as delivered from our PR firm. Serve each cluster to a different designated market area (DMA): New York, Los Angeles, St. Louis, and Minneapolis. Test every logo concept paired with each of the four marketing messages we're testing to prove the best logo/ message combination. Target everyone who lives in the DMA and is over 20 years old. Expect relatively low CTR because there is no value statement embodied in the ads, only the positioning statement. We're looking for statements that are compelling on their own. The budget is $30,000 per marketplace for one month for a total of $120,000.

KPI Prove which demographics will purchase a new product in the rollout phase and in response to which headlines and image concepts.

Facebook Ads channel tactic Create bracketed messages and images to test, making sure to try a wide range of different ideas. Serve the ads to insular geographic areas for each social segment to avoid message contamination. Measure CTR for various headline segment combinations and sales.

In most cases, the first questions we ask when an advertiser brings us headlines and body copy to deploy in ads are, "Why are you sure that this copy concept works?" and, "How have your proven it?" Many times, they have not, or the demographic research is suspect because of too small a sampling. Why trust decisions like this to anecdotal inference when absolute data is available?

Want to sell tons of detergent that takes oil and gasoline out of work clothes? Test proposed messaging to 211,000 automotive mechanics, foremen, and laundromat owners. Sell high-end sports bags? Target test ads to college hockey players, team equipment managers, used sporting goods shoppers, and people who love going to NFL games. Do you market a hot recipe website's new iPhone app that mashes the in-store grocery experience with cooking? Test the ads to those who love to whip up Baked Alaska and glazed duck.

It's simply reckless not to take advantage of Facebook's hyperactive personal modeling to study what works: what to say and to whom.

Facebook Ads and Attribution

Most conversion tracking to this point in online marketing history has been "last touch," meaning as measured from the last page a user visits before the sale, lead, or other goal occurred. We've always known by instinct that many KPIs require multiple visits before users buy, but most marketers did not have analytics technology to prove it. Now the industry standard is evolving to measure conversions by attribution models, where we evaluate sequences of multiple visits, pages touched, and so on. Time after time, we see Facebook ads prove to be first-touch "introductory" ads, which facilitate repeat visits and ultimately result in sales.

Currently, there are few Facebook Ads management tools that support turnkey attribution. Acquisio, Omniture, Marin Software, and ClickEquations are the first tools that bundle attribution into their ads platform management products. These tools are very expensive and only feasible for larger advertisers. Facebook has been patient in developing its application programming interface (API) and granting tool-makers access. We expect that more attribution tools will be created over time and released to the public.

Because Facebook grants CSV (spreadsheet) bulk upload and download to larger advertisers, some marketers have created custom applications built on spreadsheet logic engines. These spreadsheet apps, though pretty clunky, can be very effective.

It doesn't take a custom application or fancy algorithm to think this conundrum through. Facebook users are the same people who search using Google and Bing. There are so many Facebook users, common sense dictates that they overlap. Going one step further, it's reasonable to assume that users who search can be influenced prior to searching. Facebook is certainly a place to do just that. Though attribution analytics are not affordably available to most marketers as of this writing, confident marketers understand that Facebook Ads can play a role, early in a multitouch conversion process, that's potentially crucial to the ultimate conversion.

The Facebook Ad Creation UI

This chapter provides an overview of the Facebook Ads creation process. Facebook Ads represents an evolutionary breakthrough in contextual advertising. When it comes to the mechanics of Facebook's ad-building tools, though, don't worry—the learning curve is not very steep. To get started, point your browser to www.facebook.com/ads/create. *Once you've got campaigns running, you'll have an Ads and Pages link in your sidebar's global navigation area. Use your personal account or set up an ads only account. When working for clients, ask for credentials to their account, or create an ad account on behalf of the client.*

Facebook divides the ad creation user interface (UI) into three main sections: design; targeting; and campaigns, pricing, and scheduling. In this book, we're calling them modules.

3

Chapter Contents

Web UI and Power Editor
Module 1: Design Your Ad
Module 2: Targeting
Module 3: Facebook's Powerful Campaigns, Pricing, and Scheduling

Web UI and Power Editor

There are two Facebook native user interfaces for ad creation and editing. The Web UI is accessible by the, green "Create an Ad" button at Facebook.com/advertising. The second access point is by FB's "Power Editor." As of this writing, Power Editor has not been rolled out in every FB Ads account and is only available to accounts that have a FB Ads Rep'. We're including references to Power Editor, because we believe that it will have a wider rollout in the near future because it solves a few important problems. If you have access to Power Editor, you'll find a link on the left-hand sidebar.

Since the Facebook Ads Web UI is full featured for Ad Creation and Power Editor is not, this chapter will study the Web UI ad creation screen. Power Editor is essentially similar to the Web UI anyway, in how FB Ads attributes are laid out and exactly the same so far as execution within each attribute. The major difference is that the Power Editor has individual screens for each main bank of attributes, whereas the Web UI places them all on one page. That's easy to think about.

Module 1: Design Your Ad

The first step in designing your ad is to choose the destination—basically, the specific web page or Facebook page where users will end up after they click the ad or sponsored story. The destination is commonly referred to as a *landing page*. The first option is to use an external URL, which means any web page that is not part of Facebook. In the Design Your Ad module of the ad creation interface (Figure 3.1), choose External URL from the Destination drop-down menu and type the destination URL in the URL field.

Figure 3.1 Facebook advertising interface, ad creation

If you are a group, event, app, or page administrator, you have the option to link directly to Facebook assets you control. Any eligible to be advertised will appear in the drop-down menu after you select the "I want to advertise something I have on Facebook" option from the Destination drop-down menu. Choosing to promote a page or event gives advertisers options to include interactive features, such as Like buttons for pages and RSVPs for events.

In addition to using Facebook Ads, you can *sponsor stories* about your brand that have bubbled up (*surfaced*) organically in the Facebook news feed (a result of users interacting with them). Sponsored stories are not the same as ads, and they're awesome; including them in your FB campaign amplifies your target audience's actions in a natural and inherently viral way. Stories that can be surfaced include: page likes, page posts, page post likes, check-ins, app shares, apps used and games played, and domain stories.

The next step is to compose a catchy 25-character headline and some body copy (you can use up to 135 characters). Complete the ad creation process by uploading an image for your ad, in GIF, JPEG, or PNG format. Choose an image that is clearly visible when it is small because the maximum dimensions for FB ad images are 110×80 pixels. Facebook will reduce the size of larger images, but unless they are proportionally correct, they may be skewed in ways you might not like. My advice is to upload the image at the correct size so there are no surprises. We'll discuss the entire ad creation process in greater detail later, in Chapter 7.

The Suggest An Ad button* is available for an external URL and provides automated ad creation. If available, the destination page's HTML title tag becomes the headline and the meta description is used as the body copy. Unless the external web page owner has designated an image for FB to use (`meta property="og:image"`), you can toggle through images posted on the destination page. Most of the time, automated ad creation is practically useless unless the external destination URL is to a page that is set up very well.

The Select Existing Creative feature is a more recent alternative that can save quite a bit of time. Choosing this option opens a pop-up window that lists every ad in the entire account. Select an ad that would make a great starting point and click Submit. All the original ad's creative elements, including headline, body copy, and the image, will automatically populate the same attributes for the ad you're currently composing. What's cool is that you can reach into any campaign in the account you're working on, including those deleted, as a starting point to mine completed ads to clone.

Module 2: Facebook's Powerful Targeting

The next step after designing your ad is to define social segments that specify which Facebook users will see it. The capabilities are awesome, a revolutionary game-changer. In Chapters 5 and 6, we'll dig deeply into targeting strategies and how to research segments. Let's start by getting our hands dirty with detailing the form and functionality of this incredibly robust UI. The targeting interface is shown in Figure 3.2.

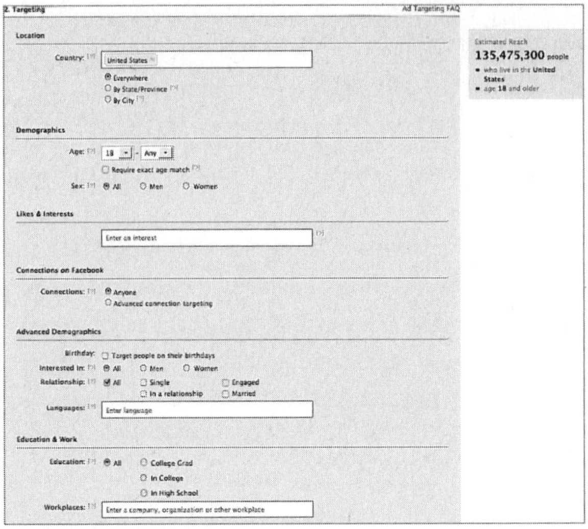

Figure 3.2 Facebook ad interface, targeting

Estimated Reach

Each of the three main modules is made up of multiple *parameters*, appearing top to bottom within each module. This chapter provides a comprehensive guide to the mechanics of the second module in Facebook's ad-building user interface: Targeting.

One of the coolest things about the UI is the Estimated Reach box, a gray rectangle that hovers to the right of the Targeting module. Scroll up on the page and the Estimated Reach box stays anchored to the top of the targeting module. Scroll down deeper into the targeting module's parameters and the box floats down the page, always in line of sight while targeting. *Reach* in Facebook Ads means how many users fit selected targeting criteria. Figure 3.3 depicts that the only targeting parameter invoked, by default, is all users age 18 and up in the United States—all $155,771,580$ of them as of this writing. The total keeps going up and up.

Figure 3.3 Facebook Ads UI with default targeting parameters

The UI's Estimated Reach box, tallying user-count predictions in real time, is an incredible demographic research tool unto itself. Arguably, this UI changed the marketing world forever because it spells out which users on Facebook are interested in what. Fluctuations—even from minute to minute or browser refresh to refresh—are to be expected, especially as combinations of parameters become more complex. Also, the Web UI can be a bit flaky, which is reasonable for technology such as this, served in a web browser. If Estimated Reach stops updating, just refresh the entire browser window. Most of the time, your work to that point will be lost, so take a screen capture of your progress so you can quickly type in any targeting ideas you've lost. Another option when the UI stops updating is to click, "Review Ad," head to the next screen, and then click, "Edit Ad" to return to the previous screen. You should not lose any work.

Targeting Attributes

Marketers finger Facebook users by choosing values on a grid of attributes in the Targeting module of the ad creation UI. Here is a text-tree outline of main sections and attributes. Make a copy of this text-tree to use as a worksheet for preproduction planning and other shredding sessions. We'll go into each of them in detail, from a marketer's perspective.

Location
- Country (attribute)
- State/province (attribute)
- City (attribute)
  - Cities within __ miles radius (attribute)

Demographics
- Age (attribute)
- Sex (attribute)

Interests (main section) Defaults to, "Precise Interests," Toggle to/from, "Broad Category Targeting"

Connections on Facebook (visible if destination is internal FB page)
- Users who are connected to (attribute)
- Users who are not already connected to (attribute)
- Users whose friends are connected to (attribute)

Advanced Demographics (main section)
- Birthday (attribute)
- Sexual interest (attribute)
- Relationship status (attribute)
- Languages (attribute)

Education & Work (main section)
- College grad (attribute)
  - College (attribute)
  - Major (attribute)
- In college (attribute)
  - College (attribute)
  - Major (attribute)
  - Graduation years (attribute)
- In high school (attribute)
- Workplaces (attribute)

And Operator

The main targeting sections—Location, Demographics, Interests, Connections on Facebook, Advanced Demographics, and Education & Work—truly work in a matrix. This means that values selected *between* each of these sections have the *and* operator in between. In other words, selecting Country: Brazil, Age: 22, and Interest: Baking means the targeted users live in Brazil *and* are 22 years old *and* also are interested in baking.

Obviously, specifying additional targeting attributes with the *and* operator reduces estimated reach because the process filters down to users who display an exact combination of those attributes. It makes sense. Adding additional criteria using *and* focuses targeting because fewer Facebook users are addressed with greater specificity. There is no way to choose the *and* operator in the UI. These decisions are made by Facebook and established as hard presets. Here's an example:

- There are 141,221,000 people (Facebook users) who live in the United States *and* are age 18 or older.

- There are 61,655,720 men who live in the United States *and* are age 18 or older. Note that estimated reach has been reduced because women are filtered out.

- There are 565,020 men who live in the United States *and* are age 18 or older *and* like NASCAR. Again, estimated reach is reduced because now, users who are not interested in NASCAR have been filtered out.

Some attributes *within* main sections use the *and* operator. For instance, choosing College Grad by itself filters users down to college graduates. Major and College become available as options upon selecting In College or College Grad. Choosing

College Grad, and then specifying College: Harvard and Major: Biochemistry aims ads only at Facebook users who've graduated from college *and* went to Harvard *and* majored in biochemistry.

Don't let this freak you out. Just remember that estimated reach is reduced with every new targeting attribute separated by the *and* operator. As we review each targeting attribute later in this chapter, we'll take note of which values are affected by preset *and* operators.

Or Operator

Some attributes *within* main sections have the *or* operator in between them. Adding targeting criteria connected by *or* increases targeting width. The Interests bucket is a great example. *Within* the Interests bucket, additional interests are concatenated with the *or* operator. Stipulating additional interests with the *or* operator in between increases estimated reach because we're adding more users who fit targeting criteria. Again, this makes sense. Adding additional criteria using *or* can reduce targeting focus as more Facebook users are addressed, potentially with less specificity. There is no way to choose the *or* operator in the UI. These decisions are made by Facebook and established as hard presets. Check out this example:

- There are 449,740 men who live in the United States, are age 18 or older, and like NASCAR.
- There are 902,040 men who live in the United States, are age 18 or older, and like NASCAR *or* bowling. Estimated reach has increased because now, we've targeted users who like either NASCAR or bowling.
- There are 2,465,440 men who live in the United States, are age 18 or older, and like NASCAR *or* bowling *or* cooking. Estimated reach has increased because now, we've targeted users who like NASCAR or bowling or cooking.

This concept is crucial. Just remember that estimated reach is increased with every new targeting attribute separated by the *or* operator. As we review each targeting attribute later in this chapter, again, we'll point out which values are affected by preset *or* operators.

And and *Or* Together

The whole stew gets even more pungent when one realizes that the *or*-separated interests in the Interests bucket and *within* some other attributes work in an *and* relationship with the other major targeting sections.

- There are 112,520 women who live in the United States *and* like opera.
- There are 7,040 women who live in the United States *and* are interested in women *and* like opera. The estimated reach has been drastically reduced because

the *and* operator is preset between the Demographics sections (where gender is selected) and Advanced Demographics (where sexual preference is selected). Remember, the *and* operator filters, refines, and requires combinations of targeting attributes within users and therefore reduces reach.

- There are 37,640 women who live in United States *and* are interested in women *and* like opera *or* like classical music. The estimated reach has been increased because the *or* operator is preset in the Interests bucket (where interests are selected). Remember, the *or* operator increases reach and, in this case, slightly reduces focus. This is key. We have not found gay women who like *both* opera and classical music. They like *either* opera or classical music. If the additional segment had been either Phantom of the Opera or Pavarotti, focus may not have been reduced, because they're both highly related to "Opera."

Start with the basic premise. The main sections have the *and* operator between them:

- Location
- Demographics
- Interests
- Connections on Facebook
- Advanced Demographics
- Education & Work

Specifying values in any of these main sections reduces reach because targeted users must meet *all* the criteria in each section, in combination. Think of each section as having targeting output determined by selections made to the attributes within.

The main sections have some targeting parameters strung together by *and* but others by *or*. Hang in there. You'll get it as we review each attribute within each main section. It may be time to start listening to music while you read.

Typing Patterns Reveal Related Segments

Throughout the UI, all values for every attribute box are preset. Typing a word in any UI box that is *not* part of Facebook's preset social graph simply will not result in a value that Facebook Ads will accept for targeting.

Fortunately for advertisers, FB goes to exceptional lengths to reveal social segments that are conceptually related to descriptive words typed into the UI. This functionality is a miracle of modern contextual targeting. For instance, typing **Boston Bruins** into the Precise Interests attributes box presents options that I never would have thought of, unaided (see Figure 3.4).

A bit of coordinated alphanumeric pattern testing surrounding key concepts yields fascinating UI typing hacks. These typing patterns help reveal a cornucopia of preset Facebook targeting attributes available to choose from. Think of it the same way as a search-and-rescue mission flown by the coast guard, scouring the sea in a grid to locate a missing ship. You literally type patterns to the point that a rhythm is established. To the privileged few given access to the Facebook Ads application programming interface (API), these testing grids can be automated. For the rest of you advertisers out there, get used to the idea of those typing patterns.

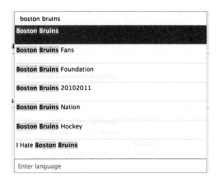

Figure 3.4 Facebook Ads suggests Precise interests similar to Boston Bruins.

This is easily illustrated in its most basic form by typing the letter *a* in the Precise Interests bucket. The following preset social-segments inventory is offered: A Prayer For Owen Meany, A Clockwork Orange, A Walk to Remember, Aaron, and so on. They seem to be roughly offered by segment size, but this is far from consistent. To explore *b*, backspace and type the letter.

It works for words, too, not just individual letters. Start with the word *boat* in the Interests bucket. Boats, Boating, Boatbook, Boat That Rocked, and Boat Trip are the first options. That's great, some good options for sure, albeit seemingly random. Facebook does not reveal its algorithm for how it selects. One can only imagine.

From the basics, things can only get more complicated as the search patterns deepen. Invoke a little trickery. Try typing in **boat a**, the *a* being the first letter of an alphabetical search pattern designed to discover more social segments not shown previously.

Now we're getting somewhere. Nuggets of interest—gold like Antique Boat Center, Andros Boatworks, and Aberdeen Boat Club Hong Kong are rendered. Try **boat c, boat d,** or **boat 1** to flesh out even more preset targeting ideas. To move through the different tests faster, copy *boat* to your computer's Clipboard. Then, execute the pattern, pasting into the Interests bucket, the results of which are shown in Figure 3.5:

- Paste *boat* / type a space and **a** after *boat* / select any presets.
- Paste *boat* / type a space and **b** after *boat* / select any presets.
- Paste *boat* / type a space and **c** after *boat* / select any presets.

Figure 3.5 Facebook Interests bucket with *boat* keywords

Once preset options have been discovered, selected, and exhausted, undertake the same testing pattern using tightly related words, which can include plurals, abbreviations, and synonyms:

- Paste *boats* / select any presets.
- Paste *boats* / type a space and **a** / select any presets.
- Paste *boats* / type a space and **b** / select any presets.
- Paste *boats* / type a space and **c** / select any presets, etc.
- Paste *yacht* / select any presets.
- Paste *yacht* / type a space and **a** / select any presets.
- Paste *yacht* / type a space and **b** / select any presets, etc.
- Paste *yachts* / select any presets.
- Paste *yachts* / type a space and **a** / select any presets.
- Paste *yachts* / type a space and **b** / select any presets, etc.

Each targeting attribute has its own idiosyncratic alpha patterns, which can be used to hack out heretofore unrevealed preset options. Some typing patterns are more Byzantine and others require some creativity. We'll take a closer look at classic patterns as we cover each attribute.

 Note Facebook Ads targeting only recognizes alphanumeric characters for targeting. "Amazon.com" becomes "amazoncom" and "I <3" (text colloquialism for "heart" or "love") becomes "I 3".

Location

The first main section of the targeting module is Location. The practice of geotargeting ads is venerable and proven. Once you've selected the country or countries you'd like to target, it's easy to further refine the audience by selecting specific states, provinces, or cities users self-identify as their location. Only locations that are within your selected countries will be shown.

Facebook Ads' geotargeting is a deeper animal than the classic IP-driven geotargeting search pay-per-click marketers have come to know over the years. Search engines typically mine a user's Internet Protocol (IP) address to reconcile location against a database of IP addresses and physical locations, including countries and cities. Facebook bases its geotargeting, for the most part, on the location users claim when filling out their Facebook profiles.

According to Facebook, "If a user has listed a current address on their profile, they may see ads targeted to that location, regardless of where they are currently located. Ads are not targeted to a user's geographic networks or any other information." Marketers are not given controls to choose between targeting users by either IP location or addresses in their profiles. Facebook decides behind the scenes.

It's amazing how accurate this really is: It can tell when you're out of town and places ads from that locale on your page. Facebook decides and seems to do a decent job understanding the difference between a road trip and a permanent move.

Facebook Mobile has been widely adopted. The 200 million active users accessing FB via their mobile devices are two times more active than non-mobile users. This portends an incredible future for advertisers, who could benefit from adding additional geographic context to targeting.

Facebook Places, a highly publicized mobile application much like Foursquare, encourages users to "check in" at an Event Page or businesses' Places pages. Obviously, users give away highly specific geolocation data, cultivated by their mobile phones' GPS signal. If widely adopted by users, this could be a treasure trove of hot-live information that is transient enough to provide data valuable for advertisers.

For instance, if an advertiser could target users checked in at a certain Laundromat, potentially with time to kill while clothes dry, the users could be targeted by a coffee shop next door offering free coffee for Laundromat patrons. It's not currently possible to target Facebook Ads by this method. However, it is already possible to "target people who 'Like' your Place page if you have performed a Page to Place merge," according to Facebook. This seems to carry the same limitations of Facebook Page marketing, where advertisers are allowed to target only their own fans, friends of their own fans, or everyone but their own fans.

In the future, we may be able to target by combinations of user profile and IP address mash-ups, and just think of the possibilities! It would be super-cool to target folks who live in Montreal, as indicated by their Places activities while visiting Nantucket. These users might be targeted by ads that tout special Canadian currency exchange rates at an establishment in Nantucket.

Country

The first attribute in the Location section is Country, which defaults to the country you register as home. This attribute is mandatory in order to move forward—if you deselect all entries in the Country section, the estimated reach isn't zero but, technically, invalid. Choosing a country is very straightforward. Like all Facebook Ads parameters, countries are preset values that populate as you type. You can't just type in the letters for some country that Facebook does not offer as a preset. Facebook does not have an All Countries setting, and you're limited to targeting 25 countries at a time. Not to worry; for tracking purposes, it's nearly always a better idea to target smaller groups or single countries in one ad.

Research-Typing Pattern One

Type **a** in the Country parameter box to see 26 countries beginning with *a*. Facebook lets us target from Afghanistan to United Arab Emirates. Type in **al** to see the countries beginning with these two letters: Aland Islands, Albania, and Algeria. This research-typing pattern works in a number of other Facebook Ads parameters boxes.

Choosing multiple countries eliminates the option to target specific states and provinces within those countries. To target specific states and provinces within multiple countries, create multiple ads targeted to each of the countries, one at a time.

Behind the scenes, Facebook Ads inserts the *or* operator between multiple countries, meaning targeted users live in any of the countries listed. While some users might have dual citizenship or claim multiple homes (think college students studying abroad), you can't target such duplicity in the Country attribute box. For practical application, each additional country adds more users to the countries bucket. Figure 3.6 shows us targeting users who live in any of the countries listed.

Estimated Reach

13,142,840 people

■ who live in one of the countries: **Burkina Faso, Democratic Republic Congo, Central African Republic, Bosnia and Herzegovina, Yemen, Namibia, Federated States of Micronesia, Haiti, Aland Islands, Afghanistan, American Samoa, Qatar, El Salvador, Albania, Denmark, Falkland Islands, Equatorial Guinea, Honduras, Jamaica, Hong Kong, Laos, Kazakhstan, Japan, Hungary or French Guiana**
■ age **18** and older

Figure 3.6 Facebook Ad targeting based on countries

State and Province

If available, based on selecting a country, the next attribute in the Location section is State and Province. If a single country is big enough and/or it actually has states, provinces, or analogous subdivided territories, ticking the states and provinces radio button reveals granular states and provinces options.

In the real world, not all countries refer to their territories as states or provinces. The key to figuring out how each country works in Facebook is to see what attribute boxes show up after country selection and what preset values are returned. For the most part, the UI is intuitively dynamic and comes close to handling different country configurations. There's some stuff that doesn't make total sense, so be sure to pay attention. The United Kingdom is actually a constitutional monarchy and unitary state, not a country. Wales is technically a country within the UK. Yet in Facebook Ads, UK is a country and Wales shows up as a state, though Wales is not technically a state.

Choose Northern Mariana Islands and watch the State and Province options disappear. Just keep in mind that in Facebook Ads, states and provinces have various configurations, handled in assorted ways, including hiding city and/or state parameters and other workarounds for less common governmental designations.

City

Another location-based option to refine your targeting is to select specific cities (Figure 3.7). Only cities within the selected countries will be shown. The Cities parameter box is super-cool. It's smart too. Choosing multiple countries eliminates the Cities option, meaning advertisers can't target United States/New York and London/United Kingdom in the same targeting scenario. To accomplish this, duplicate the ad, targeting each clone to a different country/city combination.

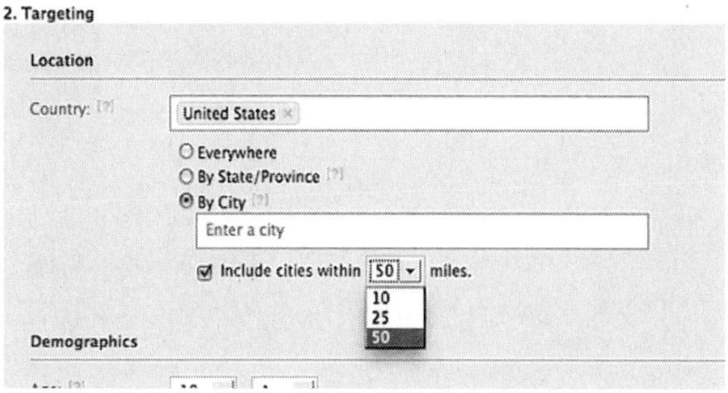

Figure 3.7 Facebook Ads targeting with city and radius criteria

Choosing cities is easy. Just start typing the name and the rest will take care of itself (Figure 3.8). Don't be surprised if a specific city somewhere is not listed. Facebook is not everywhere, though it sometimes seems that way. Another interesting feature is the ability to target users within 10-, 25-, or 50-mile radiuses of selected cities. Since it works for more than one city, this capability makes drawing circles around a collection or population centers a really useful tactic.

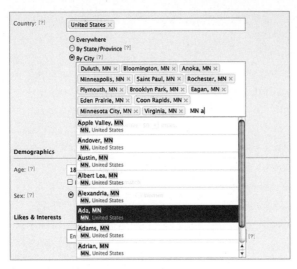

Figure 3.8 Facebook Ads targeting, expanding cities

Demographics: Age and Sex

Next up is to specify the age range of users you'd like to target. Facebook suggests starting broad and narrowing down based on the age results of initial impressions and clicks.

For sex, specify whether your ad should target both genders, just men, or just women. Keep in mind that some users do not identify their gender and can be reached only if you select All. This explains an obvious discrepancy. Men plus women don't add up to All. This is a problem across all targeting criteria except country because users aren't currently required to enter all targeting criteria. This is one of the few weaknesses of Facebook targeting. Not to worry. Most users give the information up.

When it comes to some ad content surrounding contraception, sex education, health conditions, dating sites, and related content or services, ads must be targeted only to users 18 years of age or older. Also, the Interested In targeting parameter must be applied, and a single value of either Men or Women selected.

Broad and Exact Age Match

In the Demographics main section, the age parameter defaults to Broad Match, which means that users just outside the selected age range are also targeted. In the scenario where ages 19 to 24 are selected, users who are 18 and 25 may see the ads. Broad match is cheaper. In exchange for accepting reduced focus in selecting ages targeted, Facebook offers an unspecified reduction in cost per click. Broad age match is selected by leaving the Require Exact Age Match box unchecked. By doing so, you give Facebook permission to deliver your ads to those inside the specified age range as well as those who fall slightly outside of the range, but at a discounted bid.

If you check the Require Exact Age Match box, you are essentially paying Facebook more to target only users within the age range you specify. The ads will never be delivered to anyone outside that age range, no matter how perfectly all the other targeting lines up. Facebook explains: "By allowing the system to increase delivery of your ads slightly outside your target age range, you can receive additional discounted impressions and clicks that are generally just as valuable as the impressions and clicks within your target age."

In some geographic locations, though age selection may still be possible in the UI, age targeting may actually be neutered. Facebook maintains it does not "serve ads to any Facebook user within some age groups in certain locations. The Facebook Ads user interface may allow you to set up campaigns targeting that age group, but Facebook will not deliver such ads." Certain types of advertising may not be served to children under age 18, according to Facebook TOS, including advertising for dating sites and alcoholic beverages. In the United States, the Childhood Online Protection Act (COPA) limits distribution of "material harmful to minors," defined as material that by "contemporary community standards" is judged to pique "prurient interest," including showing sexual acts or nudity. This is a much wider standard than obscenity. One assumes that FB is sensitive about and compliant to COPA standards.

World-Famous Interests Bucket

Over the last three years, the official name of this targeting attribute has changed from, "Keyword" to "Likes and Interests" just this year to "Precise Interests." We lovingly refer to the next major section of the targeting UI as the Interests bucket, or Interests bucket for short. If one parameter box exemplifies Facebook's cornucopia of targeting plenty, it's the Interests bucket. The internal algorithm that parses Facebook's social graph to presets in this box is so incredibly powerful that we sometimes refer to each interest as a "social segment." From foot fetishes to cupcake baking, this section is where the targeting rubber meets the social graph road. As we move forward, we'll refer to Precise Interests targeting attribute as the Interests Bucket, because that's what it is.

Adding additional likes and interests to this bucket does not mean that users are filtered down to those who are interested in interest #1 *and* interest #2 in combination. Instead, the *or* operator is inserted between criteria in the Interests bucket.

Here's an example: If values in the Interests bucket are Basket weaving and Botany, we're targeting users interested in *either* basket weaving *or* botany. When adding more likes and interests in the Interests bucket, in your own mind, insert the *or* operator in between interests.

Marketers new to Facebook Ads often wonder why Facebook offers only the *or* operator within the Interests bucket. Wouldn't it be an easy mathematical feature for Facebook to add an *and* option in the Interests bucket? Many believe the answer is twofold. First, when the UI was created, the sampling of users was much smaller. Allowing marketers to weave and target intricate personas revealing users who like this *and* that *and* those could quickly reduce available users to barely any. Even when the Facebook population was 50 million users, the sampling was not broad enough to support such a micro-targeting concept.

More likely, now that Facebook has around 700 million users, offering the *and* operator as an option between interests in the Interests bucket could be a privacy nightmare. Imagine if we could target users who work at Best Buy, live in Minnesota, are 19 to 21 years old, go to the University of Minnesota, like teaching *and* teachers *and* educator *and* pot *or* marijuana *or* foot fetish. The FCC would be crawling up Facebook's snoot with a microscope and the current privacy dialogue would rage even further out of control. Still, the prospect is titillating. It's a moot point because we don't get the *and* operator within the Like bucket. It's safe to say that one tiny word defines one of the most important political decisions in marketing history: *or* and not *and* in the Interests bucket.

Note The nomenclature, "Likes," "Interests," and, "Likes & Interests" opens a can of worms and inconsistent language throughout FB ads. In the Web UI, this attribute is called, "Interests," and subdivided into either "Precise Interests" or "Broad Category Targeting." Power Editor refers to this attribute as "Likes & Interests." The "Estimated Reach" target summary box in the Web UI uses the word, "Like," while Power Editor does not have a summary.

Interests, Bucketed Intent

In search marketing, we spend a lot of time doing our best to associate keywords with intent, or what the user really wants to accomplish. Sure, the keyword *caterer* is easily extrapolated to *catering*. Grab a thesaurus and it won't take long to stem outward to discover *food service* or even *party-planning*. However, the keyword *gourmet food delivery Manhattan* is very desirable because the words the user selected clearly divulge intent. *Delivery* probably means the user wants to buy now. *Gourmet* denotes a customer with finer tastes, perhaps amenable to purchasing a more expensive product. *Manhattan* not only reveals location, but also compounds the sense of readiness to buy.

In social segments, as in search keywords, users' intent is often revealed, that is, what sorts of products would at least register or, at best, seriously catch their eyes and pique emotions. Always ask, "What could we sell to users interested in X, Y, or Z?"

If ever there was a place to express creativity, intuition, and guile, the Interests bucket is it. Marketing in Facebook requires a much different sense of humor than any other channel requires. After all, we're not targeting keywords that users search. Rather, we're knee-deep in contextual or walk-by space. Think about choosing social segments that define customers' characteristics, how they live life, express themselves, tithe, what they read, brands consumed, political inclinations, leaders followed, perversions, afflictions, professions, hobbies, and many other predilections, tastes, and affinities. Stand by, as Chapter 5 and 6 will take a seriously deep dive into the social targeting ooze.

Social marketing requires delightfully sideways thinking. For instance sweatbands and water bottles to the 1,218,560 people who live in the United States; are age 18 or older; and like tennis instructor, tennis, playing tennis, i enjoy playing tennis, sanwa tennis academy, tennis club, tennis coach, i love tennis, tennis life camps, we love tennis, tennis pro, tennis player, *or* tennis runs in our blood (Figure 3.9).

Estimated Reach

1,218,560 people

- who live in the **United States**
- age **18** and older
- who like **tennis instructor**, **tennis**, **playing tennis**, **i enjoy playing tennis**, **sanwa tennis academy**, **tennis club**, **tennis coach**, **i love tennis**, **tennis life camps**, **we love tennis**, **tennis pro**, **tennis player** or **tennis runs in our blood**

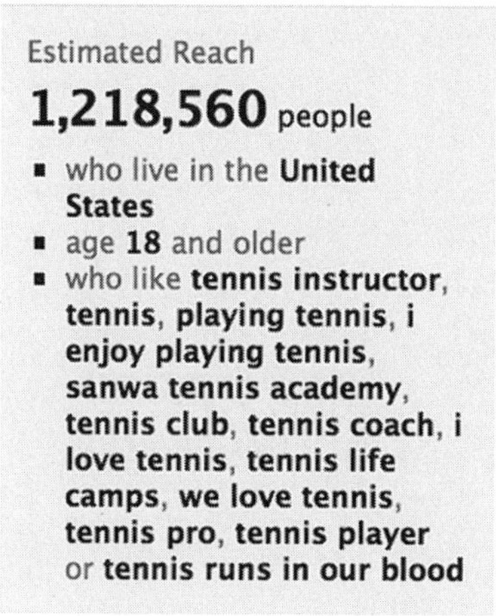

Figure 3.9 Facebook segment for tennis lovers

Sometimes, targeting can be slightly less esoteric and more literal, even though we're operating in contextual space. Could you sell Rosetta Stone language learning software to an estimated reach of 15,980 people who live in the United States, are age 30 or older, and like learning arabic, learning italian, learning spanish, speaking spanish, learning french, learning speak french, learning hebrew, learning portuguese, or learning russian?

Interests from the drop-down box that appears as you type will target your ads to users that list one or more of those things on their profiles. Facebook reminds marketers: "Not all users complete these fields, so choosing fields here will limit the targeting of your ads to only those users with one or more of these Interests."

Social Synonyms: Getting from Here to There

It's interesting that the best way to communicate social segments is still expressed by keywords, even though it's not queries that trigger Facebook ads. Therefore, when dealing with the Interests bucket, keep the intrinsic relationship between keywords and social segments in mind. Synonyms are totally your friend. Microsoft Word's inline thesaurus is an awesome starter tool to help unearth "social synonyms." We also use UrbanDictionary.com a lot to find slang that is often prevalent in Facebook.

Take the example of marketing an überhealthy granola bar with recycled packaging to a target audience comprising Facebook users who care about sustainable living.

It's easy to understand targeting 29,900 people who live in Australia, New Zealand, Canada, United States, United Kingdom, or Ireland; are age 24 and older; and like sustainable earth, sustainable living, sustainable food denver, or sustainable food.

Now put on your semantic hat, grab the thesaurus in one form or another, and giddyup with synonym discovery. It won't take long to find *natural* and *organic*. We're going to run a typing pattern in the Interests bucket. Start the process by making a list of each possible combination of our root social synonym associations. The purpose here is to exhaust every possible social segment:

- organic food
- natural food

Put on your typing fingers and execute the following pattern:

- Type **organic food** / copy *organic food* / select any presets that apply.
- Paste *organic food* / select any presets that apply.
- Paste *organic food* / select any presets / continue until there are no more applicable segments to choose.
- Type **natural food** / copy *natural food* / select any presets that apply.
- Paste *natural food* / select any presets that apply.
- Paste *natural food* / select any presets / continue until there are no more applicable segments to choose.

The estimated reach for this segment is 156,900 people who live in the United States, are age 19 and older, and like organic food, organic foods, natures path organic foods, homegrown organic local food coop, natural foods, natural food connection, bobs red mill natural foods, brazos natural foods, raw food naturals, oryana natural foods market, sprouts natural foods cafe, ians natural foods, or boulder canyon natural foods (Figure 3.10).

It's cool to note that we've found Facebook users who not only like organic and natural food, but also are also interested in specific cafés, other food brands, and Whole Foods–sorts of supermarkets. It's easy to see how treating social segments as keywords, figuring out synonyms in the semantic world, and looping the synonyms through the Facebook interest bucket can yield fabulous results. We tell our team to "always redefine the box you're outside of."

This technique is great, but organic food is a relatively long tail space in Facebook, in that there are not vast pockets of interest. That's why all we had to do was paste the major two-word combinations to find the cool stuff that applied. Shorter tail space, where there are, in fact, massive amounts of users interested in things, require more discretion in determining what is germane and more intense finger technique to run the search grid.

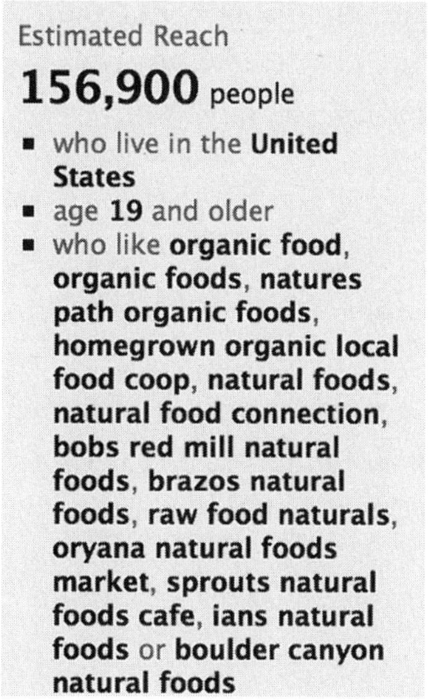
Estimated Reach
156,900 people
who live in the United States
age 19 and older
who like organic food, organic foods, natures path organic foods, homegrown organic local food coop, natural foods, natural food connection, bobs red mill natural foods, brazos natural foods, raw food naturals, oryana natural foods market, sprouts natural foods cafe, ians natural foods or boulder canyon natural foods

Figure 3.10 Facebook segment for organic food lovers

Say the assignment is to market College GameDay Fan Gear to football lovers of all stripes. First, even typing the word *football* in the Interests bucket results in suggested interests. Let's step back for a moment. *Football* actually means soccer in most places, but generally not in the U.S. We only care about obvious American gridiron football interests. Since we're in the U.S., we'll go with most of the suggestions, with the exception of England Football. Check the suggestions* you accept and hit refresh suggestions to see if there are any more obvious ones, as demonstrated in Figure 3.11.

Interests
Precise Interests: [?]
Football × Fantasy Football × NCAA Football ×
Flag Football × Michigan Football × Football Manager ×
Suggested Likes & Interests
Football Manager
Fantasy Football
NCAA Football
Flag Football
Michigan Football
England Football
Switch to Broad Category Targeting [?]

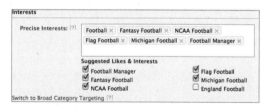

Figure 3.11 Facebook segment for football lovers

The next suggestions are all about England—Pro Evo, England Football, Match Of The Day, Liverpool Football Club, Soccer Am, and England Football Team, so we'll pass and move along.

- Copy *football* onto your computer Clipboard.
- Paste *football* / select any segments relevant to your marketing. Now we've added football factory, football games, football time tennessee, football manager 2009, football videos, or football season.
- Paste *football* / type a space and **a** / select any segments relevant to your marketing. Repeat this process until applicable segments are exhausted.

- Paste *football* / type a space and **ab** / select any segments relevant to your marketing.
- Paste *football* / type a space and **ac** / select any segments relevant to your marketing.
- Paste *football* / type a space and **ad** / select any segments relevant to your marketing.
- Paste *football* / type a space and **ae** / select any segments relevant to your marketing.
- Paste *football* / type a space and **af** / select any segments relevant to your marketing.
- Continue the pattern until all two-letter combinations for the letter *a* have been tested. If you don't want to test every single letter, the obvious second letters to test with *a* would be consonants. Just use your head. If the first letter is a consonant, the obvious second letters to test would be vowels.

This technique does a great job of testing all words associated with your main keyword. It takes a marketer's discretion to select only segments and suggested segments that apply to the marketing tasks at hand.

Going a step further, typing the first three letters of the second word is rarely warranted but sometimes worth the jag. In the football case study, typing **football su** shows Football Sunday and Football Sundays. Hmmm. I wonder if there's more to that. Of course there is. In the world of American sports, Sundays are practically gospel, sacred, the Sabbath.

Type **football sun.** Lo and behold, now we've added Sunday Funday Football Fans, Sunday football, Sun football, Sunday Night Football on NBC, Watching football on Sunday, and Joey Doyles football Sunday, as shown in Figure 3.12. Had we not followed our intuition and worked with the third letter, a treasure trove of football targets would have been missed.

Broad category targeting allows you to reach groups of people who share similar interests and traits. These categories draw from the authentic information people have included in their profiles, allowing you to easily reach your ideal audience. Browse and select from our list of categories to get started.

Broad Categories Targeting*

As previously mentioned, Facebook is famous for throwing spaghetti at the wall (no pun intended) in that they test, refine, or even remove significant tools with little fanfare. As of this writing, FB has been testing a Broad Category feature to target preset user groups sharing common demographic characteristics. Your Facebook Ads account may or may not have access to this targeting tool. If it does, you'll see a Switch to Broad Category Targeting link just under the Interests attribute, as shown in Figure 3.13. To switch out of Broad Category mode, click Switch to Precise Interest Targeting.

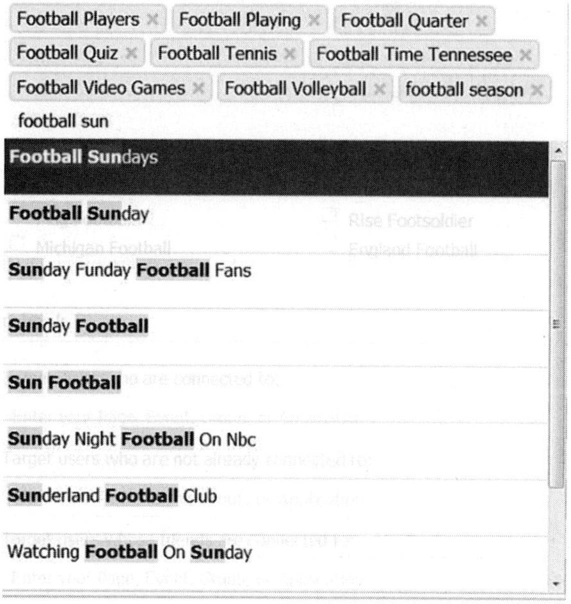

Figure 3.12 Building out the Facebook segment for football lovers

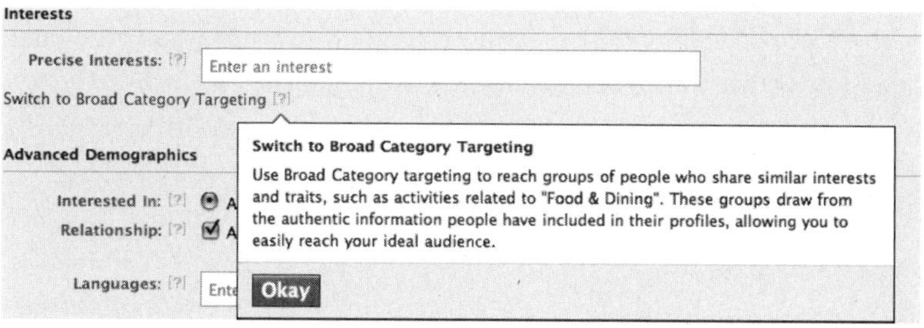

Figure 3.13 Broad Category Targeting option and FB inline help explanation

Broad category targeting lets advertises take aim at users who, in FB's opinion, share related interests and characteristics. The Facebook Ads help section states that "these categories draw from the authentic information people have included in their profiles, allowing you to easily reach your ideal audience."

Our tests indicate that these presets are effective and, in some cases, offer access to certain demographics that are otherwise difficult to target with a high degree of specificity, using the classic Interests bucket one segment at a time. Just look how easy it is to target parents who are raising children between birth and three years old, as shown in Figure 3.14. Cool! That particular targeting assignment would be nearly impossible using the Precise Interest Targeting option.

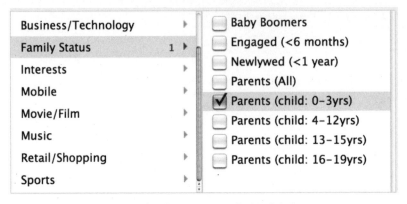

Figure 3.14 Targeting personas via broad categories in Facebook's ad platform

Other categories seem more subjective. For instance, in the United States, broadly targeting Retail/Luxury Goods results in fingering about 5 million users. What exactly does that mean? FB does not tell us for sure. Are they targeting folks who read *Condé Nast* magazines or are interested in Rolex watches? Unknown. My point is that, for some of these categories, I'd rather figure the segments out myself, using Precise Interests Targeting as opposed to using FB's presets.

Still, the Broad Category tool shows promise if FB keeps it around. Please note that this feature is not stable yet and we've seen it added to accounts only to see it removed from some and not others. Still, the capabilities are significant enough that they bear mention. Please check back to www.KillerFBAds.com for up-to-date information.

External Semantic Stemming Tools

In the keyword research universe, we call the thesaurus function *stemming*. Microsoft Word's thesaurus is only one of many tools we use to stem keywords. Here's a glimpse at aimClear's favorite tools:

- WordTracker, Lateral Stemming Thesaurus: www.wordtracker.com.
- Google AdWords Keyword Tool: https://adwords.google.com/select/KeywordToolExternal. Try phrase and broad match.
- Trellian Keyword Discovery: www.keyworddiscovery.com.
- Wikipedia can be an awesome place to stem keywords for synonyms—try following the trails from the interlinking in articles.
- YouTube, Google, and Bing search suggestion boxes. Use the ScrapeBox application (for Windows only) to easily navigate them in one UI: www.scrapebox.com.

Advanced Demographics

The Advanced Demographics section is pretty sexy, as clearly indicated in Figure 3.15. There are no two ways about it. Filter by sexuality, workplace, relationship status, and languages spoken, and even aim ads at folks on their birthday.

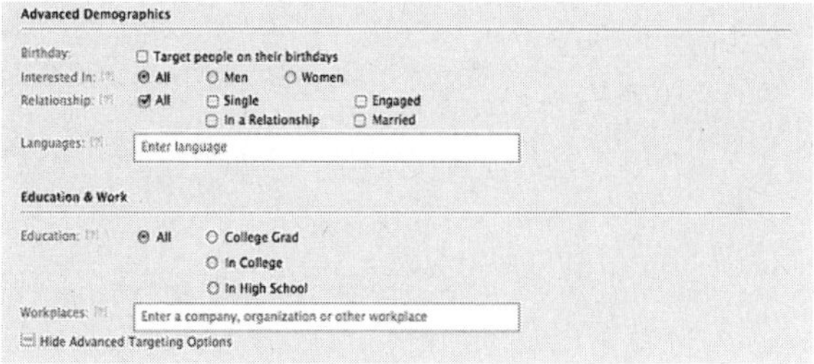

Figure 3.15 Facebook's Advanced Demographics features

Birthday

Birthday targeting allows ads to be targeted to users on their birthdays. With this option, advertisers can create highly relevant ads or highlight special offers available to users on their birthdays.

This one's easy. Checking Target People On Their Birthdays does just that, within the bounds of the overall targeting picture. Facebook suggests that "advertisers can create highly relevant ads or highlight special offers available to users on their birthdays." Right on, then!

Running ads by this targeting method for a course of days results in serving ads to users whose birthdays occur on the specific day the ads run. Facebook users with April 14 birthdays will see birthday-targeted ads only on April 14. Running the campaign over the 15th and 16th results in users celebrating their special days on the 15th and 16th seeing the ad.

> **Tip** Facebook does not provide insight as to what other ads exist for any social segment. Wondering what other advertisers are also targeting certain interests or other attributes? View your own live ads or competitors' ads simply by temporarily modifying your personal Facebook profile. For insight as to what marketers are targeting, temporarily modify your own Facebook profile's interests. Though it violates Facebook terms of services, some marketers create a shadow profile just for this purpose. Try changing your birthday to the current calendar day or modifying other aspects of your profile. Don't forget to test for geotargeted ads by changing your hometown.

Relationship Status and Sexuality

People disclose their sexual interests in their profile. Though it's not required, many people happily put out for Facebook's questions during account setup and profile maintenance. If it's publicly displayed by privacy settings, it's easy to see whether users are interested in men, women, or both. If privacy settings are locked down, all that does is hide the information from other users. It does not exclude Facebook Ads advertisers from marketing to those preferences. In combination with other elements, this information can telegraph lucrative marketplaces or users with internal contradictions.

Under Relationship, you can target All or any combination of those who identify as being Single, In A Relationship, Engaged, or Married. Some users do not specify their relationship status and can only be reached if you select All.

You can segment by sexual preference under the Interested In demographic. Select whether your ads should target all users or only users interested in men or interested in women. Like relationship status, some users do not specify this information and can therefore only be reached if you select All.

Straight up, here's American out-of-the-closet Facebook gay men, some of whom may or may not have an accent:

- There are 122,940 men who live in the United States are age 18 or older; are in a relationship; speak English (US), English (UK), English (Pirate), English (Upside Down), French (France), French (Canada), Spanish, Spanish (Spain), or Hungarian; and are interested in men.

What does sexual interest say about a persona? There are many opinions. Classic marketing suggests gay professionals have more disposable cash because there are fewer children in the household, on average. Obviously, marketing to engaged women has certain markets. Here are some other interesting segments with distinct interests:

- There are 7,900 women who live in the United States; are age 18 or older; like vegetarianism, vegetarian, vegetarian cooking, vegetarians, vegetarianvitamin-scom, vegetarian food, vegetarian wellness, or vegetarians rock; and are interested in women: gay female vegetarians.

- There are 3,166,760 men (boys) who live in either the United States or Canada; are age 13; are single; and are interested in women: teen boy love.

- There are 10,480 men who live in the United States; are age 18 or older; like republican party, republican, republican conservative, republicanconservative, republican party gop, conservative republican, conservative republicans, conservative republican party, very conservative republican, or republican party conservative; and are interested in men: gay male Republicans.

- There are 21,640 men who live in the United States; are age 18 or older; like equal rights amendment, equal rights, equal marriage rights for all, gay rights media, support gay rights, i support gay rights, nsw gay lesbian rights lobby, gay civil rights movement, international gay lesbian human rights commission, defeat proposition 8, repeal prop8, prop 8 being overturned, stop prop 8, or inspired voices against prop 8; and are interested in women: straight men for gay rights.

- There are 2,540 women who live in the United States; are age 18 or older; like construction, construction management, construction manager, construction work, construction worker, or highway construction workers; and are interested in women: gay female construction workers.

Remember to check Facebook Ads Guidelines because some products, which we previously described, have certain targeting requirements. Simply put, when marketing most adult-themed products and services, advertisers can target only users over age 18 who have specified that they're single for dating services.

Languages

If you'd like to target individuals that use Facebook in a language different from the common language for the selected location, enter that language in the Languages box. If you leave this field blank, your ads will target all users in the specified location regardless of the language they use on Facebook.

Remember, languages transcend geographic borders. There are over 30 million users who speak English who *don't* live in the United States, the UK, or Canada. Test different languages in various countries to radically expand marketplaces.

Education & Work

The Education & Work section provides a superb layer of stylish focus. We have several clients who have undertaken a years-long strategy of gently marketing to tomorrow's thought leaders. Target users by colleges attended, areas of programs and courses, and graduation year, including alumni. Since Facebook originated at Harvard and then spread, at first, among Ivy League schools, then all colleges, and then high schools, there are plenty of cool goodies here. Combine education attributes with self-reported occupations in the Interests bucket to concoct a potent shaker of uptown targeting.

To target users who are at a specific educational level—college graduate, in college, or in high school—select the appropriate attribute. Otherwise, select All to target all users regardless of education.

To target users at a specific company or organization, enter the name of the workplace in the Workplaces field. Otherwise, leave this blank.

Element boxes open automatically when some options are selected. Selecting College Grad or In College opens the College and Majors boxes, as previously described and as seen in Figure 3.16.

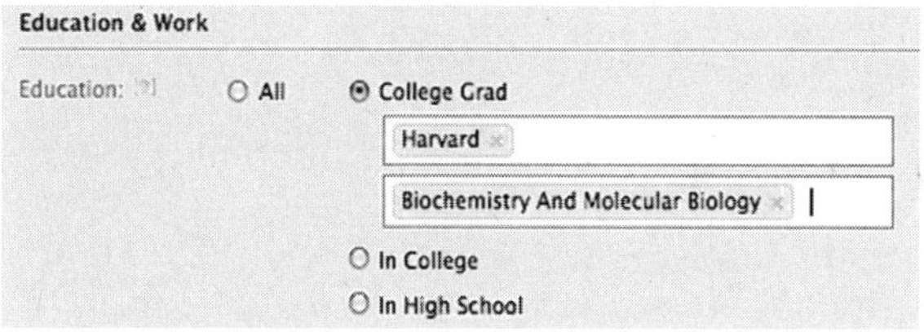

Figure 3.16 Facebook Education & Work features

It's pretty obvious that FB does not offer us the ability to select specific high schools because of the creep factor. That's probably a good idea.

Here are some targeting scenarios for your dining and dancing pleasure. We'll start with Boston-area college students who don't list the United States as their home, at least in their Facebook profiles. You get the picture.

This first segment, as shown in Figure 3.17, depicts the volume of Facebook users who list a country other than the U.S. as their current country of residence yet study at a college in Boston, Massachusetts, and list English as a language they speak:

- There are 3,700 people who live in either Canada, United Kingdom, Australia, Japan, China, France, Mexico, or Ireland; are age 18 or older; are at BU, Boston Conservatory, BC, Boston Baptist College, Boston College for Professional Studies, Boston Institute, Boston Computer Institute, Harvard, MIT, MCPHS, Mass. Art, or Mass Maritime; and speak English (US), English (UK), English (Pirate), or English (Upside Down).

Estimated Reach
3,700 people
- who live in one of the countries: **Canada, United Kingdom, Australia, Japan, China, France, Mexico** or **Ireland**
- age **18** and older
- who are at **BU, Boston Conservatory, BC, Boston Baptist College, Boston College for Professional Studies, Boston Institute, Boston Computer Institute, Harvard, MIT, MCPHS, Mass. Art** or **Mass Maritime**
- who speak **English (US), English (UK), English (Pirate)** or **English (Upside Down)**

Figure 3.17 Facebook segment for non-U.S. resident Boston college students who speak English

- There are 4,940 people who live in the United States; are at UIllinois, Indiana, University of Iowa, Michigan, Michigan, State University, University of Minnesota, UNL, Northwestern, Ohio State, Purdue, Wisconsin, or Penn State; and are majoring in mechanical engineering.

- There are 680 people who live in the United States; are age 18 or older; are at BYU, Notre Dame, Wheaton IL, Grove City, Hillsdale, Bethel IN, Azusa, Pacific, Evangel, Biola, Palm Beach Atlantic University, Judson University, Bethel MN, or Judson AL; and are majoring in vocal performance, music composition, music performance, theater arts, theatre dance, theatre arts, performing arts, fine art, studio art, media arts, fine arts, or art studio.

- There are 200 people who live in the United States; are age 18 and older; are at Brown, Columbia, Cornell, Dartmouth, Harvard, Princeton, UPenn, or Yale; and are majoring in undecided.

- There are 520 people who live in the United States; are age 18 or older; are at Cal Poly, CSU Northridge, CSU Fullerton, CSU Long Beach, Cal Poly, Pomona, CSU Chico, CSU Sacramento, CSU Fresno, California PA, CSU San Marcos, Humboldt State, S.F. State, San Diego State, San Diego, San Diego Christian,

UCSD, Point Loma, Alliant, CA Western, Art Institute of California - San Diego, Thomas Jefferson School of Law, SF Conservatory, San Francisco Art Inst., San Francisco School of Digital Filmmaking, University of San Francisco, Academy of Art, Universidad Francisco de Paula Santander, CA College of the Arts, Uni San Francisco de Quito, UC Hastings, San Jose State, or San Jose City College; and are majoring in broadcast journalism, communication journalism, communication media, mass media, or media studies.

The Workplaces element certainly does not index every company. In fact, it's pretty short tail. That said, it has been growing for years, right along with Facebook itself. Use your good alpha pattern practice, sometimes up to four letters. You know the drill:

For a snapshot of the element's depth:

- Type **a** and have a look.
- Type **al** and have a look.
- Type **all** and have a look.
- Type **all** and have a look.
- Type **alla** and have a look. Allan Industries is now visible, but was not until the first four letters were typed.
- There are 11,500 people who live in the United States in Minnesota, California, or Texas; are age 18 or older; and work at Best Buy.
- There are 2,600 people who live in the United Kingdom, are age 18 or older, and work at UK Parliament.
- There are 17,760 people who live in the United States and work at Delta Air Lines.

The power and intricacies of the Education & Work tool add a wonderful dimension to Facebook Ads. Used in clever tandem with the other main sections, every present *and* operator in between, it's easy to define personas for marketers.

Connections on Facebook

Facebook allows you to target users who have already expressed interest in your Facebook content...or not. The options are simple and powerful.

Target Users Who Are Connected

The first target-by-connections option is to target users who are already "connected" to your Facebook assets. This means they've engaged your content, for example by "liking" your page, RSVPing to your event, joining your group, or interacting with your app. Start typing in the target field and watch as it populates with these Facebook assets you've previously created.

Targeting users who are not only aware of your brand but dig it and engage with it lends certain opportunities. Consider tailoring ad copy that speaks to them as VIP members or valued customers, and offer special coupons or other incentives exclusive to your existing audience. Facebook recommends leaving this field blank unless your goal is to specifically target, or narrow, an audience consisting only of people already connected to your page, group, event, or app.

To be clear, these capabilities are available only to owners and administrators of FB pages, groups, and apps. In other words, I can't decide to target all of Starbucks's fans by this attribute. I can probably get to them by other means, however—for example, via the Interests bucket.

Target Users Who Are Not Connected

Conversely, the second targeting option for connections narrows your audience to include only users who are not already connected to your Facebook properties—in other words, users who have not yet engaged with your content (they don't "like" your page, have never been invited to an event, haven't joined your group, or haven't interacted with your app). To target these users, follow the same procedure as before—begin typing in the target field and select the Facebook properties you want to specify.

Targeting users who are not already connected to your brand's presence on Facebook also provides unique opportunities, such as advertising with the intent of recruiting new members, fans, or customers or offering promotional discounts for first-time shoppers. Facebook recommends leaving this field blank unless your intent is to narrow your target audience to people not already connected to your brand. Again, these targeting rights are available only to owners and admins.

Target Users Whose Friends Are Connected

The third and final way to target by connections is to filter your audience for users whose friends are connected to your page, event, group, or application. Same as before, just enter the name of your Facebook entity in the field and select the properties upon which you want to focus.

Cooking up ads that speak to this second-degree targeted audience can arguably require more sideways thinking than the first two target-by-connections options. Consider pulling that first-degree of separation—the user's friend who already likes your page, group, and so on—into the ad. Something like, "Hey—your friend likes [product]! Maybe you will, too!" or "Do your friends love [product]? Pick them up the latest edition for the holidays!" might catch their eye and plant an idea in their brain.

Ad Targeting Options Help Center

When in doubt, Facebook's Help Center is awesome. The Ads: Targeting Options section, which can be found at www.facebook.com/help/?page=863 (Figure 3.18), is a particularly useful resource for a wide array of questions ranging from the basic (what is birthday targeting?) to the slightly more advanced (what are the benefits of refining my targeting versus trying to reach a broader audience?).

The contents in this section are offered in over a dozen languages, including English, Italian, Turkish, Spanish, German, French, and Portuguese. There are also in-line help items within Facebook designated by small gray question marks next to certain elements in the UI. Between this book, the help section, and that in-line insight, you should be pretty well fixed up.

Figure 3.18 Facebook Ads targeting options help section

Module 3: Campaigns, Pricing, and Scheduling

The third step, after designing the ads and targeting users, is all about logistics to bid, schedule, and file the ad within campaigns. Facebook Ads offers pricing and scheduling options common to modern online ad platforms. There are a few interesting quirks, but it is otherwise straightforward.

First, create a new campaign or choose an existing one. Aside from organization, having separate campaigns is important because you can designate a budget for each. Choose either a daily or lifetime campaign budget. Choosing a daily budget distributes that campaign's ad spend throughout each day. Choosing a lifetime budget distributes the ad spend throughout the duration of the campaign. Check the "Run my campaign continuously starting today" box and ads will run at full throttle until the budget is expended, as opposed to the budget being metered out over the campaign period.

Next, select the schedule by choosing beginning and ending dates. If you checked the "Run my campaign continuously starting today" box, the ending date will be grayed out because the campaign ends when you run out of money. It's interesting to note that choosing a daily budget with continuous running does still gray out the end date, so you have to remember to turn the campaign off when you want it to stop.

CPC vs. CPM

Facebook Ads offer two payment model choices, cost per click (CPC) and cost per thousand impressions (CPM). *Impressions* means times the ad is shown. Choosing CPC means that each click, up to the amount you've bid, will be charged against your budget. To my mind, this is almost always the correct choice. Choosing CPM means that a share of your budget will be charged every time your ad is *shown*. Facebook suggests, "This is the best choice if you'd like to increase brand awareness by users simply seeing your ad." Frankly, I don't agree. When we brand, we usually still choose CPC and meter clicks by not having a call to action in the ad, bid level, and other methods. We'll discuss the technicalities of CPC vs. CPM in more depth in Chapter 9, "Field Guide To Optimization & Reporting."

Regardless of the billing method, Facebook chooses the "best ad to run based on ad performance." In my experience, FB does not give each ad enough of a chance in rotation to really make that call. Whether using CPC or CPM, the amount charged will never exceed your budget.

Pricing

How high up on the page an ad runs, if at all, is determined by your bid. It's as easy as choosing the maximum amount you're willing to pay for each click or every thousand impressions. Tax is not included in bids or budgets. Facebook suggests bids in a range, low to high (see Figure 3.19). The ranges may or may not be indicative of how much it will really cost to run the ads. Sure, it's a bid model, which means we're competing against others for ad positioning. However, there are likely other factors, analogous to Google AdWords quality score. Facebook does not disclose ad performance factors, which impact quality score. It is probably that bid + quality score = ad position, in competition with other advertisers competing for position.

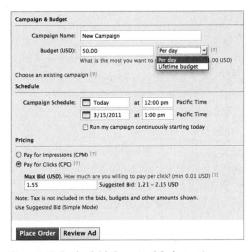

Figure 3.19 Facebook Ads Campaign & Budget options

Use Suggested Bid (www.facebook.com/ads/create/) does not offer any advantage that I can determine, except to give Facebook a blank check. FB adjusts the Simple bid range upward as competition increases, and there is no cap. Also, the only option is CPC, and CPM is not available. The option might make sense if there were a bid-to-position option, which might be available in the future.

Facebook Ads' simple design tools, targeting matrix, and pricing options, in tandem with nearly 700 million users, amount to an incredible opportunity for advertisers. Later in the book, we'll look at advanced ad design, copy, and killer targeting. Happy ads creation!

Facebook Ads Production Workflow

4

Now that you've studied the ad creation web user interface (UI), in this chapter, we'll share workflow hacks to streamline production. Facebook Ads production is extremely labor-intensive. The efficiency hacks proffered are nuggets of wisdom born of our staffs' extreme production pain over four years of boots-on-the-ground field experience.

Facebook Ads has an easy-to-grasp structural hierarchy, which has evolved out of the chaos marking earlier versions. The platform is always being updated. Every time you log in, there's a fair chance you'll notice new or withdrawn features, but fear not: The basics have remained the same for years. Let's get to work mastering them.

Chapter Contents

Power Editor
Account Structure
First Step: Wireframe Demographic Research
Second Step: Create Your First Ads
Structural Best Practices

Power Editor

Power Editor (Figure 4.1) is a relatively new Facebook Ads management utility that only runs in Google's Chrome browser. You'll have to download Chrome and install it first. That's rather ironic to anyone tracking the public acrimony between Google and Facebook. Power Editor offers much less functionality that the Web UI in many ways. For instance, there is no reporting, columns are not sortable, and Sponsored Stories are not supported.

However, Power Editor excels in other workflow matters. When it comes to duplicating ads and campaigns, Power Editor rocks. Also there is a dandy Bulk Import function that, when coupled with its sister the Export button, provides awesome tools to edit raw text from ads and campaigns via spreadsheets and to upload images.

Power Editor was released in June and was long awaited by the Facebook Ads marketing community. We'll note workflow differences between Power Editor and the Web UI more as we crunch workflow hacks in this chapter. Watch for side-by-side screen captures that illustrate the difference. Let's roll up our sleeves and rock some Facebook Ads now.

Figure 4.1 Screen capture of Power Editor, in Google Chrome Browser

Understanding Account Structure

In the Facebook Ads hierarchy, *account* is the highest-level object. Every account is associated with a specific user's Facebook account. Advertisers can grant each other access to their Facebook Ads account by navigating to the permissions management system on the Settings tab, located here: www.facebook.com/ads/manage/settings.php.

Figure 4.2 shows the highest level, which displays your account and a list of any others you've been granted access to.

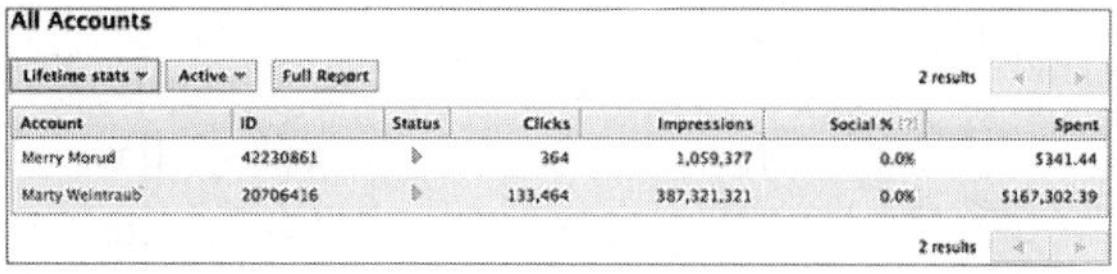

Figure 4.2 Facebook advertising interface, all accounts

Figure 4.3a shows campaigns within an account in the Web UI and Figure 4.3b shows ads within a campaign.

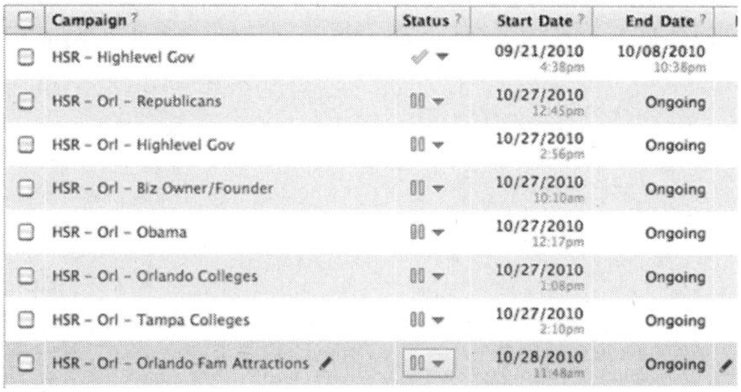

Figure 4.3a Facebook advertising interface, all campaigns, Web UI

Figure 4.3b Facebook advertising interface, all ads, Web UI

Campaigns hold ads. Any ad can only be part of a single campaign. Drill into any campaign to see its ads as illustrated in Figures 4.3a and 4.3b (above) for the Web UI and 4.4a and 4.4b (below) for Power Editor. It's pretty straight forward but go ahead and take a minute to experiment in whichever UI you're working in presently.

At the campaign level, daily budgets are assigned and the master on/off switch (run status) can be activated. Each campaign can hold any number of ads. Every ad is self-contained, including targeting elements, ad creative, bids, and duration (which refers to when the ads start and how long they'll run). There is no requirement for ads in any campaign to be related in any way. However, you'll see in this chapter that it is best practice to bucket like targeting in campaigns for a number of reasons.

Campaign		Start Date	End Date	Budget	Period	Remaining
Avatar	▷	05/27/11	Ongoing	$100.00	Daily	$61.06
Browser – Chat – Chat/Talk F	‖	11/02/10	Ongoing	$142.75	Daily	$142.75
Browser – Chat – Chat/Talk M	‖	11/05/10	Ongoing	$142.75	Daily	$142.75
Browser – Chat – New/Date/Lone...	‖	11/02/10	Ongoing	$142.75	Daily	$142.75
Browser – Chat – New/Date/Lone...	‖	11/05/10	Ongoing	$142.75	Daily	$142.75
Browser – Music – AdultPop	‖	11/02/10	Ongoing	$47.58	Daily	$47.58
Browser – Music – Classical	‖	11/02/10	Ongoing	$47.58	Daily	$47.58
Browser – Music – Concerts	‖	11/05/10	Ongoing	$47.58	Daily	$47.58
Browser – Music – PopCountry	‖	11/02/10	Ongoing	$47.58	Daily	$47.58
Browser – Music – Rave	‖	11/02/10	Ongoing	$47.58	Daily	$47.58
Browser – Music – RnB	‖	11/02/10	Ongoing	$47.58	Daily	$47.58
Browser – Music – Trance/Techno	‖	11/05/10	Ongoing	$47.58	Daily	$47.58
Browser-Music-Emocore	‖	10/28/10	Ongoing	$47.58	Daily	$47.58
Browser-Music-Mainstream-Metal		10/28/10	Ongoing	$47.58	Daily	$47.58
Browser-Music-Metal – Women/...	‖	10/28/10	Ongoing	$47.58	Daily	$47.58
Browser-Music-NewSka		10/28/10	Ongoing	$47.58	Daily	$47.58
Browser-Music-Pop-Indie	‖	10/28/10	Ongoing	$47.58	Daily	$47.58

Figure 4.4a Facebook advertising interface, all campaigns, Power Editor

Campaign ...	Ad Name		Bid	Object	Title	Body	Location	Age	Sex	Clicks	CTR %	Avg. CPC	A
Coding	Buddhist Virtual World 2		$1.65		Buddhist Virtual World	Friendly vi...	US	18–Any	All	0	0.000%	$0.00	
Coding	Graduates (programming)	‖	$0.86		Join Second Life	The world'...	US	18–Any	All	0	0.000%	$0.00	
Coding	College-Coding	‖	$0.76		Join Second Life	The world'...	US	18–Any	All	0	0.000%	$0.00	
Coding	Go To Church Online	‖	$1.67		Go To Church Online	Worship &...	US	18–Any	All	0	0.000%	$0.00	
Coding	Free Virtual Dog World	‖	$1.40		Free Virtual Dog World	Create or ...	US	18–Any	All	0	0.000%	$0.00	
Coding	Muslim Virtual World	‖	$1.14		Muslim Virtual World	Meet fello...	US	18–Any	All	0	0.000%	$0.00	
Coding	Buddhist Virtual World	‖	$1.65		Buddhist Virtual World	Virtual te...	US	18–Any	All	0	0.000%	$0.00	
Coding	Buddhist Virtual World 1	‖	$1.65		Buddhist Virtual World	Friendly vi...	US	18–Any	All	0	0.000%	$0.00	
Coding	Free 3D Haunted Houses	‖	$0.97		Free 3D Haunted Ho...	Gorgeousl...	US	18–Any	All	0	0.000%	$0.00	
Coding	3D Halloween World	⊖	$1.15		3D Halloween World	Experience...	US	18–Any	All	0	0.000%	$0.00	
Coding	I work for the Military	‖	$1.35		I work for the Military	I might ha...	US	18–Any	All	0	0.000%	$0.00	
Women	Pen Pal	‖	$0.30		Meet Interesting Peo...	Why settle ...	IE, NZ,...	25–54	Wo...	0	0.000%	$0.00	
Women	Shop Virtually Free	‖	$0.86		Shop Virtually Free	Second Lif...	US	25–45	Wo...	0	0.000%	$0.00	

Figure 4.4b Facebook advertising interface, all ads, Power Editor

Yes, the Zen of Facebook Ads organization is all about how the ads are grouped within campaigns. Because individual ads within campaigns do not have unique daily budgets, the allocation of daily *campaign* budgets is a principal consideration for how things should be laid out. Grouping ads targeted to the same demographic in the same campaign bucket makes it much easier to gauge the performance of a social segment targeted overall.

One problem here is that Facebook does not allow us to alter the rotation of FB ads within campaigns. The algorithm decides which is the "best" one. In other words, you can run 10 ads inside one campaign but there is no way to set how much of the budget each ad gets. One ad might get the entire budget and another might barely be shown. There are no settings to ensure that ads will be seen in even rotation, or at all, for that matter. FB makes the choice of which ad it "thinks" is best based on the ad's performance very quickly and early on in a campaign's life. The only way to have true control over which ad is served is to run only one ad in each campaign at any given time.

First Step: Wireframe Demographic Research

I'm a big fan of planning. Whenever it comes to nearly any type of advertising, *planning* means demographic research. Taking time in advance to explicitly spell out to whom I'm going to market is where a lot of the magic takes place.

We suggest beginning your Facebook Ads project by profiling segments for each target market and submitting one ad each for editorial review. Having target segments brainstormed in advance makes the demographic research process a lot easier than planning on-the-fly. Don't get me wrong—you'll still find interesting segments, stumble upon user concentrations, and experience "aha" moments while doing the research. That said, a little organization goes a very long way.

Begin by making a list of demographic (social) segments you want to target. It makes a lot of sense to have the ad creation tool open to play around with while brainstorming targets. A Word or Excel document is fine too, for listing the segments. Using Power Editor, you can create ads and export a spreadsheet to capture your demographic research ideas. This research should be the very first thing you do—the primary driver of Facebook Ads production. In the spreadsheet, it's important to note the size of each segment because the size will affect how many impressions there are and therefore potential traffic and cost.

Here's an example of a targeting list. Be creative here. Killer targeting concepts make for killer FB ads!

- Females, age 35 and older, who like Oprah Winfrey or Martha Stewart and live in New York or Connecticut
- Females, age 45 years and older, who like sewing, knitting, or needlework and live in Australia or New Zealand
- Males, age 50 and older, married, engaged, or in a relationship and interested in anniversary presents or birthday presents
- Males, age 50 and older, married, engaged, or in a relationship and interested in love my wife, love my fiancé, or love my girlfriend (hmmm, married and love my girlfriend?).

Second Step: Create Your First Ads

Facebook has no process to save ads without submitting them for editorial approval. This is one of the greatest drawbacks to the UI and the ad building process and a serious pain in the butt. As a result, it's most efficient to submit one version of an ad for each social segment for approval at the time of research. There's no use making all the ad variations until you know that the ad copy concepts and landing pages will pass editorial scrutiny. Once the draft ads are approved, you'll be able to tweak, duplicate, build out ad variations, and resubmit.

This is a smart approach. Should an ad be rejected by Facebook editorial, much less production time is wasted because you haven't taken the time to build out additional derivative ad versions. After the first ad in each campaign is approved, you'll go back to each of the campaigns, duplicate ads, and modify them to create additional ad variations to test.

Here's the process. Open up the ad creation tool (`www.facebook.com/ads/create/`) or Power Editor and follow these steps:

1. Designate the landing page. If the landing page has not already been determined, which is common in corporation-land, designate or create a page somewhere on any website that is relevant to the draft ad copy. The most important consideration is that the landing page, even if it is a mocked-up placeholder, must be relevant to the ad copy or FB editorial might reject the ad. Once the ad is approved, you can change the landing page and resubmit. It's easy to designate internal Facebook content you administer as the ad's destination, such as a Facebook Page or an App. We'll talk about this much more in Chapter 7, "Creating Killer Facebook Ads."

2. Create the draft ad copy. The ad title, image, and body need to be sufficiently related to pass editorial review. For Sponsored Stories, the title is preset. Power Editor does not support the creation of Sponsored Stories.

3. Enter your target research. This is the fun part. Use targeting attributes to fully define the first social segment. If demographic research itself seems a bit esoteric, don't worry. You'll catch on. Chapters 5 and 6 upcoming are entirely devoted to the process of ferreting out target markets. Figure 4.5 illustrates how ads carry both the creative (headline, image, copy, etc.) and the demographic targeting.

Figure 4.5 Facebook social demographic segment and accompanying ad, Web UI

4. Set your bid. Great! Now that the demographic research and draft ads are complete, set the bid to $.01. You set the bid so low because there's no way to pause ads until after approval. So setting a miniscule bid helps ensure that ads don't accidentally run. Changing the bids later won't require additional editorial approval.

5. Pick your campaign. If you're starting fresh in the Web UI, select "Create a new campaign." Placing the order brings you to the main ads page, where you'll see the ad you've just created. Use the breadcrumbs to navigate up a level to the newly made campaign. The "run" status is automatically active, so you'll want to pause it now. Even if you miss this step, the $.01 bid will nearly guarantee that the ads won't run. Click the little blue triangle under in the "Status" column, select Paused, and then save it.

> **Note** In Power Editor, you'll have to create the campaign first to put the ad in, by clicking Create Campaign on the Campaigns tab. For each ad created, Power Editor requires you to name the ad first.

A lesson our team has learned the hard way is that ads must strictly adhere to Facebook Ads Guidelines. If an ad is disapproved, you can go back and modify it so it conforms to guidelines. Sometimes, simply resubmitting it without changing anything works. Still, it's best to start by creating one draft ad for each demographic segment. That's the routine. For now, we're only going to create one placeholder ad for each demographic segment. After approval, we'll build more ads with common targeting within campaigns for testing.

One thing about FB editorial is for certain, and that's that little is for certain. Facebook is growing fast, and editorial discretion varies from human to human. There is also likely an algorithmic screening process based on words, punctuation, and other terms-of-service considerations. Facebook does not reveal how its internal review process works, but don't give them any reasons to disapprove your ad. Check off the basics:

1. Create a headline with correct punctuation, if it is a full sentence.
2. Use full sentences in body copy. This is the official line, but not always enforced.
3. Don't substitute symbols for letters such as "$ave Money."
4. Don't use excessive punctuation or capitalization.
5. Use relevant images that somehow relate. FB is very uneven about this.
6. Use a verifiable URL.
7. If in doubt, consult the Facebook Advertising Guidelines.

Let's continue. After pausing the first campaign, move along to the next ad. Click the green button in the upper right, Create An Ad. Go through the process again for each segment on your list until there is a paused campaign with an ad for each segment.

Now you're in a good place, having laid out your campaign structure with placeholder ads after defining your social segments. Hopefully, none of the ads will be rejected. If they are rejected, no worries, you'll go back and edit them in an attempt to placate the FB editorial gods. Don't be surprised if there is little rhyme or reason to approval and rejection. On occasion we've simply resubmitted previously rejected ads without editing them, and had them approved. Go figure.

Structural Best Practices

Next, let's discuss how we want campaigns and ads laid out. Most marketers want to test more than one ad's creative to the same target audience. While it's tempting to dump a lot of ads targeting various segments in one campaign bucket, the result can be a big mess. Unfortunately, Facebook does not currently allow you to sort results by demographic group. So you can't isolate performance of ads by gender, education level, or other criteria with a few clicks of the mouse. You have to do it yourself. Setting things up with a bit of foresight goes a long way later.

Example 1: No structure, a big mess
- Food campaign
  - Pastry ad
  - Pastry ad 2
  - Steak ad
  - Yogurt ad
  - Football ad
  - Football ad 2
  - Football ad 3
- Meat campaign
  - Steak ad
  - Pork chop ad
- Beverage campaign
  - Milk ad

Note that there need not be a uniform number of ads in each campaign. In some cases, there might only be one. Remember that daily budgets are controlled at the campaign level, not the ad level.

Earlier in this chapter, we mentioned that Facebook's algorithm determines which ads in your campaigns are served. That algorithm is more optimized for Facebook to maximize its profits than for you to get coverage across all your ads equally. Because Facebook automatically rotates through each active ad in a campaign, it's really important that the algorithm is comparing apples to apples. For that reason, we want FB to consider same demographic segment to same demographic segment.

Example 2: Best structure
- Pastry campaign
  - Pastry ad
  - Pastry ad 2

- Steak campaign
  - Steak ad
- Yogurt campaign
  - Yogurt ad
- Football campaign
  - Football ad
  - Football ad 2
  - Football ad 3
- Pork chop campaign
  - Pork chop ad
- Milk campaign
  - Milk ad
- Baseball campaign
  - Baseball ad
- Cookies campaign
  - Cookies ad
  - Cookies ad 2

The more granular approach in example 2 offers several advantages, including the ability to set separate daily budgets for each campaign and work with campaigns that group completely related targets.

For more extensive campaigns, it's fine to get even more granular for the sake of separating daily budgets and separating targets that are similar but not entirely the same. Check out the following example as a great how-to:

- Football campaign 1 (college teams)
  - Football college ad
  - Football college ad 2
  - Football college ad 3
  - Football college ad 4
  - Football college ad 5
  - Football college ad 6
- Football campaign 2 (pro teams) ages 17–33
  - Football pro 17–33 ad 1
  - Football pro 17–33 ad 2
  - Football pro 17–33 ad 3
  - Football pro 17–33 ad 4

- Football campaign 2 (pro teams), ages 13–17
    - Football pro 13–17 ad 1
    - Football pro 13–17 ad 2

At any rate, build campaigns to bucket ads built on the same targeting segments.

Creating Alternate Ad Variations

If any of your ads were disapproved, then refer to the screen captures, review FB Ads terms of service for clarification, edit the ads (from scratch), and submit again. Hopefully, the ads will be approved this time.

Now that the ads have been approved it's time to create additional versions of the ads. This might mean testing different headlines, switching body copy, or moving the same body copy around in the ad. Try different combinations of copy and pictures. We've found that it's important to test at least a couple of ads, but don't go nuts by creating a zillion different samples. FB is not going to give each ad a true chance to shine in even rotation but will quickly skew toward an ad the algorithm perceives as successful.

As you can see in Figures 4.6a and 4.6b, the process for duplicating ads within the campaign is easy.

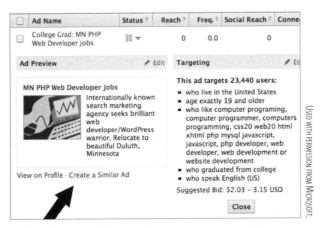

Figure 4.6a In the Web UI, click on the ad you want to copy and Create a Similar Ad.

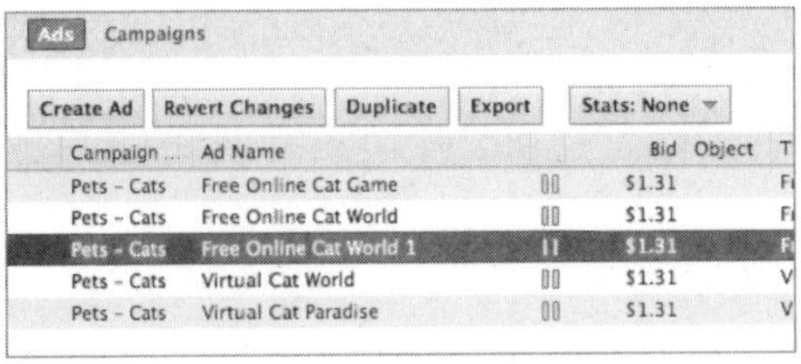

Figure 4.6b Using Power Editor, highlight the ad and click Duplicate.

The next screen should look familiar because in both the Web UI and Power Editor you arrive at the very same ad creation tool in which you created the ad the first time, only now you are editing the clone. The fields are prepopulated with the ad copy, pricing, and targeting attributes of the ad. It's an easy starting point for modifications.

Clicking the Review Ad button at the bottom in the Web UI brings up a screen in which you can rename the ad. In Power Editor additional steps are required. Go ahead and place the order using the Web UI or uploading via Power Editor. Don't worry if the bid is still only $.01. Later, when you launch the ads, you'll bid each ad out at the actual price you want to pay. As you become more experienced with FB Ads, it's reasonable to skip the $.01 placeholder bid step in the process. However, I personally still bid placeholders at $.01 because every once in a while, I thought the campaign was paused but it actually was not. We've seen expensive mistakes where draft ads ran to placeholder landing page and wasted a prodigal amount of cash. I'd rather be (in the true Minnesota vernacular) for sure for sure.

Naming Conventions

Facebook's Web UI, like that of other ad platforms, allows a marketer to sort campaigns by most columns. Power Editor does not support sorting. The All Campaigns page painfully defaults to an alphabetical sort by campaign name every single time the marketer returns back to All Campaigns, even after another sorting column was chosen previously. The same maddening reality is true within campaigns for the list of ads. This can be frustrating if you don't plan ahead for what these alpha sorts will look like.

To create Zen-like sanity within Facebook's All Campaigns page, create a standardized naming convention for campaigns such as [promotion]–[descriptive segment name] [additional targeting metric]. For example consider naming that Black Friday promotion to middle-aged women who have daughters Bfri–Have Daughters–F30-50. Name ads something like [number][headline]–[variant descriptor]. A Black Friday promotional ad might look like this: 1-GreatGifts-Alt.Body. The naming convention need not be overly complicated, just enough to communicate the essence of the demographics the ad comprises. Figure 4.7 shows simple formatting chunked out by category [HSR] [city (where applicable)][targeting].

> **Note** In the Web UI, the default name is the title of the ad. Then you can change the name of the ad without changing the title. In Power Editor, you name the ad before you create it, then you can change it.

There are no hard-and-fast rules for naming campaigns and ads. Just think ahead and create naming conventions that make sense when sorted alphabetically by campaigns or by ad names. An excellent naming convention standard is to create names that other marketers would understand with minimal explanation.

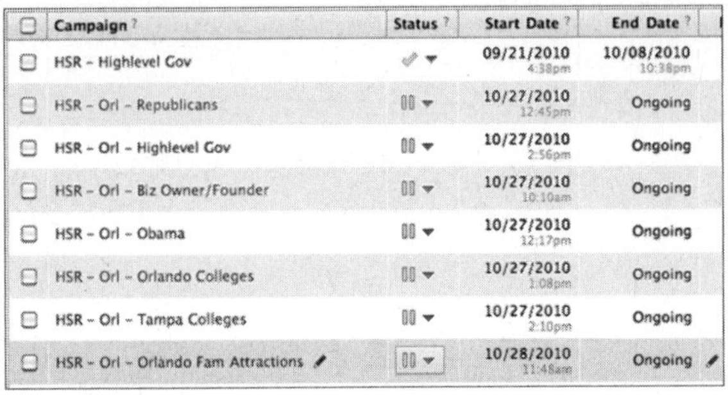

	Campaign ?	Status ?	Start Date ?	End Date ?	
☐	HSR – Highlevel Gov	✓ ▼	09/21/2010 4:38pm	10/08/2010 10:38pm	
☐	HSR – Orl – Republicans	❚❚ ▼	10/27/2010 12:45pm	Ongoing	
☐	HSR – Orl – Highlevel Gov	❚❚ ▼	10/27/2010 2:56pm	Ongoing	
☐	HSR – Orl – Biz Owner/Founder	❚❚ ▼	10/27/2010 10:10am	Ongoing	
☐	HSR – Orl – Obama	❚❚ ▼	10/27/2010 12:17pm	Ongoing	
☐	HSR – Orl – Orlando Colleges	❚❚ ▼	10/27/2010 1:08pm	Ongoing	
☐	HSR – Orl – Tampa Colleges	❚❚ ▼	10/27/2010 2:10pm	Ongoing	
☐	HSR – Orl – Orlando Fam Attractions ✏	❚❚ ▼	10/28/2010 11:48am	Ongoing ✏	

Figure 4.7 Facebook advertising interface, optimized naming conventions

The most essential take-away from this chapter is to house only ads with exactly the same targeting in each campaign. Later on, after we discuss launching the campaign and work through various optimization techniques, we'll cover moving high-performance ads from one campaign to another, including the destination campaign's targeting.

Guerilla User
Targeting Checklist

This chapter is the crux of the book. Discover how to leverage extremely personal combinations of Facebook users' traits, from professional characteristics to private predilections. Find your audience and master highly focused targeting on Facebook's social graph. We'll explain a proven targeting research system used by our team of Facebook Ads marketers since 2007. When we take on a new marketing assignment, we ask a series of questions about key performance indicators (KPIs) and potential associations to Facebook users. The checklist includes everything from magazines and books users read to occupations. Each section in this chapter offers examples of social segments.

5

Chapter Contents
Literal, Competitive, and Inferred Targeting
Occupations and Employment
Real-Life Groups and Affiliations
Real-World Publications
Online, Off Facebook
Product Categories
Classic Mainstream Interests

Literal, Competitive, and Inferred Targeting

The first step to any Facebook Ads marketing assignment is to determine the threshold for how deep you're willing to climb inside users' psyches. Are you willing to sell coupon downloads for sugary cereal to pot smokers? Trendy beach vacations to upper-crust gays? Or do things need to be more vanilla, like selling tennis rackets to users interested in tennis? Facebook Ads targeting in the hands of clever marketers can be so deep as to be considered insidious or downright creepy. Since Facebook does not police any third party's intellectual property, there may even be future legal ramifications related to certain targeting decisions.

Let's start our checklist by dividing the Facebook targeting universe into three categories: Literal, Competitive, and Inferred. Table 5.1 describes some of the advantages and disadvantages of each.

▶ **Table 5.1** The Facebook targeting universe

	Literal	Competitive	Inferred
What is it?	Targets direct relationship with the demographic segment, often keyword for keyword.	Targets competitors' fans, both positive and negative sentiment.	Targets deep personality traits of users.
Advantages	Easy to research, often better for direct-response KPIs.	Qualifies customers by known brand predilections. Killer tactic for poaching other brands' communities.	Invokes emotional response that may seed deeper engagement.
Disadvantages	Literal associations are not always realistic in FB.	May run into future legal problems. May have ethical issues now. Watch for backlash from competitors' loyal fans.	Requires a very creative marketer to map the associations.

Literal Targeting

The first stop on our checklist is to ask if there are any literal associations between our KPI and Facebook users. Literal targeting is the "vanilla" of Facebook ads targeting and is easy for most to understand. Merriam-Webster.com defines *literal* as "adhering to fact or to the ordinary construction or primary meaning of a term or expression." Literal social PPC targeting essentially means advertising to tightly interwoven combinations of a social segment and KPI. It doesn't take much imagination to theorize out that 34,900 women aged 64 and older who are interested in knitting are great targets for ads that sell knitting needles.

Targeting can be considered literal when the product, service, or other object being sold has the same keyword in its title as the Facebook segment, making the association of segment and KPI pretty much a no-brainer. That's the good news. The bad news is that literal targeting relationships between social segments and KPIs in Facebook Ads don't always exist. Sorry. For instance, *pay per click* and *PPC* are among the hottest buzzwords in the world for marketers. Still, there are very few PPC interests in FB.

Literal targeting for Facebook Ads is a stress-free way to go and usually safe ethically because it's product categories, activities, and other apparent fits we're after. There's not much left to the imagination marketing hockey sticks to young men and women interested in playing hockey. And 17- to 18-year-old girls who are interested in "Jonas Brothers Living The Dream" should be easy advertising marks to sell concert tickets for Radio Disney musical acts. These are classic examples of literal targeting.

Competitive Targeting

Our next checklist item, competitive targeting, begins the ethical and legal journey from vanilla towards cunning. Wikipedia defines *competition* as a "contest between individuals, groups, nations, animals, etc. for territory, a niche, or a location of resources. It arises whenever two or more parties strive for a goal, which cannot be shared." Williams-Sonoma might easily market cutting boards to Facebook users interested in Pottery Barn or Crate and Barrel. Apple should be able to market MacBooks to Dell PC laptop lovers, and Kellogg's Corn Flakes can take on General Mills' Cheerios for a larger spoonful of the breakfast cereal market. These brands and thousands of others can all be targeted in Facebook Ads.

There has never been a more fertile killing field for systematically picking off competitors' customers and fans than Facebook Ads. While there have already been a series of definitive appellate decisions surrounding uses of service-mark-protected keywords on websites and search engines and even in metadata, social targeting is the freaked-out Wild West of online marketing. Get it while it's hot! As of this writing, there is no case law to limit marketers, lawyers, and judges as to the propriety of targeting users who express positive or negative interests in other companies' protected brands. We doubt this frontier mentality will last legally.

But meanwhile, let us reiterate: Get it while it's hot! When targeting, keep in mind that brand interests can carry important customer qualifiers. For instance, consider luxury brands, especially if the marketing task involves high-quality goods. Those interested in luxury items tend to prefer the finer things and are willing to spend. Brands such as Mercedes-Benz, Burberry, Swarovski, Chanel, Pottery Barn (see Figure 5.1), and Van Cleef & Arpels are great examples and well represented on Facebook. From Rolex to Cartier, take aim at big spenders who are interested in the very best. Later in this chapter, we'll have a look at other potent qualifiers. Read as much as you can into what it *means* for a consumer to demonstrate "Precise Interest" in a competitor's brand.

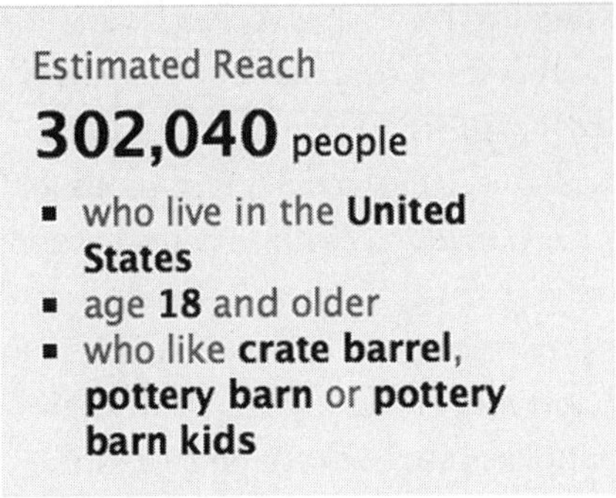

Estimated Reach

302,040 people

- who live in the **United States**
- age **18** and older
- who like **crate barrel**, **pottery barn** or **pottery barn kids**

Figure 5.1 Pottery Barn customers are ripe for picking.

In highly focused niche spaces, it's possible to target FB users interested in competitors without directly targeting competitor interests themselves. For instance, in the Internet marketing conference space, those marketing the Search Engine Strategies conference series can reach Facebook users interested in Search Marketing Expo and Search Insider Summit conferences by targeting "SEO," "PPC," and "social media marketing" interests. That's because all of the above-mentioned conference series attract attendees surrounding the same topical areas: SEO, PPC, and social media.

Negative Sentiment Toward Competitors

Colorful expressions of negativity make powerful fodder for marketers for a couple of reasons. First, we have a pretty good idea that these users are or at least were once interested in the actual products, bad experiences aside. Second, it's reasonable to extrapolate that these unhappy people may be in the market for an alternative, which we're only too happy to offer up. We'd tell Microsoft to market its underachieving Zune music player to Facebook users who hate iTunes. Don't be put off by the syntax of targeting statements. Users who express a precise interest in "[brand] sucks" mean that those users strongly dislike [brand] (see Figure 5.2).

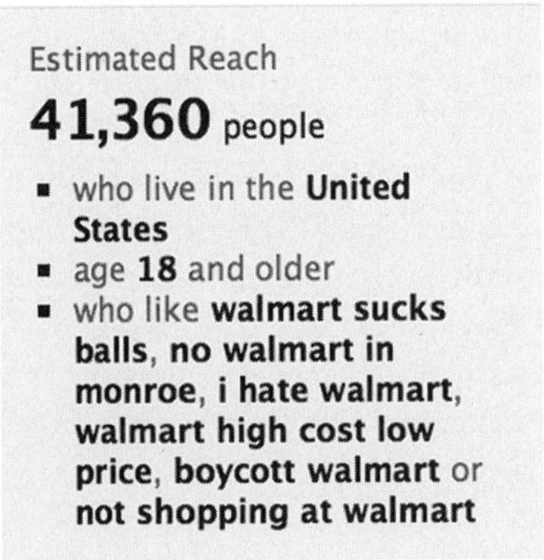

Estimated Reach

41,360 people

- who live in the **United States**
- age **18** and older
- who like **walmart sucks balls, no walmart in monroe, i hate walmart, walmart high cost low price, boycott walmart** or **not shopping at walmart**

Figure 5.2 Targeting users who dislike Walmart can be useful for marketing locally owned businesses.

Such negativity can easily be exploited with well-written ads. We've seen ad headlines that say "[Brand] Alternative," and "If You Hate [Competitor Brand], You'll Love [Our Brand]," as well as ads with other full-frontal assaults. If you're not comfortable directly challenging the opposing brand by name, there are more insidious and equally or more effective approaches. Try pushing users' buttons surrounding the *reasons* that fuel their negativity. Market Ford sedans to Toyota haters with ads reading "Gas Pedals That Don't Get Stuck" (see Figure 5.3). Try using the same keywords that users reach for in your ads. If the segment includes the word *blows*, it stands to reason that *blows* is a great word to use in the ad, even if the usage is sneakily presented as "Blowing the door down."

Are Toyotas Safe?

The 2011 Ford Ranger, Best-in-Class Fuel Economy & Big Towing Capability. Made American Safe.

© ISTOCKPHOTO.COM/GRAFISSIMO

Figure 5.3 Fictional Facebook ad for Ford targeted at people who dislike Toyota

Marketing to competitors' disenfranchised customers is nothing new, and Facebook offers lush ground to mine negative sentiment. As in life, community members are more than willing to explicitly share what bothers them about brands, including general hatred. Try typing *sucks, suck, hate, terrible, horrible, f_ck, f_cked, blows,* and other obvious negative sentiment keywords into the Precise Interests attribute box (see Figure 5.4). Use your good alpha patterns by following with a space and single letter. You'll be astounded at the cornucopia of angry consumers making their feelings known on Facebook. Keep in mind that the inconsistency of Facebook editorial comes into play as more obvious hyperbole is used in attacking other brands.

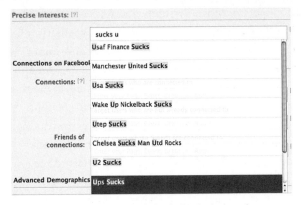

Figure 5.4 Angry consumers revealed in the Precise Interests box

Legal Considerations

Ford would probably not be willing to run the ad shown in Figure 5.3. Not only could there be a backlash from Toyota lovers, but legal action from Toyota could very possibly follow. It is reasonable to expect future litigation to define ground rules. Right now, if you're the owner of a protected mark, it's nearly impossible to police marketers who trash your brand's good name in Facebook Ads. Between the three parties—brand owner, marketer, and Facebook—the brand owner is literally the only party who does not know for certain that their brand has been invaded, unless they have extremely sophisticated reputation-monitoring tools in place. Facebook has no mechanism for brand owners to request that users' "interests" in the brand be excluded from the Facebook Ads targeting matrix. Users themselves usually have no idea they've been targeted to promote product B because of their interest in product A.

We tell our clients to expect future regulation and, therefore, to consider taking complete advantage of the ability to target competitively *now*, before the opportunity disappears. *Consider* is the operative word here. Wherever the jurisdiction to which your ads are targeted, local laws apply. Therefore, understand local laws (where you're marketing from to) and how they apply.

We have a number of clients who are simply unwilling to target competitors' brands, which we certainly support. Additionally, it's sensible to question whether such tactics are ethical, even in light of how the law might be applied. If you have any questions, check with your friendly trademark attorney.

The same legal concerns probably apply to targeting both negative brand sentiment and those interested in brands in a positive way. There is little or no case law out there to guide lawyers and marketers in making good decisions. The conservative choice is to not do anything you would not do in public. Would your lawyer feel good about you placing an ad in the newspaper that says, "We're giving customers who totally hate [brand] a 10% discount"? Maybe not, but some business people *are* inclined to undertake cutthroat tactics, or more subtle versions, under the theory that it's better to ask for forgiveness than permission. We don't presume that the ability to undertake these tactics will be possible forever, in a flurry of expected litigation. Consult with counsel. Follow the law. Remember that what Facebook does and does not allow has little to do with the law or what you can be sued for.

Inferred Targeting

Next on our checklist is inferred targeting. Inferred targeting ranges from milk-and-cookies normal to highly aggressive or even predatory. Facebook users' personal predilections are so powerful, providing such a deep glimpse at what makes them tick, that it seems like nearly an unfair advantage. To marketers, though possibly distasteful at first blush, understanding users to this great extent amounts to a deep opportunity to brand and sell things. There are many products in this world that are an easy sell to various flavors of extreme people. Just be aware that targeting deviant corners of human "interest" crosses the line for some marketers and/or their clients.

We sometimes call trips to the dark side "predatory" targeting because admittedly, we "prey" on users. That might be an extreme term, but at the very least, we certainly use available insights to profit from people in an exploitative manner. If you've ever heard "She feeds on his insecurity," "He's blinded by [keyword]," "Love junkie," or other expressions describing "slave to [something]," you understand the basis of this type of demographic targeting. Suffice to say there are very few limits to what people express to a great enough extent that Facebook identifies them as "interested" in what has been expressed. Let's go on a magic carpet ride of targeting fun, looking at segments we know tend to perform well in Facebook Ads.

General Things People Dislike

Things users dislike or even hate are not limited to brands. People are people, and most people don't like *something*! When conducting demographic research for your marketing campaigns, don't forget that disdain is a potent motivator. The University of Phoenix could tap into 2.7 million student-age young adults who hate waking up for school. These Facebook users might be cool prospects for work-from-home online university degree programs. I'd test it as in the mocked-up college recruitment ad shown in Figure 5.5.

Hate Waking Up For Class?

University of Phoenix® Official Site. Degrees Designed for the Real World. Get Started Today.

Figure 5.5 Fictitious Facebook ad for online college courses targeted at people who dislike waking up for school

© PHB.cz/Fotolia

Facebook users hate many things. Sell to people who dislike their neighbors' privacy fences and motion detector lights. Believe it or not, many men and women even hate Valentine's Day! Pray these poor, jilted souls find love, and market antiromance or lonely-person products like calendars with hot pictures, celebrity-anything, or even the local Fox station's reruns of *Cheers* and *M*A*S*H*.

Conflict and Violence

Some clients are surprised to see this on our list. We ask, "Is there anything about the KPI that leads us to believe that folks with violent interests might bite?" There are many products and services based on semi- or outright violent metaphors.

Think about it. Football, one of America's great sports, is based on systematically beating the tar out of the other team within certain rules, all in the name of claiming physical territory measured in yardage. Look at the popularity of movies and television that feature gratuitous violence. When I was a kid, I played games called "Battleship" and "Rock 'em Sock 'em Robots." Appealing to those who express an interest in violence, from the World Wrestling Federation to the whack-a-mole game on the Minnesota State Fair midway, is an "in" that often works. Interests like these abound en masse on Facebook.

We've found it's relatively easy to sell certain types of video game downloads to Facebook users interested in "killing terrorists" and "probation workers" and wish "killing was legal." Believe it or not, as of this writing, there are 14,600 Facebook users who give this information up to the targeting engine. As a disturbing aside, 7,220 of them are only 13 years old.

The video-game social segment is not the only game in town when marketing to those who love violence. We've found that such personas can be converted to a number of KPIs, including junk-food coupon downloads, lead generation for football team season tickets, paintball marketing, bars recruiting for softball teams, boxing event promotion, and many of the multitude of products and services based on violent metaphors.

Targeting examples don't even need to be as sensational to push physical-confrontation buttons in users. There are 5,240 people interested in "arm wrestling" and 1,154,140 women who are interested in "fighting." Of these women, 229,640 are over 55 years old! Do you think these older ladies might be fertile branding and direct-response sales territory for marketing divorce attorneys, facelifts, or spa services? There are 143,960 men interested in "violence." It sure might be easy to sell these guys ultimate kickboxing cable packages or football jerseys or to advertise the local butcher shop's raw hamburger promotion. Look even further to the side for inferred targeting. Figure 5.6 shows a demographic segment that certainly portends violent tendencies.

From drug lords and Crips to Emilio Escobar interests, any demographic segment that indicates conflict yields excellent insight to marketers offering products with features that either alleviate stress or feed conflictive personality traits. When we're doing demographic research to define market segments, we usually think about whether conflict and violence, either physical or psychological, may be a dynamic that could influence potential customers. Predatory? That's up to you.

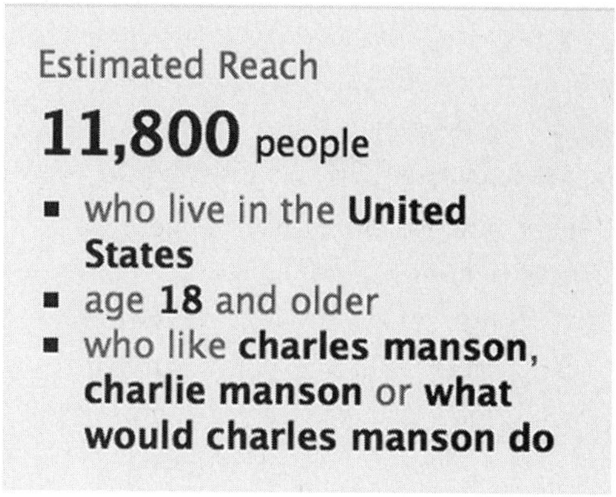

Estimated Reach
11,800 people
- who live in the **United States**
- age **18** and older
- who like **charles manson, charlie manson** or **what would charles manson do**

Figure 5.6 There are 11,800 people who live in the United States, are age 18 or older, and are interested in Charles Manson.

Legal Drugs and Medical Conditions

What can we say about people who use legal drugs? That they're uptight, wound, stressed, or challenged? Or does using legal drugs imply that people are thoughtful, taking good care of themselves, and making great choices? Only testing can tell if it's useful to market whatever you're selling to these segments, and it's often worthwhile. What we do know is that, in some circumstances, drugs and medical conditions tell us a lot about what sales pitches users may be susceptible to. For instance, there are plenty of Facebook users interested in Valium and Diazepam. Try marketing meditation music, self-help books, or any product that has escapism overtones.

Read between the lines and matriculate illness interests with gender for intriguing insights. As of this writing, 7,360 females who live in the United States are very interested in topics related to prostate cancer. Women don't have prostates, so there's an interesting cross-gender empathy here for boyfriends, husbands, sons, or fathers. So, if you're the marketing director of a hospital wondering how Facebook Ads might aid in community outreach or sales, here's your chance. Obviously, there are tons of users who have somehow been touched by illness. Tap into them for a range of marketing purposes, from charitable fundraising to promoting outpatient therapeutic radiation services.

Some medical circumstances fall into the realm of literal targeting. Diaper brands, cribs, and minivans are obviously easy products for marketing to pregnant women, men who are interested in "pregnant," and those who hate being pregnant.

More Incredible Things Users Reveal

The radical array of highly personal traits people reveal on Facebook never ceases to amaze me. The ability to target deep predilections is a godsend for marketers so much of the time. In many cases, Facebook community members "tell" the targeting algorithm things they might hardly tell another person. The following examples range from deviant to colorful. Enjoy! We're all adults here.

Advertise teasingly tantalizing images of pizza, Chinese food, or any other takeout services that deliver to the demographic segment that loves all things marijuana. Figure 5.7 includes interests of 809,740 American users. There are over one million more Facebook (author clears his throat) "users" we've identified just in the United States. We could not fit them on this page. Sell them sugary cereal late at night.

Figure 5.7 Facebook interest in all things weed

People admit to crazy things. Brand your client, the criminal defense attorney, to users who are interested in shoplifting, stealing, and larceny. Our slogan is, "Get 'em before they become criminals." Market skateboards and condoms to more than 800,000 20-year-olds who present very strong indicators that they are underage drinkers. There are so many illegally drunk students that, using the Education & Work tool, it's quite easy to separate out exactly which universities have the worst student drinking problems. Try Googling "March Madness! Which NCAA Conference Has The Worst Underage Drinkers On Facebook?" and you'll see what I mean.

Occupations and Employment

The next item on our checklist is to ask, "Are there certain occupations and places of employment that indicate a Facebook user may be interested in our KPI?" If the answer is yes, occupations can be an extremely potent targeting attribute. Next to family, profession is one of the most powerful components of an individual's identity. Occupation targeting is all the rage, especially for business-to-business (B2B) marketing, one of the classic inferred targeting techniques.

LinkedIn gets all the publicity as a *business* platform, while Facebook has been typecast as the *personal* platform. The reality could not be further from the truth. Even though in January 2011, LinkedIn finally upgraded its DIY ad platform to include specific-place-of-employment and job title targeting, we've been targeting workplaces and occupations on Facebook fruitfully for years. As far as girth, LinkedIn has about 100 million users globally on the PPC targeting grid. Facebook has about 700 million.

We work with a lot of B2B clients. One thing nearly all of them have in common is that they openly question the value of Facebook Ads for marketing to professionals. It's true that many business places block Facebook from employees. However, we serve hundreds upon hundreds of millions of impressions to off-duty professionals, who clearly are coming from a work-minded perspective as far as their identity goes. We've mined clicks by hundreds of thousands and achieved countless KPI conversions of many types.

My wife is an attorney and she tells me that even when she's off duty, she's still an attorney, legally. Legally or not, I know it's true when she tosses and turns at night about a case or a partner who's bugging her. When she reaches for her laptop at 2 a.m. to surf the latest Facebook feed updates from her sister or the kids, those sidebar ads are marketing to an off-duty attorney and are no less compelling than if she saw them between 9 a.m. and 5 p.m. Facebook Ads are insidious that way.

So, it stands to reason that if these users are not accessing Facebook during business hours on their official work computers, perhaps it's at home after hours. Hmm, must be. No matter how you slice it, business people are using Facebook at *some* time in their daily cycle, on some computer, and they're raw meat for marketers. Personally, of all the targeting attributes, I get the most excitement out of occupation targeting, because it's like getting a special "in" during professionals' personal time.

Interests Bucket Occupations

A fascinating dynamic of the Precise Interests attribute is users' propensities to self-identify their occupations as "interests." After years of testing, we've verified this phenomenon over and over. For instance, we recognize that a solid majority of the 24,660 people in the United States who are interested in music teacher, teaching music, elementary music teacher, vocal music teacher, or instrumental music teacher are actually music teachers themselves. In fact, earlier versions of FB Help pages, way back when "Precise Interests" were still called "Keywords," FB flat out revealed that a component of keyword targeting was "Job titles that users list in their Facebook profiles." Obviously, it still is. Figure 5.8 offers a classic example, electricians revealing their trade.

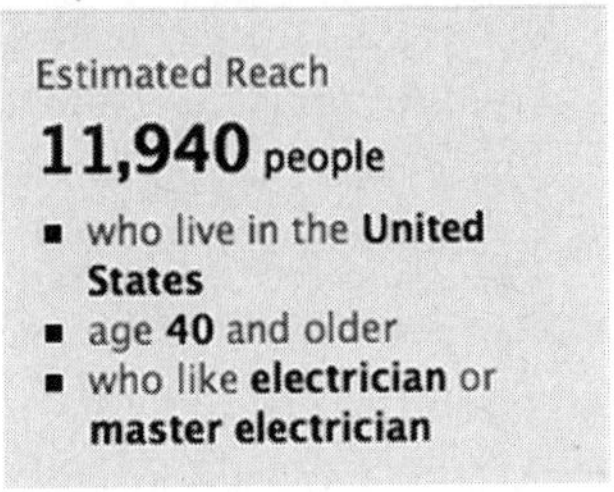

Estimated Reach

11,940 people

- who live in the **United States**
- age **40** and older
- who like **electrician** or **master electrician**

Figure 5.8 One of FB's great Easter eggs is the ability to discern occupations in the Interests bucket.

Years ago, I first discovered this surprising phenomenon by successfully signing up users in droves interested in "master electrician" or "master plumber" for free online Yellow Pages products by serving up ads that read, "Free Internet Listings for Your Plumbing Business." It did not matter that these plumbing business owners did not have Facebook all day in the field. Who cares? Maybe if they're not at work, they have more time to notice and be attracted to ads. Since then, the approach has worked over and over. Figure 5.9 is another great example.

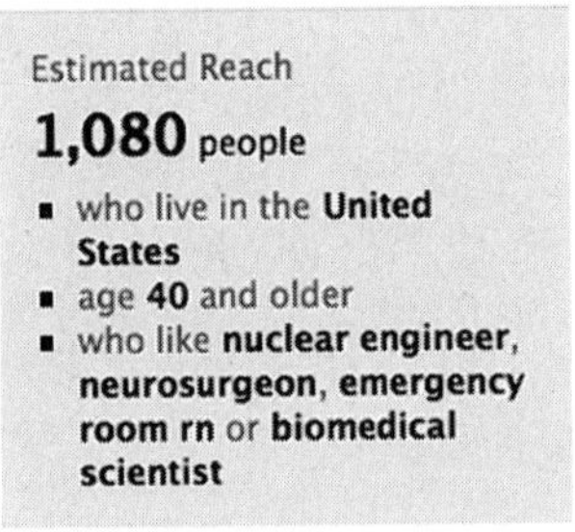

Estimated Reach

1,080 people

- who live in the **United States**
- age **40** and older
- who like **nuclear engineer, neurosurgeon, emergency room rn** or **biomedical scientist**

Figure 5.9 Mine segments targeting top-shelf professionals.

Approaching Facebook Ads targeting from this perspective provides utterly fantastic marketing tools given the site's massive penetration. In addition to the obvious—the opportunity to market tools of the trade—just think about the possibilities. For one thing, inferences can be made as to income categories. Consider the 273,360 bartenders and waitresses who probably don't have tons of money and therefore may be susceptible to budget brands or propositions.

I'd tell Foiled Cupcakes, a famous Chicago-based killer-cupcake baker, to blanket executive assistants with "Impress Your Boss with Christmas Cupcakes" at holiday time. Yep, there are 600 people in Chicago who are interested in executive assistant, executive administrative assistant, executive assistant president, and other indicative social segments. You get the picture.

The Interests bucket holds an out-and-out universe of job titles. Sell auto technicians and young machinists Metallica memorabilia, synthetic motor oil, and fishing lodge weekends. Cosmetologists are great for hawking cosmetics to. These examples only scratch the surface. Millions of people self-identify their occupations in the Facebook Ads Interests bucket. Make sure, as you create the demographic targeting grid for your marketing assignment, to ask if there are any occupational affinities that might help your KPI to success.

Places of Employment: Education & Work

Facebook users in massive numbers give up their places of employment. When targeting workplaces using the Education & Work tool, nothing is left to the imagination. When the tool first rolled out, there were not many companies available in the workplaces attribute field. Now there are tons. We've done straight-up comparisons with LinkedIn's recently released company targeting features. Facebook's ability to finger users by where they're employed is as evolved in its own way, with many companies available to marketers. In Chapter 6, we'll discuss work and education targeting with interests and other demographic attributes. For now, let's acclimate to available user data in the Education & Work tool.

Figure 5.10 shows a small sampling of the tens or nearly 100,000 Facebook users over 28 years old who work at real estate agencies around America. There are many more. Real estate agents are often real go-getters. Market products like productivity software, easy-upload video cameras, or magnetic signs for their cars. These highly aggressive professionals also need computers, snow plowing, cars, and phone service, and hey, they are also interested in going out to eat. Real estate employees are a terrific segment for many marketing applications.

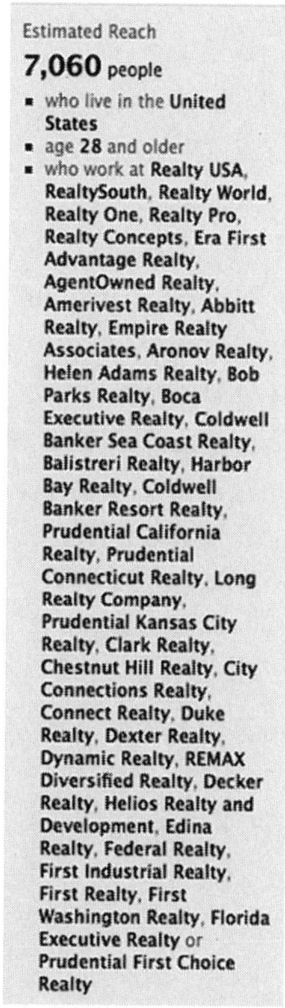

Estimated Reach

7,060 people

- who live in the **United States**
- age **28** and older
- who work at **Realty USA, RealtySouth, Realty World, Realty One, Realty Pro, Realty Concepts, Era First Advantage Realty, AgentOwned Realty, Amerivest Realty, Abbitt Realty, Empire Realty Associates, Aronov Realty, Helen Adams Realty, Bob Parks Realty, Boca Executive Realty, Coldwell Banker Sea Coast Realty, Balistreri Realty, Harbor Bay Realty, Coldwell Banker Resort Realty, Prudential California Realty, Prudential Connecticut Realty, Long Realty Company, Prudential Kansas City Realty, Clark Realty, Chestnut Hill Realty, City Connections Realty, Connect Realty, Duke Realty, Dexter Realty, Dynamic Realty, REMAX Diversified Realty, Decker Realty, Helios Realty and Development, Edina Realty, Federal Realty, First Industrial Realty, First Realty, First Washington Realty, Florida Executive Realty** or **Prudential First Choice Realty**

Figure 5.10 There are 7,060 people who live in the United States, are age 28 or older, and work at various real estate agencies.

Speaking of computers, it's easy to target folks who make, sell, ship, and support them. I'm talking about 68,880 people who live in the United States and work at Dell, Hewlett-Packard, Gateway, ASUS, Apple, Compaq, Lenovo Group, Acer Inc., Samsung, Sony, or Toshiba.

As I work on this chapter in the Detroit airport, I can't help but smile a wry smile when I think that within a few minutes, I could deploy ads aimed squarely at the Facebook accounts of 17,680 people who work at Delta Air Lines. Facebook reveals that 138,180 people identify themselves as UPS, United States Postal Service, FedEx, or DHL employees. Sell these people Sketchers Shape-ups and Dr. Scholl's custom-fit orthotics.

Interested in international B2B? Take square aim at English-speaking Facebook users living in Austria, Denmark, Germany, Sweden, or Norway who work at Siemens. You may find this fertile territory for branding KPIs. When we at aimClear visit our English-speaking B2B clients abroad, we sometimes gently market to their FB accounts for weeks ahead of time so they understand our reach and reputation before we get there. Of course, this is only the tip of the iceberg when it comes to Facebook's targeting database of employment places. I doubt most users understand how this data is used and parceled out to marketers. From B2B lead generation to literal, competitive, and aggressive business-to-consumer (B2C) KPIs, harness the muscle of this capability for fun and profit.

Real-Life Groups and Affiliations

Next on the list is to correlate real-life groups with Facebook interests. In physical life, folks cluster in groups that surround personal interests and inclinations. They interact, share, shout, complain, organize, and otherwise mingle, usually on topic. Facebook groups are fundamental to many users' experiences.

As of this writing, Facebook Ads lets you target users who belong to only groups you own and not groups owned by others, unless you are a designated administrator. If that's the case, you may ask, "Why are we discussing Facebook groups as part of an advanced targeting manifesto?" The answer is that we use groups as a metaphor for clusters of people that have real-world grouping analogies. Figure 5.11 shows the search engine results page (SERP) in Facebook for "boy scouts," revealing that there are not very many Facebook groups about Boy Scouts.

The Facebook Ads platform reveals that there are many people, age 30 and older, who are interested in "Boy Scout awards," "Boy scout leader," and other related segments. While these folks might or might not hang out on Facebook in groups, per se, we think of them as groups for the purpose of describing physical world clusters that define a social demographic.

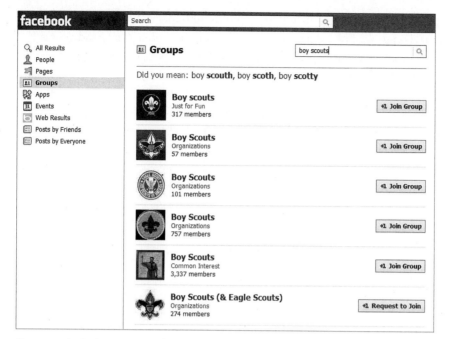

Figure 5.11 Facebook groups SERP for "boy scouts"

Just think of what we can market to tens of thousands of people who are all about Alcoholics Anonymous. Try selling these good people coffee clubs, self-help books, dating sites, smoking cessation plans, candy, and just about anything else that may be a "safer" addiction than booze. It's also easy to get AA-going Facebook users to try gym memberships, tweetups, and energy drinks. Use your imagination. You'll find those in various types of recovery useful to many marketing assignments (Figure 5.12).

Figure 5.12 Facebook ad for fast food targeted at people interested in "Alcoholics Anonymous"

Don't forget trade groups, including unions. Hundreds of thousands of Facebook users belong to commercial trade organizations of some type. The key here is to start with what we know about physical life and the institutions that people define themselves as part of. Think about what it means to belong to Rotary or Kiwanis. Rotarians literally are not allowed to miss meetings without making them up or paying. These are committed folks. Figure 5.13 shows trade group members who are typically very well connected in the community and are especially predisposed to participating in, if not organizing, charitable and volunteer events. Businesses often sponsor their employees by paying dues for these types of organizations. Do your homework to understand identifying traits for each real-world group as well as the large-scale community events each group sponsors. More and more, even these old-school groups are using Facebook events, fan pages, and other tools as promotional tools. Since the Facebook Ads targeting tool is great at picking up what users are really interested in, the more Facebook tools used by Rotarians and Lions Club members, the more their annual events can be targeted via the Interest.

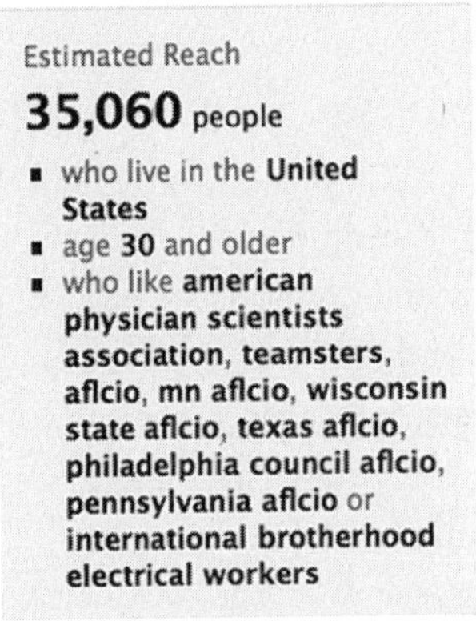

Estimated Reach

35,060 people

- who live in the **United States**
- age **30** and older
- who like **american physician scientists association, teamsters, aflcio, mn aflcio, wisconsin state aflcio, texas aflcio, philadelphia council aflcio, pennsylvania aflcio** or **international brotherhood electrical workers**

Figure 5.13 Trade groups are an excellent place to target professional affiliations.

I love the pesticide-free foodies for inferred targeting fodder. They're eager to consider anything that feels natural. From environmentally friendly clothing to ecotourism, no pesticides are used when we advertise to those interested in "Maine Organic Gardeners Association," "Michigan Farm Bureau," or "National Farmers Union." There are tons of geo-specific intent implied in such segments, with city and state names included. When these Facebook users come up from their root cellars to connect with fellow earth people, sell them any "goodness" brand, food, or product feature you can think of that is somehow organic in nature.

Animal rights groups are a rabid and committed bunch. From PETA to the Humane Society, these are people who come from a place of serious values, sensitive about balance and keenly aware of justice. Play on their empathy. Consider sales pitches where, instead of offering a $.50 coupon on a $3.85 box of Koala Crunch cereal, you tell them that for every box of cereal sold, you'll donate $.25 to the

Save-the-Something-or-Other-Tree-Fish-Bark-or-Wilderness-Amazon fund. It'll cost you half as much as coupons, they'll be twice as happy to purchase, and no dolphins will be harmed in the implementation of this campaign.

Speaking of groups, sons and daughters, there is no shame in marketing to those who love Jesus, Buddha, or L. Ron Hubbard. Throughout the history of mankind, legions of fanatically driven people have marched from one end of the earth to the other, all in the name of their faith. If Facebook users love their religion enough to register on Facebook's social graph, their feelings are probably intense enough to lend inferred marketing insight.

Those passionately interested in religion can often be shepherded toward solutions fitting with their values, which we've seen evidence of over the years. Coming from a "commitment" standpoint works, too. One thing's for sure: Saying "Jesus" in an ad gets the attention of people who are passionately committed to Christ.

Also, subtly (or not so subtly) quoting visual icons from various faiths can be incredibly effective. We've served ads with subtly watermarked Jewish stars, guys with beards and white shirts, and semi-Buddha-looking round-bellied fellows with Wayfarer sunglasses. A word of advice: Be very respectful or fully understand potential ramifications of the irreverent tack you're embarking on because backlashes can occur. Be careful, have fun, live long, and prosper.

Though there is no "faith" attribute with which to target users, it's easy to locate the following American religious proclivities:

- 903,800 Catholics
- 310,340 Mormons
- 77,120 Muslims
- 215,480 Jews
- 70,600 Buddhists
- 19,720 Hindus
- 12,520 occult

Real-World Publications

As part of demographic research, we always ask, "What do your customers read?" Magazine and book interests present wonderful opportunities for marketers because, by their very nature, such publications are focused topical hubs. Sports lovers read *Sports Illustrated*, entrepreneurs read *Inc.*, and well-off travelers read Condé Nast magazines.

This level of topical aggregation portends communities that are predictable in their interests. Finding lovers of magazines and books in Facebook offers yet another level of user targeting that the shrewd demographic researcher should not miss.

Popular search engines Google and Bing can play an important role in the discovery of books and magazines. Say my marketing assignment is to market equestrian items. If not for a Google search of "Horse Riders Magazine," I would not know to check the Interests bucket for *Horse & Rider* magazine, a publication that interests over 9,000 people in the United States.

Magazines

Most mainstream magazines and periodicals are franticly trying to crack the Facebook code, somehow attempting to participate. Magazines try several common approaches. Figure 5.14 shows how the efforts can be turned to targeting users who follow a magazine onto Facebook, some of whom you might not be able to target otherwise.

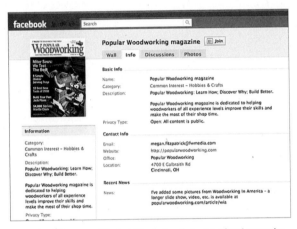

Figure 5.14 Get around the inability to directly target others' groups by marketing to users who are interested in the publication.

Most magazines push a certain percentage of their content to their Facebook Wall, start a fan page, or otherwise attempt to leverage the fact that their readers are probably on Facebook. Some just put up a brochure-type page and run little promotions to get their readers to fan it. Whichever way, it's a double-edged sword. The publication gets the benefit of users who flock, mingle, share, and interact with each other, often with the magazine's community manager. Marketers get bountiful access to users who are aggregated under a nice topical umbrella.

As a rule, Google and Bing are great friends to the Facebook demographic research process. In this case, Google and Bing are great places to find magazines. A quick search for "woodworking magazine" is easy pickings, in both the ads at the top and organic search results below (see Figure 5.15).

The first Google results I found are super-easy to cross-reference for Facebook Ads targeting. Figure 5.16 shows how search engine results can guide marketers to real-world magazines. It's easy to follow the SERPs into FB Ads to see if there are any interested Facebook users. It's nearly comical (or at least ironic) that the harder these magazines work at search engine optimization (SEO) to show up higher in Google and Bing SERPs, the easier it is for marketers to locate and target their fans in Facebook!

Figure 5.15 Google search engine results page for the query "woodworking magazine"

Figure 5.16 Targetable FB users who are interested in themed offline publications, as discovered in search

Figure 5.17 reveals that people in this world still love paper magazines. Lots of them hang out on Facebook.

Figure 5.17 Magazines are not dead by a long shot.

There are thousands of magazines in the Facebook Interests bucket. To find them, use those good alpha pattern skills you learned earlier. To find specific magazines, type the word **magazine**. Yes, make it singular. Then type other letters—first **A**, then **B**, and so on. To go deeper, type vowels after consonants and vice versa. Facebook Ads give up particular magazines pretty easily. Start with the word **magazine** and then start typing keywords that define the marketing niche you seek (see Figure 5.18).

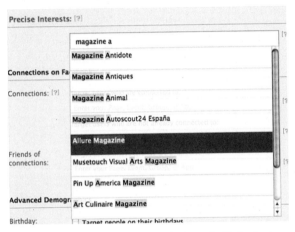

Figure 5.18 Building our Interests bucket for "magazine" in Facebook

Don't only be literal when thinking about magazines; rather, reason out the activities and personal traits that surround the niche. Hunting magazine readers don't just buy camouflage clothing and boots. They might also be interested in video games, pickup trucks, beer, and snowshoes. The key here is to get inside the heads of topic-specific readers. Here are some representative lines of thinking.

Boating magazine readers probably have money or they could not afford to have boats to be enthusiastic about. They also likely live near water, are out in the sun, enjoy fishing and/or waterskiing, and have to clean the boat's deck. Boaters need places to dock the boats as well as to store them in the winter if they live in a northern region. They need to sleep when they take breaks if the boat is not a sleeper and usually drive their car to the water, take a bus, take a taxi, or pull their boat trailer with a big car they own. There are *a lot* of products embodied in the end-to-end experience of being a boat enthusiast. Think about that in light of 2,120 people who live in the United States; are age 25 and older; and interested in boating magazine, powerboat magazine, yachts magazine, or yachting magazines. I know! Sell them nautical-themed scarves and Nantucket placemats.

Musicians and recording engineers who read magazines are a technology-savvy and creative bunch, often expressive by way of countercultural activities, and are killer targets for digital distraction products, like games. Sell 'em iPad cases because musicians tend to be early adopters of technology. Many musicians are mostly broke from buying those iPads and portable digital recorders, so marketers can offer them discount oil changes, gas coupons, movie ticket bulk discount plays, online video rentals, and anything "bargain" early adopters might love.

When it comes to muscles, there are many people who read bodybuilder magazines. These readers' bodies are their temples, so come on, brothers and sisters, let's pray! Target these beefcakes to market suntan oil, vacations on volleyball beaches, singles cruises, and cool sunglasses.

Let's practice using Bing and Google to find real-world magazines. A quick Bing search for "body building magazine" helped me find *Iron Man Magazine* (Figure 5.19). Figure 5.20 exposes 1,760 people who live in the United States, are age 18 and older, and are interested in *Iron Man Magazine* on Facebook.

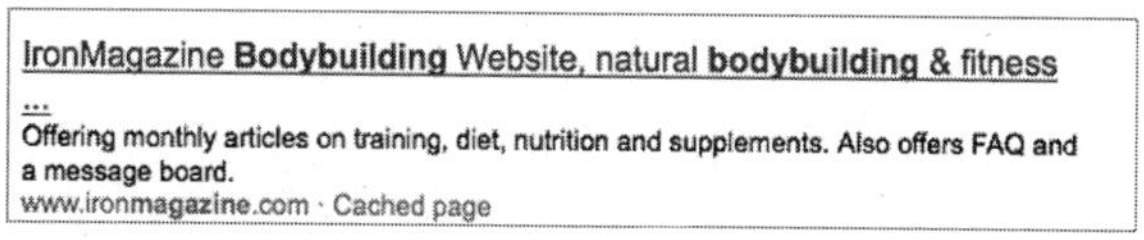

IronMagazine **Bodybuilding** Website, natural **bodybuilding** & fitness
...
Offering monthly articles on training, diet, nutrition and supplements. Also offers FAQ and a message board.
www.ironmagazine.com · Cached page

Figure 5.19 Check Facebook Ads to see if search engine results are reflected in available demographic segments.

Estimated Reach

1,760 people

- who live in the **United States**
- age **18** and older
- who like **iron man magazine**

Figure 5.20 *Iron Man Magazine* as an interest in Facebook

Google and Bing often make suggestions at the bottom of the SERPs. Figure 5.21 shows how I found *Flex* magazine, which interests 4,600 people who live in the United States, age 24 and older in Facebook.

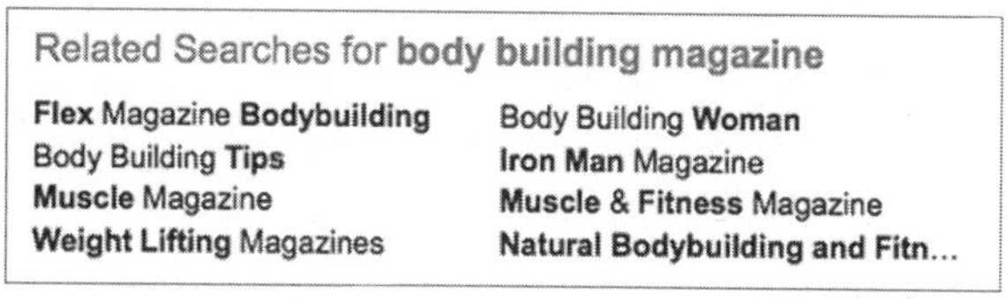

Related Searches for **body building magazine**

Flex Magazine **Bodybuilding**	Body Building **Woman**
Body Building **Tips**	**Iron Man** Magazine
Muscle Magazine	**Muscle & Fitness** Magazine
Weight Lifting Magazines	**Natural Bodybuilding and Fitn**...

Figure 5.21 Bing related searches for "body building magazine"

Magazines come in all flavors. Magazines about parenting, writers, travel (Figure 5.22), equestrian, gourmet food, snowmobiles, and pop music are just a few examples of the thousands of category-specific publications discoverable in the Facebook Ads targeting tool. The periodicals that Facebook users read are a rocking data point to help marketers spawn ideas for category-based demographic segments.

Estimated Reach

14,160 people

- who live in the **United States**
- age **18** and older
- who like **travel magazine, sidetrip travel magazine, conde nast traveler magazine, wanderlust travel magazine, costa rica traveler magazine, travel agent magazine, travelife magazine, baja traveler magazine, travelgirl magazine, travel around world magazine, business traveler magazine, travel club magazine, liberia travel life magazine, ultimate travel magazine, travel plus magazine, voyage travel magazine** or **travel magazines**

Figure 5.22 Users interested in travel as expressed by interest in magazines are easy to hunt down using FB Ads.

The fact that these periodicals still exist in the physical world and that users feel strongly enough to express the interest literally on Facebook means that some community members must have a strong bond with the topical space. We always ask ourselves, "What magazines do our customers read in the physical world?"

Books: Subjects and Authors

Favorite books are also a known targeting attribute, as admitted in previous versions of the Facebook Ads section. Users also give up favorite authors in the Interests bucket. As such, book interests are essential instruments in the marketer's toolbox. Since books are also intrinsically about *something*, they're terrific topical hubs, gathering points that serve as clear signals to those willing to follow clues. Here are some examples to start your explorations.

Travel books from Frommer's, Lonely Planet, and Berlitz reveal a lot about Facebook users, especially the geographically specific editions. It's easy to sell airfare, hotels, and guide service with the destination of Rome to readers of *Rick Steves' Rome*. As usual, aim to get past the literal. Travelers consume many products and services aside from the aforementioned, which stem directly from travel itself. Sell elegant or rugged luggage sets, travel accessories such as airplane neck pillows or noise-canceling headphones, foreign-language software such as Rosetta Stone, or even recipe books for ethnic cuisines.

Legal-novel consumers enjoy intrigue and intellectual stories. In the United States alone, there are nearly one million faithful John Grisham readers. Filter them by age and education status for maximum effect. Law schools can dangle early registration and the prospect of becoming a badass prosecutor in front of die-hard Grisham fans in their senior year of pre-law at select international universities. In the United States, there are 471,460 Facebook users under the age of 25 who are Grisham fans.

We've had a lot of luck targeting romance-novel readers. Might as well face it, those addicted to love are suckers for certain marketing approaches. There are nearly 700,000 American ladies explicitly interested in romance novels and authors including Danielle Steel and Nora Roberts. Sell these women slightly tacky yet popular designer products, such as Vera Bradley accessories, Brighton jewelry, bedazzled bookmarks, and Mary Engelbreit calendars, planners, and stationary. We might also sell them books, blogs, classes, and audio books on finding the right partner or improving relationships (because I *guarantee* their personal love life isn't living up to those books). Facebook reveals that 24,180 men have the same interests! Hmmm, what can we sell *these* guys?

Those interested in reading self-improvement books are probably open-minded or, at least on some level, seeking brutal truths, like it or not. These propensities can be leveraged with a little thought. Sell them gym memberships. There are a lot of Facebook users attracted to inspirational books such as *Chicken Soup for the Soul*. Sell these people classes or seminars led by motivational speakers, blogs, and other books about family values and inspirational memoirs.

There are so many categories of books that we nearly always include exploring them as part of our targeting checklist. Here are a few more ideas to start your journey.

- Smart investing books
- Oprah's Book Club books
- Epic fantasy novels
- Cookbooks
- Books by Stephen King and Dean Koontz
- Erotic literature
- Alternative classics (Gen Y)
- Books Gen Y loved as kids
- Motherhood and pregnancy books

Online, Off Facebook

Facebook is not the only website on the Internet. There's a world of websites that community members frequent when they're not using Facebook. Ironically, Facebook users express the significance of off-Facebook sites they're interested in *on* Facebook. Mashable, a leading social media blog, has the interest of 225,660 users, as indicated by the Facebook Ads Interests bucket.

Specialty websites that are about searchable databases of information, e-commerce storefronts, and mashups of both are outstanding resources to inspire

Facebook targeting. Why? These users are not just out to consume content, as customary in the old-world magazine model. They choose sites to find actionable information and are ready to seek, preview, select, and purchase. *Purchase* can mean consume free content after the user locates it. In other words, they have their conversion pants on.

Recipe sites are a great example. Users visit them for the last-minute Shrimp Pad Thai recipe or to figure out oven time for a turkey. They search the sites with keywords, select the recipe, and, well, get cooking. They come to the recipe site ready to act—print it off, bring the laptop into the kitchen, send the recipe to Mom, or, otherwise, bookmark it.

Many Facebook users are interested in AllRecipes.com or MyRecipes.com. Trust me, they're suckers, given the right pitch, for kitchen supplies and pots and pans. Penzeys would have an easy time reminding them to refill the spice rack with Adobo or Barbeque 3000. Throw in free shipping as part of the ad and they'll whip out the credit card, clicking to the landing page for a one-touch conversion.

Another great example is travel sites. There are 10,080 people in the United States, age 30 and older, interested in Orbitz. From airport parking to extra chargers for the iPhone or Evo, travelers are in spending mode as they plan trips and hit the road. It's possible to tell a bit more about the trips Facebook users might take by targeting those interested in niche sites that focus on European travel interested in Dohop .com or Venere.com. International travelers are a slightly different bunch. Tailor the ads to push global buttons for products like antimicrobial wipes, single-serving coffee bags, or online currency-exchange calculators.

Eight Ways to Brainstorm New/Creative Targeting Options

Here's an outline of key targeting ideas from this chapter, for easy reference. They represent themed topical hubs, which reflect social constructs humans tend to cluster around. Don't forget to use Google and Bing to locate these gathering places.

1. Occupations

2. Publications customers read

3. Websites customers consume

4. Traditional groups and affiliations

5. Trade affiliations

6. Places of employment

7. Education and degrees

8. Books and authors users read

9. Users' personal predilections (inferred)

Beauty product e-commerce websites attract fanatical buyers. Stay literal and sell them every beauty product under the sun, from mascara to mud facials. Cross over into spa vacations by marketing to 54,260 females interested in TotalBeauty.com, BeautyTicket.com, or Beauty.com. Note that such e-commerce verticals are rife for competitive tactical marketing. TotalBeauty.com, BeautyTicket.com, or Beauty.com could easily market to each other's Facebook customers.

Again, Google is a good friend when looking for e-commerce sites. Figure 5.23 shows internal search results for "cosmetic sites," *within* a site I found on Google. The listings give up great ideas for beauty sites I'd never heard of. I'm a guy, after all! A trip through the Facebook targeting tool quickly revealed tens of thousands of users interested in LoveToKnow.com or Sephora.com. Right on!

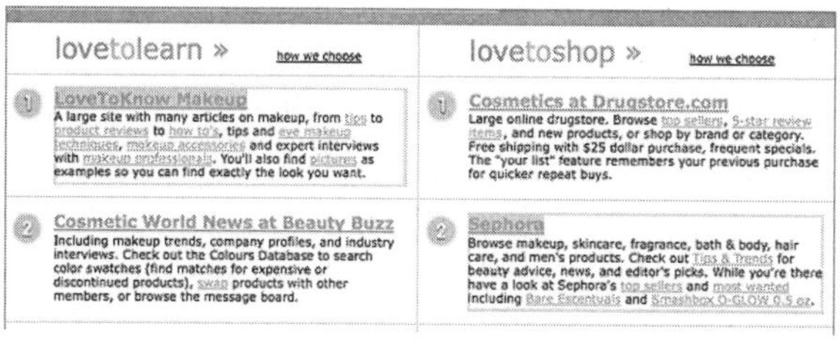

Figure 5.23 Site discovered in SERPS for "cosmetics sites," gives up list of cool site ideas

Website fans rock as demographic segments for marketers. Pitch wedding clothing, stockings, veils, centerpiece ideas, honeymoon ideas, and DIY invitation applications to MyWedding.com lovers. Cracked.com users are easy marks for other lowbrow/humor/time-waster sites and videos. Find hard-core DIY fanatics who seek out websites for insight as to how things are built or fixed. From streaming music to arts and crafts, targeting users based on sites they're interested in is an awesome strategy for Facebook Ads marketers.

Applications

Users who download and otherwise install applications to Facebook or their local desktops demonstrate a willingness to engage and (duh) use applications! Identifying consumers of specific applications is a great research node for Facebook Ads marketers. This is especially useful if the product you're marketing happens to be an application itself.

The pool is very large. Facebook reveals that 7,277,760 people in the United States age 24 and older are interested in Farmville; 4,618,960 people are interested in Mafia Wars or Mafia Wars Stone Cold Pimps (Figure 5.24). We already know these users are willing to download an application and use it. We have every reason to believe that they're willing to download and use another application.

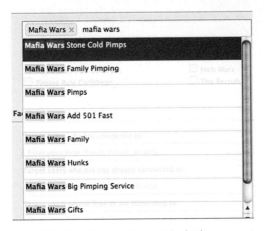

Figure 5.24 Mafia Wars as an interest in Facebook

The style of application says a lot about the user, adding more definition. Users who play the What Rapper Are You? app are a much different lot from those who play (Lil) Green Patch or Fairyland. There are apparent targeting ideas for users of Wedding Calculator or fashion applications. Games are applications, too, and are great targeting fodder. Over 3.7 million American users play or covet pet games like PetVille and Pet Wars. From book applications to travel maps and mobile Twitter clients, look to web applications for targeting insights.

Product Categories

Product categories are a more general manifestation of particular brand names. Marketing to categories is fruitful because we can sell products and services that are related to the categories. As opposed to finding folks interested in Monopoly, which is a specific product name, the product category might be expressed as liking board games.

Wine and wine tasting are other great examples. Clearly, this is a fitting segment for Zagat or any winery for marketing. For perspective, there are about 1.2 million Americans interested in wine, wine tasting, good wine, good bottle wine, or good wines. Don't forget varietals (Figure 5.25) and your favorite wineries. There are 24,920 people in the United States who are interested in cabernet franc, cabernet sauvignon, merlot, pinot days, pinot grigio, or pinot gris. Trust me. I can tell you from experience that nearly every varietal is represented on Facebook. You can sure find wine lovers on Facebook, and selling to them is both fun and profitable.

Figure 5.25 Various wines as interests in Facebook

Another example is motorcycles. With over 1.6 million people in the United States directly expressing their enthusiasm for motorcycles within Facebook, the segment is outstanding territory for many KPIs. Sell them heavy metal concert tickets, leather chaps, helmets, and bug strainers for their teeth (just kidding!).

Power tool interests are terrific clues that tend to indicate that users like taking on self-directed tasks (Figure 5.26). Don't forget the ladies. In the United States, there are 10,900 females interested in power tools. These women are any DIY company's dream, from HGTV home repair shows to recruiting for Home Depot's Home Improver Club. They probably own their own home, too. Also, with some hunting, there are granular power tool categories to discover.

Precise Interests: [?]

Pneumatic Drills ✕

Figure 5.26 Pneumatic drills as an interest in Facebook

There are tons of product categories, and it's standard for us to include investigating them as part of our targeting worksheet. Here are a few more ideas to start your voyage:

- Home decorating
- Punk rock
- Snowboards
- Fabric and sewing
- Gay travel

Product Usage Examples

One of the easiest targeting hacks in the world is to zoom in on what the product you're marketing is used for. Sure, it's a no-brainer that tennis ball manufacturers can market to those interested in tennis. It's important to be creative with product categories. For instance, if the marketing assignment is to market 10-inch Calphalon frying pans, target users interested in family meal planning, cooking, and family meals. Look to the use of products for obvious marketing segments to leverage.

Here are some other examples of targetable product categories:

- Scrapbooking
- Pets
- Cooking
- Baking
- Gardening

- Cleaning and organizing
- Photography
- Painting

Software

We look to commercial software brands for clues about what products a person might buy. Interest in software can reveal many things about a Facebook user, including hobbies, interests, methodology, profession, and, sometimes, family role.

Use of Adobe Photoshop, an expensive and high-end graphics program, usually means we're working with a student or professional artist who's a cool blend of creative, technological, and commercial. Otherwise, the user would not invest in such an expensive and specialized package. Avid Audio's Pro Tools is a professional audio-recording software package used in conjunction with specialized hardware. Only serious hobbyists, audio students, or professional musicians use Pro Tools.

The secret, again, is to look past the literal and into associated characteristics of the persona. Users of voice-recognition software like Dragon and MacSpeech are early adopters, often interested in new concepts, especially technological ones. If your brand is one of the many promoting video contests, make hay with Facebook users interested in video-editing software like Final Cut Pro and Windows Movie Maker. Users interested in RootsMagic genealogy software may be moved by history and susceptible to FB Ads fundraising to save your town's historic building.

Classic Mainstream Interests

Of course, there are tons of "normal" folks that use Facebook. We call them "Leave It to Beaver" segments because the following social groups speak to timeless values. We're talking about interests that you could tell your sweet grandmother about.

Cooking/baking from scratch, canning/preserves/jam, picking flowers, star gazing, making soap, weaving, tatting (lace making), and chopping wood are examples of classic "value" interests. Others can be categorized.

Leisure Activities

The activities that users participate in can reveal quite a bit about what advertising lures they might gnaw on. To start, there's literal inventory like the tools needed to participate in the endeavor. There's usually some type of related inventory. Bocce ball, camping, pool, and horseshoes are great examples.

Sports are a dominant force around the world. Aside from the actual equipment used, many sports have rituals attached. From tailgating to schnapps at the ol' ice-fishing hole, target sports lovers with marketing campaigns in Facebook. Don't forget to get out of the literal and into the sideways when targeting.

Another interesting dynamic surrounding sports lovers is the distinction between attending sports as a spectator and actually playing the sport. A sports clothing manufacturer probably can't sell athletic shorts to a 65-year-old NBA fan, for example. So, in these cases, you'll have to combine targeting criteria to make sure you hit the market segment you want.

Facebook users often reveal whether they're spectators or players for you. It's reasonable to extrapolate that those interested in "olympics" or "american league baseball" are onlookers. Reciprocally, someone interested in "playing hockey" or "wrestling coach" probably likes to rough things up. Look for such distinctions.

Pretty much any sport you can think of is represented in Facebook, by both fans and players. Segment by age and educational status to find sports fanatics of all stripes, from girls who play high-school soccer to NHL players. As examples, there are 764,520 U.S. users interested in lacrosse, 161,800 in field hockey, 348,300 in kickball, 1,340 in dogsledding, and 1,774,380 in softball.

Don't forget that it's easy to aim for specific teams and players, both college and professional. We like targeting individual players' endorsement deals and products associated with them. For instance, it's a great trick for sneaker brands to target Michael Jordan fans because MJ is so deeply enmeshed with the Nike brand.

Entertainment and cultural activities are huge to many Facebook users. They're interested in television, movies, concerts, board games, casinos, libraries, and going out to eat. Make sure to associate the specifics with the leisure categories. For every movie, there are actors, there are specific casinos like Harrah's and MGM, and concerts have styles such as classical and musicians such as Sting and Pavarotti.

Use this information as leverage for marketing efforts by choosing images you know will appeal to each segment and micro-segment and words you think users will relate to. Classical music lovers may react well to the word *sonata*, and the 8,000+ users interested in "Lincoln Center Theater" probably get to New York from time to time and have disposable cash. Find any insight possible. Leverage it in your marketing.

Political Orientation and Pundits

From Arizona militia members to Mothers Against Drunk Driving, political viewpoints can be excellent data points for marketers and their wares. The world is so polarized now, and communication is so global by way of cable television and social media, that viewpoints abound. From mainstream to radical, the cornucopia of political inclinations and the figureheads who prattle on about them is astounding.

Millions of Facebook users can be targeted by their political affinities by way of the Interest, from Glenn Beck and Ann Coulter to Chris Matthews and Rachel

Maddow. Here's the checklist we run as we ask the question, "Do certain political interests make these Facebook users susceptible to our KPI?" Here are some ideas to start your journey:

- Conservative broadcasters such as Rush Limbaugh
- Progressive broadcasters such as Ed Schultz
- Comedian and political revolutionary Jon Stewart
- The moderate, middle-of-the-road voters
- Conservatives and Republicans, such as Sarah Palin lovers
- Liberals and Democrats for instance, President Bill Clinton or President Barack Obama

Figureheads

Figureheads are not limited to politics. There are many leaders—notable, political, and other types—who impact our world in various ways. Their followers tend to be on Facebook and can lend insight to savvy marketers.

For instance, if you're the advertising agency for the Memphis Orpheum Theater showing a production of *For Colored Girls Who Have Considered Suicide When the Rainbow Is Enuf,* there are a dismal 240 people in Memphis interested in that specific show on Facebook. However, try targeting people who are interested in the inspiring memoirist Maya Angelou. That ups the reach to 10,980 Facebook users within 50 miles of Memphis.

Say you're the marketing director for Gap Adventures looking for people who love adventure travel. Sure, there is inventory for a variety of "adventure travel" interests, but consider targeting a bit more abstractly; 23,380 people in the United States are interested in Sir Richard Branson, billionaire, humanitarian, and adventure travel junkie.

From Marc Cuban to Julian Assange to Smokey the Bear, figureheads make for killer Facebook Ads targeting.

Family Roles

There is little else as compelling to humans as family relationships. While Facebook Ads does not have a "family role" targeting module per se, we can glean a whole lot of insight about who's who from the Interests bucket with a little research. Most advertisers don't seem to think about the Facebook Ads gender-bender phenomenon.

Some ladies just say straight out, "I'm a mother" on Facebook, and likewise for some dads. It's fairly easy to filter the gender of their children from the Interests bucket. This makes a difference to marketers because of subtle dynamics—stereotypically, in how product owners feel parents interact with children of either gender. Though far from absolute, surely some family stereotypes come from somewhere.

As a father of two daughters, I'm about as progressive as they come, and I certainly have done different things, on average, over the years than my counterparts who are raising boys. How do I know this? At figure skating classes, ballet academy, dance line, jazz dancing, Red Cross babysitting classes, and a number of other activities, I simply did not see very many boys. Also, sports are segregated by gender as kids get older, and often, girls use slightly different equipment. Girls have different biological equipment, also. I'm fairly confident that (remember, I'm talking on average here) not many moms and dads take little Johnny, Billy, or Dave out to buy first bras, tampons, eyeliner, and Victoria's Secret panties.

There's no doubt that marketers sell differently to children based on their gender. The ability to identify parents raising boys and parents raising girls is a fantastic perk if it happens to matter to the marketing assignment. Figure 5.27 illustrates how easy it is to keep these kinfolk functions in mind when looking for market segments.

Why Not Spoil Them?

Go ahead & spoil your nephew and niece! Find the toys they'll go nuts for here.

© Pavel Losevsky/Fotolia

Figure 5.27 Facebook ad for aunts who love their nephews and nieces

With a little creativity, it's no trouble to figure out precise family roles:

- Women who "love being mommy" or "love being mom"
- Moms interested in "playing with my sons"
- Moms interested in "playing with my daughters" or "taking care of my daughter"
- Men interested in "being dad" or "being a great dad"
- Dads interested in "my son plays baseball" or "my son is my life"
- Dads with daughters, males who are interested in "I love my daughter" or "playing with my daughter"
- Grandparents interested in "my grandchildren"

Family roles get even more granular and include various combinations of grandmothers, grandfathers, grandsons, granddaughters, aunts, uncles, nieces, and nephews. At holiday times, these highly focused segments are mighty powerful tools for e-commerce jockeys selling gifts.

Also, don't forget FB's new Broad Category targeting feature, which allows Facebook advertisers direct access to Family Status:

- Baby boomers
- Engaged (<6 months)
- Newlywed (<1 year)
- Parents (all)
- Parents (child: 0–3 yrs)
- Parents (child: 4–12 yrs)
- Parents (child: 13–15 yrs)
- Parents (child: 16–19 yrs)

Ideas, Ideals, and Beliefs

Human beings are a passionate lot, likely to go to the mat for ideas, ideals, and beliefs they deem crucial. Qualifying users as potentially disposed to a marketing pitch, based on deeply held inclinations, is the stuff of serious social media PPC marketing. As part of the research process, ask what you can sell Facebook community members passionately interested in these ideas, ideals, and beliefs:

- Traditional marriage
- Euthanasia
- Pro-life
- Pro-choice
- Abolish death penalty
- Stem cell research
- Support troops
- Pro same-sex marriage
- Equal rights
- Human rights
- Homelessness
- Salvation Army
- Haiti support
- Save Darfur
- Mental health initiatives
- Stop hunger
- Autism
- General philanthropy
- Community activism

Of all the segments we've marketed to over the years, "green" is a group we've come back to over and over because they are willing to buy so many products based on peripheral aspects like packaging, country of origin, and pure ingredients. We've successfully advised clients with marginally valuable products to focus on the green aspects, which subsequently spun semi-crap into gold. That's how powerful these social segments are.

By and large, users don't really seem to understand exactly what claims of natural, organic, sustainable, eco-friendly, and other bytes for which companies do or don't require various degrees of government certification to make the assertions. It's bad marketing to not seek out product characteristics that potentially meet the needs of these users who are out there in force. Remember that it's not even necessary that products be green. It's often just as effective to have the appearance of being green, under the guise of supporting green initiatives.

Many products and services are fractionally green, allowing marketers to share truths about components that meet factual criteria to support the claims. "Natural sugars" and "recycled packaging" don't say much about the other ingredients or the disgusting fleet of diesel trucks that deliver the products to stores. Reciprocally, the "environmentally responsible shipping program" tells a customer little about the marginal junk the product is made up of. Big brands usually have "claims" documents with legally approved messaging regarding aspects of the products and services. However, we often need to remind our clients that there are "ins" to be had in the marketplace and to consider what aspects of their products might warrant another look.

Believe it! There is a veritable universe of creative targeting ideas for marketing. Take in the examples provided and chew on them. Much more important than the specifics of the few segments I've highlighted, I hope you're inspired to look deeply at contextual targeting in a whole new light. This chapter is meant as a starting point for your own creative explorations and uses, mining the bottomless personal interests of nearly 700 million users—the largest online sampling of humans in history.

Mastering Compound Targeting

Now that we've taken Facebook's ad creation tools for a tactical targeting spin, let's explore more complex combinations of attributes to achieve an even higher level of demographic focus. This chapter is meant to spark creativity by adding more layers of targeting. For instance, we'll combine things users are interested in with their location, workplace, and age to clarify possible susceptibility to marketing propositions.

So, fasten your seatbelt and let's find creative combinations of attributes to gain even more insight into clusters of Facebook users. Let this be the start of your compound targeting adventure.

Chapter Contents

Age, Interest, and Gender Mashups
Workplace and Precise Interest Amalgamations
Education and Interest Amalgamations
Sexuality, Relationship Status, and Interests
Country + Language + Interest Combinations

Age, Interest, and Gender Mashups

As men get older, the toys get more expensive.

—Marvin Davis

You know you're getting old when all the names in your black book have M.D. after them.

—Harrison Ford

Stacking attributes in combination puts the personality in personas. There are 11 high-level targeting attributes available to Facebook marketers, including age, sex, precise interests, connections, birthdays, interested in, location, relationship status, languages, education, and workplace. Each attribute is especially powerful on its own and in combination with others. Unless you find a magic Broad Category, precise interest targeting is the way to go. As deep as the universe of creative targeting concoctions is, this chapter will only scratch the surface. It is my hope that the examples herein serve as a jumping-off point for your own creativity.

Say it's Chanukah time and you're marketing an e-retailer. Targeting Alzheimer's disease interests might make a lot of sense, including the interests in Figure 6.1. In the United States, UK, and Canada, among English speakers, there are about 79,000 users interested in Alzheimer's disease, be it by associations, societies, a cure, research, or information. This requires a little imagination, so let's roll up our sleeves and indulge in some fun inferred-targeting speculation.

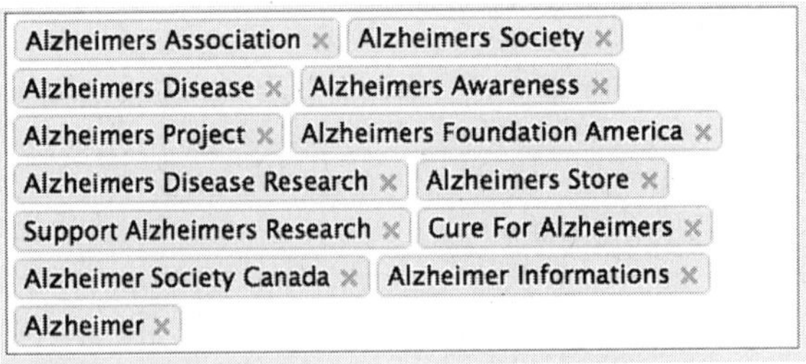

Figure 6.1 Facebook Interests bucket: Alzheimer's disease interests

Only 540 13-year-old Facebook users are interested in Alzheimer's, which stands to reason. Not many 13-year-old kids have parents who suffer from Alzheimer's. Their grandparents may be too young, on average, to be afflicted, or the situation might not be on these teens' radar. Also, 13-year-olds don't have credit cards or buy things online themselves. Alzheimer's disease interests, filtered by 13-year-olds only, are not a particularly inviting segment to marketers.

However, there are more than 12,000 users who are 20 or 21 and interested in Alzheimer's. Is there a "why" we can infer from this age filtering? Well, not many of these Facebook users are married or have kids of their own, so we're not talking about spouses or offspring yet. Unless it's early-onset, it's unlikely the Alzheimer's interest is about a parent. More likely, a biological or adopted grandparent, older than their parents, is top-of-mind for this interest/age combination. The point here is that it's reasonable to infer that these users feel emotional about an older person in their lives.

The premise is that if a 20-year-old person is sensitive enough to care about Alzheimer's, then they won't want to forget older loved ones at holiday gifting time. A 20-year-old is old enough to buy online but young enough to be tardy in gift buying and, on average, broke. At holiday time, advertise products that might make a sweet gift for grandfather/grandmother types, and make sure to use quirky pictures of older people with an instant-gratification-low-budget-by-email pitch, like those in Figure 6.2, because all or most of these factors should resonate to maximize the possibility of a sale.

Email Grandma's Gift Now!

Late with that holiday gift? Email the perfect mushy gift to make grandma swoon. 58 instant gifts for under $20 bucks

Forgot Grandpa's Gift?

Nooo, Late with that holiday gift? 58 instant gifts for under $20 bucks. Email Gramps' the perfect mushy gift to make him swoon.

© Yuri Arcurs/Fotolia

Figure 6.2 Fictitious Facebook ads for grandparent gifts

Chanukah gifts aren't the only product or service for which the Alzheimer's interest would prove useful. Let's say the assignment is to market an assisted living facility. For example, 38- to 55-year-old users interested in Alzheimer's might be facing the reality of helping their older parents through the end of their lives. Filter the segment further by only marketing to folks from Beverly Hills, California; Burbank, California; Brentwood, California; Palm Springs, California; Sausalito, California; Napa, California; Sonoma, California; Nantucket, Massachusetts; Minnetonka, Minnesota; Miami Beach, Florida; Boca Raton, Florida; Captiva, Florida; Steamboat Springs, Colorado; Vail, Colorado; Vale, North Carolina; Hilton Head Island, South Carolina; or Manhattan, New York. The communities in these cities are rather affluent, so it's reasonable to assume that the users have enough money and would consider solutions that involve significant expense. This segment may well be susceptible to "Do the right thing for mom and dad"–style messages for KPIs branding upscale assisted living homes, concierge services, home health care, or a bonded private nurse service.

The 67-year-old and older Alzheimer's-interested Facebook users who live in affluent communities may be thinking about an ill spouse or friend, or even the end of their own life. I would tell the Mayo Clinic or Massachusetts General Hospital to undertake very sensitive branding, offer free one-on-one informational phone calls and other supportive services to these older users. Most hospitals need endowments to flourish. Market unconditional care and love to the senior community. You never know, users may remember to bequeath money in their will.

Serve an ad like that in Figure 6.3 to widowed female users 66 years and older who live in expensive communities and are interested in any type of serious cancer or illness, which is fatal a high percentage of the time. If the husband has passed, there is a great chance that the disease that killed him is the cancer expressed in her profile. At age 67+, she won't live forever and might consider leaving money in his name. If he's currently dying, the request still works really well. She may be interested in discovering the services Mercy offers, which will lead to a greater relationship over time.

In Your Heart He Lives

Mercy Hospital offers free Outreach programs to Families dealing with liver Cancer. Bequeath so that We can help others in His Name.

© Andrew Gentry/Fotolia

Figure 6.3 Facebook ad for Alzheimer's disease Interests bucket

As a rule, age and gender are terrific clues as to what roles human beings play and to motivations. The 73,000 males under age 17 who are interested in topics related to "boy scouts" and "boy scout patch trader" are probably scouts themselves (Figure 6.4). This is the REI demographic. These boys are good marks for KPIs ranging from Outward Bound summer programs to ROTC training for college scholarships. There are 8,820 users of both genders in the 30–55 age group who are probably parents of scout-age teens or were in the Boy Scouts themselves. Ask yourself, "What does being the middle-aged parent of a Boy Scout *mean*?" The 1,040 55- to 64-year-old females interested in "boy scouts" may be either the proud grandparents of a Boy Scout or, well, cougars (older women who are interested in young men). All kidding aside, grandparents of responsible kids tend to buy savings bonds, airplane tickets to come visit, and computers for high school graduations.

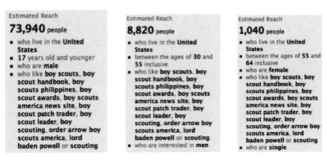

Estimated Reach
73,940 people
- who live in the **United States**
- **17 years old and younger**
- who are **male**
- who like **boy scouts, boy scout handbook, boy scouts philippines, boy scout awards, boy scouts america news site, boy scout patch trader, boy scout leader, boy scouting, order arrow boy scouts america, lord baden powell** or **scouting**

Estimated Reach
8,820 people
- who live in the **United States**
- between the ages of **30 and 55 inclusive**
- who like **boy scouts, boy scout handbook, boy scouts philippines, boy scout awards, boy scouts america news site, boy scout patch trader, boy scout leader, boy scouting, order arrow boy scouts america, lord baden powell** or **scouting**
- who are interested in **men**

Estimated Reach
1,040 people
- who live in the **United States**
- between the ages of **55 and 64** inclusive
- who are **female**
- who like **boy scouts, boy scout handbook, boy scouts philippines, boy scout awards, boy scouts america news site, boy scout patch trader, boy scout leader, boy scouting, order arrow boy scouts america, lord baden powell** or **scouting**
- who are **single**

Figure 6.4 Facebook segments for Boy Scout interests

The takeaway here is that in its most simple presentation, age alone is a reliable qualifier. There are more than 13,000 Facebook users in the United States, of all ages, interested in "biomedical scientist," "biomedical engineering," "biomedical research," and similar endeavors. As you learned in Chapter 5, the Interests bucket can be a strong indicator of what users' professions are. Obviously, the grown-up crowd would be a better age segment to brand biofeedback, neurofeedback equipment, and supplies. They could be the supervisors or teachers. I don't think there are a lot of 14-year-olds in the market for EEG, qEEG, EMG, temperature, GSR, and heart rate products.

Finally, mashing geographic location can be more than just playing rich city/poor city. Rochester, Minnesota, is home to the Mayo Clinic. While there are other medical centers in Rochester, Mayo is by far the biggest, employing thousands of physicians. There are 40 people in Rochester over age 25 (old enough to be a fellow) who are interested in "cardiologist," "journal invasive cardiology," or "cardiology fellow." These individuals are very likely Mayo doctors and their fellows. As a side note, all of them identify themselves as married.

Workplace and Precise Interest Amalgamations

LinkedIn gets all the ink about business, but Facebook can be a fertile place for high-impression, super-focused professional touches. While LinkedIn only recently baked in advertisers' ability to target in a grid of job titles and companies, we've been doing it for years with Facebook Ads, working between the Workplaces bucket in the Education & Work attribute and the Precise Interests bucket. In other words, select a workplace and mash in a precise interest. Since it's the *and* operator in between, you're locating users who work at a specific company *and* have a clarifying interest.

Targeting Politicians

Up for some snazzy political lobbying? As Figure 6.5 shows, there are exactly 100 Facebook users who self-disclose they work at the United States Congress, are at least 39 years old, and are interested in "senate." That's striking because there are exactly 100 senators in America, two from each of our 50 states, and the youngest at the time of this writing (Mike Lee) is 39 years old. A coincidence? Whew, talk about micro-branding!

Estimated Reach

100 people

- who live in the **United States**
- age **39** and older
- who like **senate**
- who work at **United States Congress**

Figure 6.5 Facebook segment for the Senate

Targeting Media Influencers

Facebook Ads rocks public relations media outreach. The notion of targeting influencers in the form of journalists is just an awesome idea. There are 92,300 employees of

Gannett, *USA Today*, the New York Times Company, or *Chicago Tribune*. Sixty of them reveal they're interested in screen actors guild foundation, Roger Ebert, Pauline Kael, Screen Actors Guild, online film critics society, "film criticism, or film review.

These interests speak to such an entertainment insider focus that we can common-sensically speculate that these users are entertainment-reporters and critics. This is another terrific example of a micro-segment that would be brilliant for media relations KPIs. How much is a good review worth in *USA Today* or *The New York Times*? Before a show can be reviewed, journalists must be made aware of it. Try reinforcing the press release announcing the summer concert tour or new movie release by foreshadowing the event quietly to reviewers.

Occupation Targeting (Facebook's Hidden Jewels)

LinkedIn gets all the attention for occupation targeting (as mentioned earlier), even though it's roughly one-sixth the size of Facebook globally. Though there's no official method to target occupations in FB, we know users reveal their job titles in the Interests bucket. This can be incredible useful for B2B marketers. Have a look at Figure 6.6. I've typed the word *manager* into the precise interests attribute, followed by the letter *g*. Try this with the other letters and words following the word *manager* for an excellent glimpse of users revealing their occupations in the Interests bucket.

There are 281,040 Facebook users in the United States who reveal that they work at Walmart, Target, Kmart, or Sam's Club via the Education & Work tool. Of them, 14,880 identify as a type of manager via the Interests bucket, as shown in Figure 6.7. Combining Interests bucket occupations with places of work in the Education & Work tool is a classic Facebook Ads B2B targeting technique. From human-resources-hiring campaigns to brand-brainwashing campaigns for senior buyers, this targeting tactic is a winner. Facebook is remarkably juicy toward the lower end of the job title food chain. Assistant managers, for example, are users who might not hang out on LinkedIn. There are only about 50 million users in the United States using LinkedIn, but over 140 million in Facebook. There are certainly job title/workplace combinations to be targeted in Facebook that can't be mined in LinkedIn.

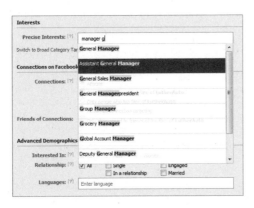

Figure 6.6 Users give their occupation with specificity in the Interests bucket.

Figure 6.7 Facebook segment for manager types

Check out other job title words as well. There are more than 164,000 flavors of receptionists in the Interests bucket. Receptionists don't make a ton of money, so they're great plays for seasonal budget items. With more than 90,000 U.S. users over the age of 40 identifying themselves as CEO, CEO founder, CEO owner, or chief executive officer, there are some monstrous advertising opportunities available. Sure, cross-referencing these power users with company names like Raytheon, HP, or Starbucks will yield you targeting clusters that are fewer than 20 people. Great! Well, what do you expect? Companies don't have many executives of this station. Microtargeting is the new black!

Mashing up the Interests bucket with the Workplaces attribute is good for more than just identifying job titles. Some workplace affiliations are somewhat implicit in the job description by their very nature. Out of the 240 users who self-identify as working for the Food Network, 120 of them are interested in "cooking shows" and "cooking channel." Promote your McMinnville, Oregon bistro to this killer microsegment with soft-touch branding ads every few days over the course of a couple of months. Thank customers for the recent tasting win in San Francisco or the Beard Award nomination. The good workers at the Food Network control an incredible amount of America's perception of what restaurants are worthy. A notable feature of this strategy is that marketing to a 120-person microsegment is extraordinarily inexpensive.

There are many construction companies, contractors, high-tech companies, defense contractors, hard-core industry firms, public institutions, and just about every other type of company you can think of in the Workplaces tool. From science teachers, foremen, club tennis pros, and nuclear physicists to opera singers and prostitutes, the Interests bucket has it all. Use your ingenuity to define personas by mashing up the two tools. Dial in geographic attributes and age for greater clarity, à la Figure 6.8.

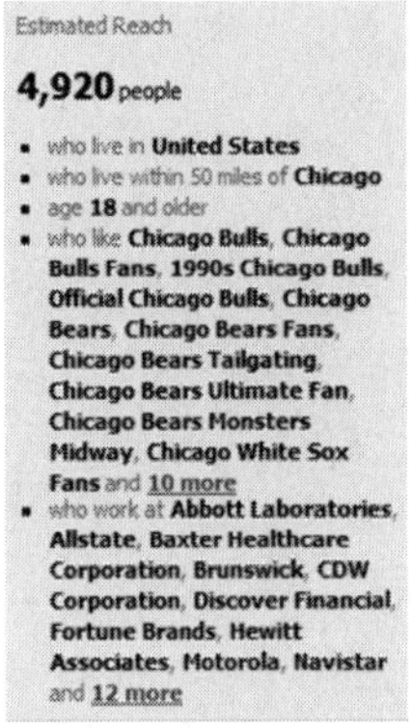

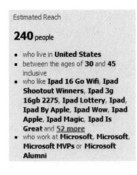

Figure 6.8 Facebook segment for Chicago sports lovers with mashup qualifiers

As with all Facebook targeting, think about the ecosystem surrounding workers. What products do they use? Forty-seven-year-old drivers traversing the frozen northern plains need road snacks, gloves, lock deicers, and lip balm, and they might be ready to upgrade their GPS. A women's varsity soccer coach in Alabama (works for the school system and interested in "varsity soccer coach") uses deodorant, wicking clothes, and water bottles.

The only limit to combining segments by this method is the sampling size. The estimated reach gets low pretty fast, so plan on working with very large workplaces or long lists of smaller ones, such as the example in Figure 6.9. Don't be surprised if it's not always possible to segment any further than the workplace and interest combination. That said, happy hunting out there in workplace land!

Figure 6.9 Facebook segment for Apple lovers who work at Microsoft

Education and Interest Amalgamations

Facebook was born to and among college students, so it stands to reason that the community is stuffed with college-related data. As the site expanded to high schools and, later, to anyone, "anyone" came to include students at all levels of education, professors, teachers, and alumni. The education targeting attributes are located in the Education & Work area.

High School Students

Ironically, some of the least specific targeting available to advertisers is high schools. Facebook has seemingly neutered our ability to reach specific high schools by making it impossible to identify individual schools. One would assume that this decision was made by Facebook brass to avoid criticism about privacy and young teenagers. Even if you could target specific high schools using the Education bucket, this isn't necessarily the most reliable way to access that demographic. Not to worry—it's fairly easy to narrow targeting down to an individual high school and its students, subdivided by what class they're in.

Looking at the demographics makes me suspicious. There are 23,080 13- to 14-year-old kids who self-identify as being in college. Fewer than 100 of them are interested in "mesa," "calculus," "math," and "science," which I would expect. Clearly, there are issues targeting this group. There are 340 14- to 18-year-old high-school kids in my boyhood hometown of Chelmsford, Massachusetts. Hmm, that's for all *four* classes. CHS has over 1,000 students. Fewer than 20 17- to 18-year-olds in Chelmsford are in college, so what gives?

Probably the rest of the high-school-age kids in Chelmsford don't have Facebook accounts, don't designate the school they attend, or lie about their age. You decide. At any rate, the point here is that you don't need a "high school" option to generally target high-school-aged kids. Just targeting the age and geography is enough for marketing purposes. In fact, choosing "high school" from the Education tool is more likely to limit the users you see. I don't care whether they're in high school if they're the age I'm looking for.

Let's get back to marketing. The younger the person, the more impressionable they are. However, many underclassmen don't have credit cards, so e-commerce and any KPIs requiring immediate use of a credit card are not usually real. Eighteen-year-olds are most likely to drive and have jobs, so they're potentially susceptible to a wider range of commercial KPIs.

High-school-aged demographic segments, which is what we should focus on, are potent when it comes to generating leads for colleges, specialized trade schools, universities, summer camps, driver education, clothing brands, free applications, concert tickets, and many other items. Within 50 miles of Chicago, there are 7,000 kids between 14 and 18 interested in "playing guitar," "singing in band," "writing songs," "writing music," "songwriting," and other such things. These kids are raw meat for a Minneapolis-based music and audio recording post-secondary school willing to serve ads that offer to help prospective students "Become Your Inner Rock Star."

College Students

College is an entirely different game. Students have their parents' money and, in many cases, earn their own. Think about your own experience when you were college age. So many college students think they're the smartest kids in the world about pretty much everything, believe they are indestructible, are focused (in many cases) on the biological drive to reproduce, and are experiencing the first true independence of their lives. Nearly all of the standard literal, competitive, and aggressive Facebook Ads targeting tactics apply, along with some add-on goodies.

First, college kids are seasonal creatures, even more so than adults. Their lives rotate on a quarterly, semester, and annual basis. It's easy to sell Daytona Beach hotels in advance of spring break to about 150,000 single college kids between the ages of 19 and 21 and interested in "spring break"–related things. Take a different approach and market the same destination and products to "bikini babe" interests to males in the same college-age group and "hot guys with abs" to the reciprocal female group. College kids are all hormones, which seem to be even more pronounced when they're single.

Another classic approach to college-student marketing centers on the academic experience itself. There are 141,880 Facebook student users in the Ivy League who are at Harvard, Yale, Princeton, Columbia, Cornell, Dartmouth, Brown, or the University of Pennsylvania. The targeting tool lets us choose a range of graduation dates. About 37,560 are scheduled to graduate with the class of 2012.

While Facebook allows us to enter a major to filter the graduation class by program of studies, usually individual or small groups of colleges are not a large enough sampling, and the results are under 20 people. However, head up to the Interests bucket and you'll find hundreds of Ivy League undergraduate seniors interested in "premed society," "journal invasive cardiology," and "surgeon." We've seen a biomedical engineering device manufacturer committed to a long-term branding program to impact these future physicians' perception of certain technologies and products. Use ads to offer these students resources to assist their career passage and bond with them for life.

Facebook is the HR recruiter's heaven. A timeless advertising play is to target specific programs of study across all colleges, sometimes segmented by geography. Out of 6,286,420 college students who graduate in either 2011 or 2012, 137,200 are studying to become nurses. Roughly 680 of them are studying at an institution in New Orleans, 260 of them are single, and within that single segment, 200 are men. Obviously, that gives super insight for HR recruiters looking to relocate graduates. Remove the graduating class restriction to include all four years and there are a couple hundred students fitting the other criteria that are also interested in cold-weather activities like skiing, ice skating, snowboarding, and ice fishing. This may betray a predilection to recruiters from northern states. I've seen this approach work over and over. How deep are you willing to go?

Alumni

It's also possible to target college graduates by the school they attended, program of studies, and of course, other Facebook Ads attributes such as age, geography, and interests. There are 80 women over age 30 who are interested in women and graduated from Yeshiva University (rabbinical college in New York). These are radically intellectual and spiritual women who could easily be the nucleus of a grassroots viral campaign.

We often use paid social advertising to light organic fires in Facebook, where a seed group of targeted users ignites a viral blaze. These rabbinical lady-leaders may well be amenable to any product that is about justice and heart, such as fair-trade coffee, organic products, social justice events, and political books. Tap this segment as a potent nucleus. As proven by the Egyptian uprising in early 2011, a *single* Facebook user is enough to spark a revolution that changes our planet's course. Use the Education tool in conjunction with other attributes to define core target groups to seed viral campaigns.

Let's not miss the forest for the trees. If I'm Zingerman's, the iconic Ann Arbor mega-deli, the 184,360 people who graduated from University of Michigan look like pretty tasty bits. Zingerman's might consider capitalizing on former students' sweet memories of hot-pastrami sandwiches and caramel brownies by marketing mail-order treat boxes at holiday time.

Finally, in the Education & Work bucket, it is technically possible to combine education and workplace for über-filtered results. In many or most cases, samplings are way too small to build even microsegments of any use. Still, there are 260 college students who identify themselves as working at the New York Times Company, the *Washington Post*, the *San Francisco Chronicle*, or the *Boston Globe*. Are they interns? There's no way to be sure, but I'd be totally interested in hiring grads who have experience at big-city newspapers.

Sexuality, Relationship Status, and Interests

There is a lot to be said regarding relationship status, sexual preference, age, and interests. The targeting implications are limited only by astuteness, as advised by stereotypical clichés and reality. The truth is that there are truly humans of every stripe. Being male, female, straight, gay, married, engaged, or single may or may not be markers for anything. I know married gay people who love to travel more than straight people... and vice versa. There are responsible and reckless heterosexuals and homosexuals who have precise thrill-seeking activities-interests and those who don't. Even if a Facebook user hides relationship status on their profile, that user's data is still in the targeting grid for marketers. Facebook targeting, while not empirical, reveals intrinsic user characteristics. Please keep in mind that nothing in this book is meant to take a position on anyone's sexual orientation. Everybody's beautiful, in their own way.

Interested In (Sexual Orientation)

One of the most compelling usages of sexual orientation expressed as "Interested in" (not to be confused with, "Precise Interest targeting" or the "Interests bucket") is our ability to tailor ad creative to its recipient. Men who prefer men may be more amenable to pictures of hot guys who are slightly younger...or older in ads. College women who prefer men and present precise interests that include reggae music and Bob Marley may be susceptible to messages that say "Ya' man" and feature zoomed-in glamour shots of Rastafarian dudes with dreadlocks. Sell these ladies coconut-flavored lip balm, hemp products, swimsuits, incense, maxi dresses, beaded curtains, soy candles, big fuzzy leg warmers, portable tents and chairs for concerts, and organic skin care.

Usually, we test to learn whether users in social segments have a proclivity for images that are distinctly similar to or from different their personal affinities. If branding a high-tech office product to 53-year-old male logistics professionals, it's hard to speculate whether a picture of their female administrative assistant in a pretty dress is the image that will push buttons as opposed to an image of another middle-aged dude or someone who looks like Jesus.

The Selig Center Study (African-American, Hispanic, and Asian-American buying power), U.S. Census estimates, Witeck-Combs Communications, and MarketResearch.com (GLB buying power) indicate that the gay and lesbian market is the most affluent and loyal group of all. The thinking goes that they are statistically less likely to have children and associated expenses, especially dual-household-income gays in relationships. Target 2,640 women who prefer other women, are 24 years and older, are in a relationship, and have "food wine," "wine," "wine tasting," or "wine spectator" precise interests. You may find this to be a fabulous microsegment for KPIs surrounding travel, cooking classes, salsa-dance lesson DVDs, and designer body sprays.

Relationship Status

There are roughly 8 percent more women users on Facebook in the United States than men. Yet there are only 1,583,640 men versus 2,369,060 women who admit to being engaged! Is this embodied in gender stereotypes, that men don't want the world to know they're taken? This may or may not be true, but in my experience, it's usually not men who are deeply involved in selecting wedding gowns, bridesmaid dresses, and hair salons. Obviously, cliché male and female heterosexual roles define what sorts of products can be marketed to this crowd. Men tend to be susceptible to pitches invoking his love for her, and women for ideas for pampering her special man. Couples getting married usually go on some sort of honeymoon, which is not always planned at the time a user changes their profile to read "engaged."

Age comes into play in choosing appropriate targets. There are 54,440 women and men over the age of 62 who identify themselves as being engaged. It's sweet to note that about 26,000 of each gender own up to being engaged, meaning older guys are happy to record their committed status as part of their profile. Again, the difference is far greater than the 8 percent male/female differential in FB. Sell engaged couples honeymoons, wedding cakes, and self-storage. Older couples might be interested in classified listings for garage sales, realtors, and movers since they may be consolidating two homes into one.

About 8,860 single women over age 45 are interested in "not getting cheated on," "cheaters are not real men," or "real men don't cheat or lie or abuse women." It stands to reason that these ladies may have had a difficult experience in a relationship. This segment might be a good prospect to market daytime television personalities like Oprah Winfrey, self-help gurus like Dr. Phil, books, motivational tapes, and quickly prepared meals for one.

For real insight into the power of mashing up relationship status, interest, age, and gender, all we need to do is look at those same interests through the eyes of a very different targeting set. There are 7,520 married men over the age of 30 who are absorbed in exactly the same "real men don't cheat" interests. Obviously, this presents a much different type of individual. Perhaps they are defending their wives' honor by expressing themselves as defenders of virtue. These men might be interested in religious retreats, yard tractors, power tools, purity books, and golf clubs.

Country + Language + Interest Combinations

We live in a brave new connected world, where physical separation is no longer a barrier to many marketing activities. If Facebook were a country, it would be the third-largest on Earth. For the purpose of segmenting marketplaces, we can now market to everyone who speaks a certain language worldwide. At aimClear, we're fond of saying that we're going to market to the "Country of [Language]," the "Country of Spanish," for example. Targeting populations of similar-minded users who speak specific languages and share common interests is now as easy as a few hours of research and production. Marketers can compare the creative and cost-effectiveness of various bids and sales pitches to similar populaces spread across the globe. Gosh, it's an amazing time to be alive.

Iconic pop culture brands that don't require translation are fabulous targeting assets. What could we sell to the "Country of U2/Spanish," shown in Figure 6.10? There are 115,200 Spanish-speaking Facebook users who are interested in "U2," "U2 fan," or "U2gigscom," and live in the United States, Spain, Mexico, Chile, El Salvador,

Argentina, Costa Rica, Belize, Honduras, Colombia, Panama, Uruguay, Paraguay, Ecuador, United Kingdom, Dominican Republic, Canada, Guatemala, Peru, Bolivia, or Nicaragua. It does not take much imagination to sell U2 accessories, but how about Bono-style sunglasses or edgy T-shirts about human rights?

Facebook limits the amount of countries we can bucket to 25 entries, I suppose to limit our ability to easily target users globally all in one shot.

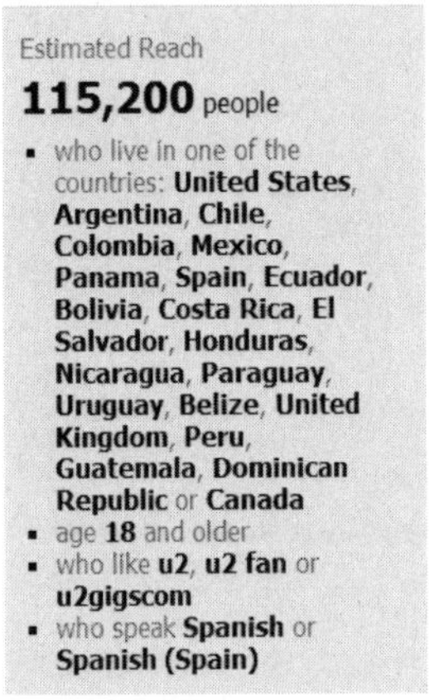

Estimated Reach
115,200 people
- who live in one of the countries: **United States**, **Argentina**, **Chile**, **Colombia**, **Mexico**, **Panama**, **Spain**, **Ecuador**, **Bolivia**, **Costa Rica**, **El Salvador**, **Honduras**, **Nicaragua**, **Paraguay**, **Uruguay**, **Belize**, **United Kingdom**, **Peru**, **Guatemala**, **Dominican Republic** or **Canada**
- age **18** and older
- who like **u2**, **u2 fan** or **u2gigscom**
- who speak **Spanish** or **Spanish (Spain)**

Figure 6.10 Marketing to the "Country of Spanish-speaking U2 lovers"

Not to worry! Just create campaign and ad structures to accommodate splitting countries. You'll find it's an advantage to track cost and performance by individual and/or clusters of countries. There are a number of different approaches. We separate by either language or country, depending on whether we target multiple languages in a single country or not. This is how we handle segmenting by language:

Spanish campaign
- Spanish ad 1: Mexico
- Spanish ad 2: Mexico
- Spanish ad 3: Mexico
- Spanish ad 1: Spain
- Spanish ad 2: Spain
- Spanish ad 3: Spain

Italian campaign
- Italian ad 1: Italy
- Italian ad 2: USA

The alternate approach is to segment campaigns by country as opposed to language, as follows:

Mexico campaign
- Spanish ad 1: Mexico

- Spanish ad 2: Mexico
- Spanish ad 3: Mexico

United States campaign
- Spanish ad 1: USA
- Spanish ad 2: USA
- Spanish ad 3: USA
- English ad 1: USA
- English ad 2: USA
- English ad 3: USA

There are over 35 million Facebook users who profess to speak perfectly fine English, who do not live in the United States, UK, or Canada. Sydney, Australia, bustling cosmopolitan jewel of the southern hemisphere, boasts over 2.5 million English-speaking Facebook users alone. Brisbane and Melbourne have another 3.4 million, and New Zealand has a small but vital English-speaking population of 1.8 million. All over the world, there are English-speaking pipe fitters, recording artists, search marketing professionals and monolithic insurance companies. Facebook ads tend to cost a bit less outside the United States, in Australia in particular. If the product you're selling is something that can ship internationally, consider amplifying your sales internationally.

There are 1,640 English-speaking users interested in various types of small aircraft like Cessna, Cirrus, and Piper who live in Australia, New Zealand, United Kingdom, Iceland, or Greenland. Market the latest modular avionics, handheld GPS devices, and cars that drive really fast. If I worked for the CIA, I'd make recruitment inventory lists of nuclear scientists around the world, as in the segment depicted in Figure 6.11.

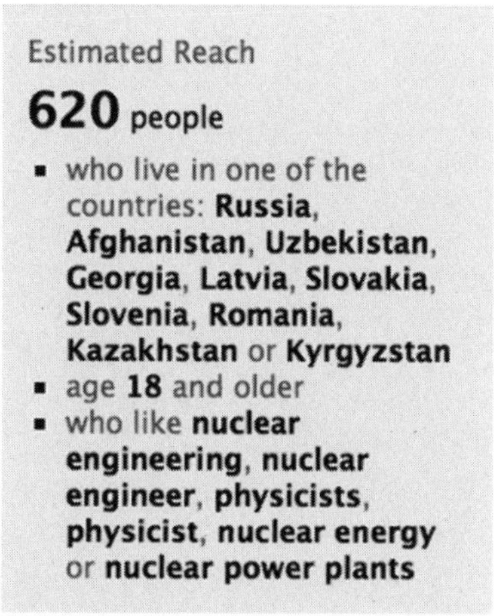

Estimated Reach

620 people

- who live in one of the countries: **Russia, Afghanistan, Uzbekistan, Georgia, Latvia, Slovakia, Slovenia, Romania, Kazakhstan** or **Kyrgyzstan**
- age **18** and older
- who like **nuclear engineering, nuclear engineer, physicists, physicist, nuclear energy** or **nuclear power plants**

Figure 6.11 Russian nuclear energy Interests bucket

Compound targeting is as complex or simple as you want to make it. Here are a few dos and don'ts to guide your explorations:

- Don't add layers just for the sake of adding layers. Let your guide be whether there is actual clarity added to the targeting scenario.

- Do take whatever time is required to handle the job. However, start with base targeting and ads. Then segment further. For instance, prove the general message with more generic targeting and pictures in the ads, and then segment the winning ads to deeper targeting. Segment targets and messaging for men, women, age, and geography. It's hard to optimize base messages when they're already spread out with incredibly granular segmenting, so start broad and go deep.

- Do try B2B marketing, at home and internationally. Occupations, education, and workplaces, both in the Interests bucket and the Education & Work tool, are powerful all over the world.

- Don't believe all the stereotypes you've heard. Prove them wrong or right with data from testing.

- Keep cultural differences in mind. *Mate* in Australia means friend. In the UK, Mate is a kind of condom that was a failed brand a few years ago. Be aware of cultural differences.

- Remember the targeting types: literal, competitive, and inferred. They apply to compound segments too.

Combining attributes in layers puts the personality in personas. Happy social-segment hunting, marketers!

Creating Killer Facebook Ads

Now that we've set KPIs and targeted users, it's time to build ads that resonate. Though writing ad copy and choosing images for Facebook involve similar processes to those for other advertising channels, Facebook ads are a special animal unto themselves. This chapter focuses on creating ads that get the job done by rising above the noise and clutter to push emotional buttons. Visit `www.KillerFBAds.com/chapter7` *for color renderings of the images in this chapter.*

Chapter Contents

The Five Levels of Brand Clarity
Headlines
Ad Images
Putting It All Together with Body Copy

The Five Levels of Brand Clarity

Sure, I know what you're thinking: The chapter about composing ads should be all about headlines, images, body copy, and other creative elements. Yep, we'll get to that straight away. Before we get started with those classic creative elements as applied in Facebook Ads, let's spend a moment talking about brand clarity. What's that, you ask?

Brand clarity is a term aimClear coined internally to describe how much about our client's brand we reveal to FB in an ad. Do we show the logo? How about the company name? Or, is the ad "blind" in that we display a picture of the product in action, mention keywords associated with the product, and let the user find out exactly who the brand is on the landing page? Each approach has its merit.

For instance, if the assignment is to serve Rachael Ray ads to Martha Stewart's audience, do we show Rachael's picture, or even say that the ad is for her show? Or, do we show a picture of Baked Alaska along with a headline that says, "Amazing Dessert Recipes"? Between the headline, body copy, and image, we essentially reach for one of five major combinations of brand transparency in each ad that we create. Most often, we test permutations across the continuum.

One killer feature of Facebook Ads is that it's possible to serve massive quantities: huge bucket loads of impressions. If you're going to serve tens or even hundreds of millions of impressions to focused demographic segments at such a relatively low cost, it's worth considering the potential branding impact, no matter what the KPI is. A timeless truism of the marketing biz is that it's way easier to sell if everybody knows the brand. Therefore, it's usually a good idea to take the opportunity to help ingrain the brand's logo and positioning statement in the psyche of the Facebook community.

We've done extensive testing on the difference between ads that present corporate logos versus ads that feature pictures of various stripes. The fact that logos tend to perform a little below, in most cases, speaks to Facebook not being a commercial place per se. On the continuum of transparency in ads, there are basically five levels of clarity in explaining to users exactly what the ad is about and what company it's from.

The first level of brand clarity shows the logo so everybody knows where the ad is from. The headline and body copy clearly explain the marketing pitch. The result of an ad such as this should usually be a click, toward the goal of converting a user or firmly injecting them into the attribution cycle. It's common to also state branded terms using ® (the registered trademark symbol) and other service marks. Ads like these sometimes don't perform as well as versions that don't sport the logo and are more ambiguous as to the sales pitch. That generality, of course, is dependent on many variables and should be tested.

The second level of brand clarity also presents a logo, so everybody knows where the ad is from, but the headline and body copy don't explain the product being marketed. There may not even *be* a product marketed. This is one of my favorite methods of advertising because the advertiser regulates the click-through ratio (CTR)—and therefore, the cost per thousand impressions (CPM)—downward by not calling the user to action. Often, the objective is not to generate a click. This is a straight-up branding play, and ironically, users who do click anyway tend to spend a long time on the landing page because they're actually interested in the brand. Test magnanimous messages of gratitude such as "aimClear Thanks Duluth," or give white papers away without being too syrupy. In B2B spaces, try headlines like "Celebrating [Industry]" and "20 Years Strong in NYC." Any message that is not a direct-response KPI, especially those typically associated with PR (media relations, for example), works well. Think of the second level of brand clarity as semi-free advertising, centered on brand.

The third level of brand clarity does not use a logo. The ad's picture clarifies the marketing pitch along literal or sideways lines. The objective is a click. The headline and body copy clearly explain the product being marketed and clearly mention the brand. In our experience, because Facebook users are somewhat leery at times about brands, this type of ad often outperforms logos. This approach tends to work well in competitive space because it seems that an approach that is less branded is easier for competitors' followers to swallow. Try multivariate testing against ads at the first level of brand clarity. The main difference is the logo, and the results may surprise you.

The fourth level of brand clarity is the same as level three, but it does not mention the brand at all. The objective is a click. It's totally blind in that users know what advertisers are trying to sell, but not the seller until they get to the landing page. This is an effective tactic for brands that have a mixed reputation or are completely unknown. Testing this approach against ads at the third level of brand clarity can yield insights as to the brand equity in Facebook. Also make sure to test engagement and conversion on the landing page. This is data every brand should have.

The fifth level of brand clarity is similar to level two but does *not* present a logo, nobody knows where the ad is from, and the headline and body copy don't explain the product being marketed. This approach is an excellent method to tease a marketing pitch prerelease. The CTR, and therefore the CPM, is relatively low because we don't call the user to action. Often, the objective is not to garner a click. This is a straight-up out-in-front-of-the-campaign branding play, and paradoxically, users who do click anyway tend to respond to more specific campaigns, which come later.

At any rate, in an environment that is all extremely focused targeting, *high impressions* is a relative term. If the targeted segments add up to 5,000 users and we serve 35,000 impressions, that's a lot of cake. If the targeted segments add up to 300,000 users and we serve 10 million impressions, that's a heap of inventory as well. Either way, consider multivariate testing across the first four levels of brand clarity to determine which style works. Since blind approaches could be polluted by ones that have greater clarity, separate the deployment of each tactic by geography for a cleaner read.

At the end of the day, Facebook ads have to be good—very good—because there is fierce competition for users' attention on the page. The advertiser is competing with many elements that have graphic, social, and even emotional weight. If there is a secret sauce, it is that all elements work together to form a user's perception of the advertisement.

Any marketer who understands the Tao of social segments, headlines, and images and how they work with the body copy is shrewd indeed. Many Facebook users are not on the site to be commercial, and some even get angry at the notion of advertisers in their space. Be real with your KPIs and minimize overt selling tactics in favor of a more patient approach. Finally, study other marketers' work incessantly, in Facebook and other channels. There is no need to reinvent every wheel when so many others have gone before, tendering killer results. Remember that we're marketing to people here, not statistics. Get inside their heads and speak to their hearts and motivations.

Headlines

Facebook headlines need to be good. Very good. My friend, conversion optimization specialist Tim Ash, famously says, "Your online visitor has the attention span of a lit match!" His observation could not be truer in my experience. Not only are advertisers competing against each other, they're also facing off against huge amounts of clutter on pages, many of which include elements that stimulate users from emotional and familiar places, including messages from family and friends. Your headline, in tandem with the ad image, needs to reach out from the right-hand sidebar and speak directly to whatever is inherent to your targeted users. Mark Zuckerberg's genius revolves around his uncanny knack for understanding what it means to maximize the compelling familiarity of objects that appear on users' pages. To win with a Facebook headline, you've got to be that good.

Cultural Sensitivity and Facebook

In my experience, Facebook users in the United States, Canada, and the UK are, for the most part, not hanging out on the social network to buy things. They're there to be social! This is not the case for every culture that uses Facebook. For instance, in some Asian cultures, job and personal identities are more intertwined, both on- and offline, so users are more amenable to a hybrid social and sales environment. Also, different cultures have distinct taboos and hot buttons. I learned this the hard way. It did not take long to discover that while *fag* in the United States has a somewhat derogatory tone in referring to gays, in the UK marketplace, it means cigarettes.

For the sake of staying on the same page, we'll remain compliant with Western sensitivities in discussing copy and pictures. Just keep in mind local semantic, visual, gender, social, and cultural idiosyncrasies when building ads for consumption in other parts of the world. The 162,960 Facebook users living in Afghanistan may have strong opinions about how women are represented visually. Though the 5,336,920 users living within 50 miles of Ahmedabad or Delhi, India, have varying degrees of cosmopolitan orientation, traditional values are deeply rooted in every culture. That's *not* to say that we shouldn't mess with people for fun and profit for marketing purposes, only that it's crucial to understand the fire we're playing with.

The art of composing an effective headline transcends Facebook Ads. It's all about boiling down the value proposition or tease thereof to a few short words and packaging it in the right tone.

Later in the chapter, we'll get specific about choosing and treating images. For now, just keep in mind the creative implications of pictures because we need to consider pictures to discuss headlines. It is said that a picture is worth a thousand words. The right image serves to fill in the gaps and facilitates leaving words out or using copy to lend perspective to things the picture has already communicated.

Headlines are inexorably bound up with associated images and are a crucial part of imparting information, lending perspective, and infusing humor, angst, or other emotions. For instance, an ad that shows a picture of a 17-year-old girl clutching a prom bouquet and looking euphoric already communicates a lot: She is happy, has flowers, and is of a certain age range.

It's important to fully understand what needs to be communicated before attempting to package it. Otherwise, time may be wasted on spin and tone without a clear vision of what needs to be imparted. Start by writing out what you want to communicate in as long a sentence as necessary, without worrying about style, vernacular, or length. Like a lawyer planning the crux of a court case, we spend some time blocking and tackling concepts, or as we call it, "crafting the headline theory."

> **Note:** One bit of headline housekeeping: You can't control the headline if you are targeting a Facebook page for which you're a designated administrator. That's set by FB and can't be modified. So, if your ad's destination is an internal FB asset chosen from the drop-down menu, you won't have any control over the headline. The workaround for this is to send users to your page using the external URL option. For instance, after choosing External URL for the destination, route the destination URL to `http://www.facebook.com/aimclear`. Then, you'll have the opportunity to write a customer headline instead of FB's hardwired headline. We've had external URLs aimed at internal Facebook pages rejected by FB editorial in the past. However, after resubmitting a couple of times, the ads were accepted.

Literal Headlines

Literal headlines say what the ad is about in clear terms, without metaphor or allegory. Let's say the ad is from a national telephone florist offering a 20-percent discount on corsages and boutonnieres, targeted to teenage users in the month preceding senior proms. Start with the headline theory, "Florist offering 20% discount on prom corsages and boutonnieres." Don't worry about length or creativity. This is simply a place to begin. We don't want to put any pressure on the creative process by forcing ourselves to think of ideas at only 25 characters at a time. We call this initial rendering of an idea the *headline theory*, a statement of any length stating what the proposed headline means. The next step is to refine our headline theory into the bite-sized package to actually use in the ad.

Now that we have our headline theory starting point, let's dig in. Obviously, the theory is too long for the 25-character limit (including spaces) that Facebook imposes on headlines. I've taken note that "corsages and boutonnieres" adds up to 25 characters exactly. Perfect! Headlines, like targeting, come in literal flavors. Since the image will be of beaming boys and girls dressed in prom clothes and coveting flowers, a simple statement of what the product is just might work, though it is a tad boring. The user, who we already know is a teen at prom time, will understand that the ad is about prom flowers from the headline and picture. The body copy will clarify further. The literal headline might work so we'll test "Corsages And Boutonnieres" in our campaign, for sure.

It's usually a great idea to create multiple headlines to test because different ad copy will yield distinctive results. Go ahead and create other literal headlines, and when you launch your campaign, you can compare the results. Marketers call such testing *A/B testing.*

Often in social pay-per-click (PPC) space, as in other channels, using headlines with a hook works well. A *hook* advertises a specific benefit of the promotion. At first look, the 20-percent discount is the major hook. Every kid going to prom needs flowers, and most teenagers don't have access to unlimited funds. Since a discount is the reason we're running the campaign in the first place, we'd be remiss not to consider headlines such as "Prom Flowers Savings," "20% Prom Flowers Discount," "Prom Flowers 20% Off," and "Prom Flowers 20% Savings."

Let's go further and speak to the target demographic segment's motivations for finding the right flower vendor. Because we have the ability to target by gender in Facebook, we can combine both the literal and the savings hooks, served to the appropriate gender. Consider serving the boys headline permutations such as "Corsages For Her 20% Off," "Great Prom Corsage Deals," or "Sale On Prom Corsages." Serve ads pimping boutonnieres to girls, for their boyfriends, along similar lines. You get the picture.

Let's run another scenario constructing literal headlines from a headline theory. Say the marketing assignment is to sell time-tracking software to logistics professionals. The theory for the hook we want to promote is that "[Software name] features seamless integration of workflow, scheduling, and time tracking." Sure it's long, but the purpose of a headline theory is to put things out there without any pressure.

To come up with a headline that is 25 characters or less, we need to boil things down. To start, take the theory statement and try to express it in as few words as possible:

- "Seamless workflow integration, scheduling, and time tracking."
- "Seamless workflow integration, scheduling & time tracking."
- "Seamless workflow, scheduling, time tracking."

Although we're still over the 25-character limit, now that our theory has become much less verbose, it's becoming clear that the whole shooting match is pretty much about workflow. Surely, time tracking, scheduling, and integration pertain to and further define workflow, but these could be saved for the ad body and left out of the headline. The word *seamless* happens to be the client's adjective to describe the software's benefits, not mine. It's not an essential technical keyword like *scheduling* or *time tracking*. A quick trip through the thesaurus uncovers excellent alternatives such as *unified* and *faultless*.

Now we're getting somewhere. Let's find a picture that incorporates a clock as a businessperson's head. Figure 7.1 shows the fruits of our labor when we follow the adjective trail with a pinch of snark.

Seamless Workflow Tools

Time tracking and scheduling unified. Goodbye stupid tools. Hello faultless integration.

Figure 7.1 Sample Facebook ad for time-tracking software

© iStockphoto.com/sirup

Sideways Headlines

Sideways headlines are logical extrapolations of inferred targeting. The ad's copywriter needs to summon a well-steeped understanding of both the product and its target market. Instead of being literal in the headline concept, a sideways headline reaches for a snippet that could appeal to users' personalities, perspective, or sense of humor or an inside joke that only users of the product will fully understand. The premise behind these sometimes-snarky headlines is that advertisers don't need to get the whole message across in only the headline. It's enough to attract the gaze of users, and if the ad is compelling, they will stick around to read the rest. At aimClear, we've done a lot of side-by-side testing of literal headlines versus edgy ones. Oftentimes, it's not literal headlines that grab users' attention. The latter often wins. Why?

Twisted variations and humor can cover the same ground while they intrigue and attract. Turn the previous integrated workflow example on its head for a radically different approach. I know firsthand that many professionals can't stand their suite of productivity tools. Though the ads shown in Figure 7.2 do not have anything specific about workflow in the headline, the picture of a clock, stuck unceremoniously on a businessperson's head, serves to communicate the essence of the ad. In other words, the user will understand on a visceral level that we're talking about stupid *workflow* tools.

Take things even further outside the box for added impact. Testing will tell which type of ad will resonate best with users.

Figure 7.2 Sample Facebook ads for time-tracking software, testing edgy headline
© iStockphoto.com/sirup

Let's return to the prom flowers example to build some sideways headlines, from theories to completed headlines. To rise above the noise on an average Facebook page, sometimes there just needs to be a certain level of perspective or humor. Ask yourself how to prognosticate and leverage the user's motivations in conjunction with the hook that brought you, as a marketer, to the table. It's not that the literal headlines won't work. They may perform well. However, we nearly always test headlines that push limits by mashing up classic advertising motivations with what we believe to be the deeper motivations of users.

Buyers, in general, want to feel as if they're cool, sexy, on time, knowledgeable about everything, independent, and master of most things. Proms are sometimes as much about making out afterward as they are about going out to dinner and dancing.

Again, we usually start with headline theories so as not to put any pressure on ourselves to make first renderings of headline ideas short, packaged, or otherwise shiny. The goal of a headline theory is to fully understand what it is we're trying to say. I prefer to run a number of creative options and choose which ones are worthy. The following theories illustrate headline theories that came out of a headline theory brainstorming session:

Headline Theory 1 "Get him/her prom flowers, corsage, or a boutonniere that gets you sex and for a great price" (image of a hot-looking target's opposite gender with flower)

Headline Theory 2 "Get him/her prom flowers, corsage, or a boutonniere that is cooler than other kids have and for a great price" (image of winking target's same gender with flower)

Headline Theory 3 "Don't be late in getting him/her prom flowers, corsage, or a boutonniere and for a great price" (image of target's same gender reaching out for a flower)

Headline Theory 4 "Get him/her prom flowers, corsage, or a boutonniere that proves you're the grown-up and in charge" (image of target's same gender driving a car with flower on the steering wheel)

Now that we have such insightful ideas, it's time to choose which theory we want to boil down to a 25-character headline. Since sex usually sells, especially to teenagers, let's work with #1. You know the drill. Boil the theory down to fewer words of more concentrated essence:

- "Prom + Flowers = Kisses"

- "Prom Flowers = Kisses"

- "Flowers, Hot Like Her/Him"

- "Hot Flowers = Lucky Dude" (to guys)

- "Get Her a Hot Corsage"/"Get Him a Hot Boutonniere"

- "Hot Corsage, Hot Date"

Figure 7.3 Sample Facebook ads for prom corsages, testing edgy headline

Classic Headline Approaches

I was taught marketing and PR by a bunch of marvelous gray-haired men and woman who cut their teeth during the *Mad Men* era on Madison Avenue. They taught me to form my headlines first by writing out a long-form theory, along with both literal and sideways thinking. There are additional headline-writing twists that have worked for generations and can enhance both literal and sideways thinking. The thinking is timeless. From newspapers and billboards to magazine ads and placards over urinals, some headline vehicles are eternal. Most classic headline slants work great as either literal or sideways statements. Whether marketing by obvious literal associations or coming from deep left field, remember the archetypal headline constructs presented in the following sections.

Speak Directly to the Demographic Segment

Obviously, if the mission is to market hair extensions to 14- to 18-year-old girls interested in "hair extensions," it makes sense to test headlines that say, "Hair Extensions?" or "Yes! Hair Extensions." It's clear that these users somehow, you know, are interested in hair extensions, so reflecting their interest in the headline deserves testing.

Reciprocally, negative interests can play well in headlines. There are 19,560 Facebook users who are interested in "I hate Walmart." I might test headlines for the downtown store getting reamed by the big-box behemoth that read "Wall + Mart = Not," "Walmart Alternative," "Not Walmart Reason #356," or "Walmart, Really?"

In cases where the connection is less literal, try speaking to the root interest. When marketing GORE-TEX boots to users who love camping in the Rockies or canoeing, try headlines like "GORE-TEX Camping Boots," "GORE-TEX Canoeing Boots," or "Breathable Canoeing Boots."

Questions with "?"

Headlines that are questions, complete with a question mark, engage by design. Questions by nature request responses, and humans are hardwired to feel compelled to offer one up. Start question-style headlines with the classic question words: *Who, What, Where, When, Will, Is, Are, Can, Why, How,* and so on. Question headlines work well for Facebook Ads because they're easy to craft as short little nibbles. They're also really fun headline fodder when quoting clichés such as, "When Pigs Fly." Consider answering the questions with body copy:

- "Why Eat Junk Food?"
- "Where Is The Love?"
- "Will Grandma Groove NYC?"
- "Can Tacos Be Radical?"
- "When Will Stuck Pigs Fly?"

Questions That Are Really Answers

Using classic question words without question marks forms an interesting and common advertising headline vehicle. This interesting literary juxtaposition starts with an explanation that somehow feels like a question and leaves users waiting for clarification in the body copy:

- "Why Pilates Rules"
- "If Diapers Didn't Smell"
- "When SEO Works"
- "When Monkeys Can Fly"

Tout the Benefits

Encouraging an audience by highlighting all good things that will happen upon lending a click is an everlasting headline tactic. Enthuse, reinforce, support, impassion, or stimulate users with an uplifting statement of positive encouragement. This construct often begins with a verb such as *get*:

- "Beat the Dating Odds"
- "Outmaneuver Mere Mortals"
- "Win the Clogged Drain War"
- "Boost Sales Immediately"
- "Leverage Offshore Labor"
- "Find the Perfect Wife"

Negative Consequences

Depending on the marketing assignment, sometimes emphasizing the bad things that will happen if users *don't* act is an effective play. Words such as *evade, avoid, circumvent, dodge, sidestep, elude escape, skip, lose, ditch, stop,* and *prevent* work really well in the 25-character short-form headline:

- "Don't Be That Nasty Guy"
- "Ditch Contact Lenses"
- "Avoid Embarrassing Zits"
- "Escape from Bad Pizza Mtn."
- "Stop Macular Degeneration"

Leverage the Power of Clichés

Every kid learns the phrases "A penny saved is a penny earned" and "All the world's a stage." From *Aesop's Fables* to Shakespeare, sitcoms to board games, piggybacking on top of statements already ingrained in users' psyches can be quite effective. Because folks already have the essence of the cliché in their brains, a headline can seem familiar on first impression. It's not necessary to rhyme or otherwise quote the absolute phonetic of the original. However, doing so can augment the effect. Cliché parodies can take many vernacular forms, including positive, negative, literal, and sideways:

- "1 + 1 = Tooth Decay"
- "All the World's a Steak"
- "Get Out of Spam Jail Free"
- "Eat Carbs or Be Eaten"

Memorable Phonetics

This traditional headline technique takes a page out of the song-lyricist playbook. I recommend *Writing Better Lyrics* by renowned Berklee College of Music professor Pat Pattison (Writer's Digest Book, September, 15 1995). He teaches how to lace together similar phonetics, rhymes, cadences, and repeated words. The technique is especially effective using multiple hard consonants in a row:

- "Do Be Do Be DK's Donuts"
- "Jewelry For Dandy Divas"
- "Terrific Tires, Save 20%"

Attention [Demographic Segment]

Since the dawn of advertising, when the baseball-game scorecard had "Attention Baseball Fans" as an ad's headline, advertisers have been calling out the target demographic in headlines. Words like *Attention*, *Calling all*, and *Are you a*, have always been go-to concepts for headline writers. The concept of shouting out to your targets, highlighting who they are, is almost always worth testing.

Figure 7.4 Example of a headline that calls out to the demographic target, in this case, me

Be a Headline Ninja

The headline categories and examples included in this chapter only begin to scratch the surface. Yes, the categories we've included are commonly used conventions, but in reality, there are no hard rules. At the end of the day, the best headline is the one that accomplishes the KPI, within the allowed 25-character count. The best way to determine which headline works best is to undertake multivariate testing.

One fantastic way to grow as a headline writer is to tweet. I've grown so much with Twitter—tweeting, retweeting, repackaging content, and observing the mob's instant reaction. Sure, ads in Facebook provide fast feedback, but not nearly as rapid as in Twitter. Next time you tweet a link, instead of simply pasting the existing title of the content you're sharing, repackage the link's destination content with a new title you create.

For example, "Free eBook from Google: AdWords Textbook" might play better tweeted as "Teach New SEM Employees to Use AdWords Right." A title like "Social Media Marketing Tactics & Resources" may get a better response repackaged as

"Luminaries Reveal Social Media Marketing Tactics & Resources." For an interesting taste of how 25-character headlines might work, test concepts on the front of retweets.

Finally, study other advertisers' headlines and how they work with images. In Chapter 9, you'll learn how to set up Facebook profiles to actually see the advertisements you deploy, making it easy to watch others marketing to your segments. Use tools from other channels—such as SpyFu for search PPC—to study ads (shown in Figure 7.5). The ads are in a different format, but the concepts are the same. In SpyFu, it's easy to see the progression of ad copy that advertisers have tested. The graph of search PPC expenditures is color-coded to indicate when creative was changed. Long stretches of unchanged creative coinciding with steady expenditures of cash probably indicate that the creative works for the keyword. For any marketing assignment, take the time to learn what has worked for other marketers in other channels, keeping in mind that social space is different.

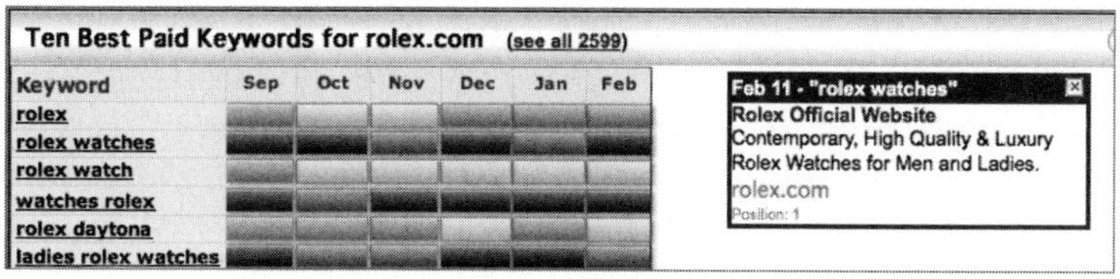

Figure 7.5 Screen capture of SpyFu, used to glean competitive intelligence for PPC ads

Additional Tips

Here are some tips to help you comply with Facebook Ads' TOS:

- The headline can make only limited reference to Facebook, only for the purpose of clarifying the destination of the ad.
- Ads must use grammatically proper capitalization, like capitalizing the first letter of all proper nouns in the ad's title.
- Acronyms have to be capitalized, like DOA.
- If the headline is a complete sentence, it has to end with one punctuation mark. Sentences can't end with dashes, ellipses, and so on.
- Exclamation points are forbidden in headlines.

In addition, here are some don'ts that we follow at aimClear:

- Don't sell gratuitously. Facebook users are there to be social.
- Don't make promises the landing page does not keep.
- Avoid over-the-top hyperbole. People can see through exaggerations from a mile away.
- Don't forget the KPI and the purpose of the ad.

Facebook headline writing is an art form unto itself, but its principles are rooted in classic advertising message-building. Always keep in mind that headlines work with pictures to capture and earn users' attention with words and imagery.

Ad Images

The first role of the image (aka picture) is to somehow cut through the clutter of an average Facebook page template. Usually, that objective can be accomplished by informed and clever use of color, zoom, cropping, and other fun tricks to highlight and enhance the image's content, which should somehow speak to the social segment. Job one: Images need to be a poke in the eye, attracting the user's attention.

The second major job for images is to lend context to the headline or vice versa. The headline "Feeling Blue?" builds an entirely different literal meaning when the image is of a St. Louis Blues hockey player, B.B. King playing guitar, or Blue Man Group. The headline "Get Ready To Rumble" is clarified when the picture is of either a monster truck or two hockey players. In each case, the picture offers crucial perspective to the precise intent of the ad, filling in the critical meaning. It is not necessary to tell the entire story of the ad in just the headline or the image. They work in unison to communicate vital literal context. Figure 7.6 demonstrates this.

Figure 7.6 Really effective images can communicate a lot of an ad's meaning.

Pictures can also impart shades of social meaning, both obvious and subtle. Let's assume the assignment is to market an occupational therapy degree program to 16- to 18-year-old single women who are interested in "occupational therapy" or "occupational therapist" and prefer men. The headline is "5 Year OT Degree." An image of a younger female occupational therapist working on an attractive and muscular male's shoulder might resonate. We know she's single and likes men. Even though she is pursuing a highly professional career where personal predilections don't matter, she's young and we're all human.

There are thousands of Facebook users over age 31 who are interested in kayaking and are from Minnesota, Florida, or Washington State. Assume I'm a kayaking outfitter hailing from one of those three states and serving a headline that teases "Kayak Bliss, Just Add H2O." Minneapolis users should receive ads featuring flat terrain and boreal forest fauna. Fort Lauderdale residents may relate better to pictures that include dunes in the background or a close-up of a pelican on the sea kayak's bow.

Sea kayakers from coastal Washington are likely more accustomed to rainforest-type terrain on the Olympic Peninsula. That said, try serving Minneapolis kayakers the headline "Defrost Your Kayak" in February when Minnesota is frozen solid. Use the pelican and dunes photo to enhance the effect.

Maybe it's because Facebook is such a social place that pictures of people tend to work so well. Look to the segment and consider what real people who belong to the segment might actually resemble or fancy looking at (more on this shortly). Consider your target's age, geographic location, interest, gender, sexual preference, and, of course, interests.

Deciding whether an ad's image should reflect what our segment looks like as opposed to what it likes to look *at* can be tricky. Should we market the audio-recording degree to 17-year-old females who sing in a band with a picture of a rock-star female singer or the hot guy playing the guitar? There's no way to know for sure unless you test, which is what we always suggest. The 55-year-old upper-management male consumer of business-travel car rentals probably won't be amped by pictures of much younger businessmen looking not-gray-haired behind the wheel. Testing may tell us our older professional gent wants to see the female car rental agent's pretty face or someone more similar to his own likeness.

Sometimes, the image doesn't need to speak to the product at all but rather to the segment. Figure 7.7 shows an ad with a picture that has little to do with the product, except that the female shown is holding money.

Figure 7.7 Facebook ad images don't have to be literal to resonate with the target audience.

Don't forget humor. After all, we're serving ads to a social community that's there to share and be entertained by others. Try random illustrations that are fun and attract attention, such as the one in Figure 7.8. aimClear's Lauren Litwinka (@beebow on Twitter) is a master of the three-minute Microsoft Paint illustration. These types of illustrations can be very effective.

Figure 7.8 Don't underestimate the power of a really sideways Facebook ad image.
Bit.ly/DeepCereal

Image Size and File Type

Facebook ad images, like headlines, have size limitations. Pictures should be sized no larger than 110 pixels wide by 80 pixels in height, with an aspect ratio of 4:3 or 16:9. File size for upload must be less than 5 megabytes. If you upload an image that does not fit these specifications, Facebook will automatically crunch the image to fit them. The result is not always pretty.

Also, Facebook doesn't support animated GIF or Flash, so don't bother. Due to the fact that Facebook will skew your images if the aspect ratio is incorrect, best practice is to handle the image in an external editor and export it precropped, sized, and ready to go. My personal-favorite program is Adobe Fireworks, but different people choose different software. One of the most popular free programs in our shop is GIMP, or the GNU Image Manipulation Program. It runs on Mac and Windows alike and does a fine job. Any program that can size and crop images will do. However, there are advanced hacks, which we'll cover a bit later in this chapter.

Colors and Color Hacks

In terms of color pallet, Facebook makes the template a pretty easy canvas to cut through. The main color on Facebook page templates is dark blue (hexadecimal 3A5896). It is accented by a lighter, nearly powder blue (637BAE). The third predominant color is gray (EFF0F7), which is used to frame conversations. Take a look at Figure 7.9 to see the colors laid out.

Dark blue   Gray   Powder blue

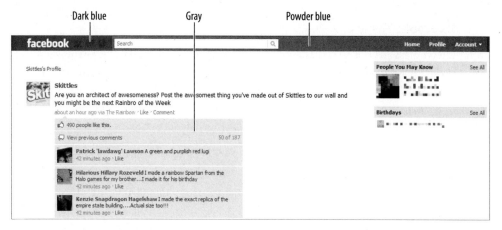

Figure 7.9 Color scheme of basic Facebook layout

Though there are some reds, yellows, and teal accent colors throughout the page and even some oranges, for the most part, Facebook leans toward the blue/gray feel, with lots of white space and relatively low contrast. The wild card presented is the rainbow of colors that show up on Facebook pages other than the site's templates. Newsfeeds, friends' avatars, and a myriad of other thumbnails clutter the page with color swatches.

The net result is that using bright, high-contrast colors that don't otherwise exist in the Facebook page template gives advertisers a greater chance of being noticed.

> **Tip:** Use colors that stand out from the Facebook page template as opposed to blending in with it. Stay away from powder blue, navy blue, and gray.

Of course, not all objects can naturally be represented in bright yellows, oranges, reds and other crazy-bright colors. One great hack to get around this is to place a border around the photo. I've had Facebook reject such borders, but they are nearly always accepted after resubmitting a couple of times. Pure primary colors are rare in the natural world, so they tend to stand out among all the naturally colored objects in Facebook. The ad shown in Figure 7.10 is one I often see from Frank Kern. He shows it both ways and is obviously testing to measure the border's effect.

Figure 7.10 Testing colored-border enhancements on Facebook ad images

Borders don't need to frame the picture or be square. As shown in Figure 7.11, this Facebook ad's image has a thin circular target grid. The green color is rather unnatural and stands out in the ad and on the whole page on which it is displayed.

Figure 7.11 Testing colored-border enhancements on Facebook ad images

Here are some other classic image-treating hacks:

- Push the image's color saturation to just below where things look unnatural. As background, zero color saturation means black and white. Boosting saturation generates an effect sort of like cranking the "color" control on your 1990s-era TV set.

- Boost the contrast to make soft edges harder. This can be particularly effective hand in hand with pushed saturation.

- Selectively paint artificial colors to highlight certain features. Turn normal eyes into luminous blue lasers that bore right through users. Create halos around objects or outline shapes with thin out-of-context colored lines.

- Be radical. Turn things on their side or upside down. Invert colors in certain image zones or for single objects.

- Change the color game. Use images in which you create your own background, which takes up the entire square. Try layering your light image on top of your dark background.

Zoom and Cropping

Because the images are so small, being zoomed in enough for the user to easily understand is important. Check out the ad for the Summit Ridge apartment complex in Duluth, shown in Figure 7.12a. In the ad I found online (Figure 7.12a), it's nearly impossible to tell what's happening. The advertiser wants us to read the sign and see the apartments in the background. The trouble is that the zoomed-out picture needs to be so small for FB Ads that we can't tell what it is. An improved approach would be to either zoom in on the sign or, better yet, show representative features of the lifestyle, like the pool or pool table. By the way, I did not write this ad and, yes, it is an example of a lame headline as well as an ineffective image.

Original as found in FB, too zoomed out

Figure 7.12a Original, as found on Facebook, too zoomed-out

Better, if bent on using the sign

Figure 7.12b Zoomed-in image of apartment sign

Better, if bent on using the sign.

Figure 7.12c Image of woman relaxing

© Liv Friis-larsen/Fotolia

Way better, touting the actual luxuries.

Figure 7.12d Image of entertainment activity

© Dimitar Marinov/Fotolia

I tell Facebook Ads trainees that I want to be able to stand five feet away from the computer monitor and be able to easily discern what the image is. Otherwise, in my mind, the image is too zoomed out. Standing that far back, there should also be something, be it an outline or other color treatment, that draws my eye to the page within the first two seconds. Every other part of all the ads from all the advertisers on the page is standardized. All the headline fonts look the same, as does all the body copy. The image is the only edge you have to attract users and entice them to continue reading.

Hyperzoomed effects can rock the house as well. Zoom in on a person's eyes, hands, mouth, or ear. Crop the face in half with a colorful background where the missing half should be. Zoom and crop in asymmetrical ways that capture attention for the "wrongness" of the approach. Just don't make the classic mistake of being too zoomed out, to the point where users can't really get the effect you're after or, worse yet, can't even tell what the picture is supposed to be.

Image Sources

Facebook is no different from any other channel in that images need to be copyright-cleared for usage. It's not okay to surf Google Images or Flickr and grab images that don't belong to you. Use your normal sources such as Corbis, Getty, or iStockPhoto.

com. Make sure to pull the appropriate license, which allows for this type of commercial usage.

Creative Commons is an organization that supports various types of open-source licenses (http://creativecommons.org/licenses). It is arguable that the Attribution CC BY license—which lets you distribute, remix, tweak, and build upon another's work, even commercially, as long as you give credit for the original creation—is acceptable.

Public domain is the most bulletproof and totally free way to find images. When a work is in the public domain, it is free for use by anyone for any purpose without restriction under copyright law. Public domain is the purest form of open/free because nobody owns or controls the images in any way. Here are a few low-cost or free image sources to consider when pulling pictures for Facebook ads:

Google Advanced Image Search Google Advanced Image Search now filters for free CC-licensed or public domain works. Before reusing a picture that you find on Google, you should confirm that its license is legitimate and check specific terms of reuse as stated in the license. Google has no way to certify if the license is real, and big G doesn't make any promise that the images are lawfully licensed.

Everystockphoto.com This site, shown in Figure 7.13, searches over 4.3 million public domain and Creative Commons photos, including photos from Wikipedia and NASA. Bestphotos.us and Gimp-savvy.com offer similar functionality.

Wikipedia Head on over to http://en.wikipedia.org/wiki/Wikipedia:Public_domain_image_resources for a massive list of public domain image resources. Some of them are junk, but there are links to many incredible meta tools and other resources from which to cull totally free images.

Figure 7.13 Public domain photo archives are a great place to hunt for Facebook ad images.

Clip art Don't forget clip art, like the images bundled with Microsoft Word (see Figure 7.14 for an example). Sometimes, quirky illustrations work really well in FB ads.

Hiring .PHP RockStar
aimclearblog.com

Internationally known MN online marketing agency seeks full time LAMP, WordPress jock. Rails or Cake a plus. St. Paul & Duluth offices.

Figure 7.14 Tap into the MS Word clip art library for a giant sample of public domain images.

Your own photos We're big fans of taking our own pictures. There seems to be an antiproduction sentiment in Facebook that probably goes with the social territory. Grab your cell phone or digital camera and start shooting. Be creative and climb outside of the typical advertising box. We've used pictures of everything from body parts to vending machines. There are no royalty restrictions on pictures you take yourself.

Putting It All Together with Body Copy

I think body copy might be the easiest of all ad attributes because we've already got the user's attention if they're even reading it. After the ad's image and headline attract the user's gaze and interest, the body copy's job is to close the deal, moving the user toward whatever KPI is on the table. At 135 characters, there's a ton of room to fill in any missing pieces of the messaging and then reinforce, amplify, and otherwise frame the ad's meaning.

Body Copy Best Practices

Regarding the body field of ads, Facebook suggests, "Use this section to further explain the product or service that your ad is about. Emphasize benefits to the user, unique qualities of your product/service, and any special offers. End with a clear call to action that users should take if they like your ad." For the most part, this is great advice, though overly simplistic. Not every ad needs to cover all those bases, that is, state a product's defining qualities, explain offers, and scream out to users with action calls. Best practice is to use body copy as a detail utility to complete whatever context is put forward in the unified statements of headline and image.

It is also a great idea to clarify and complete the headline and image. Most ads should have some combination of user benefit, an offer, and a call to action. Let's break it down and look at examples of what FB is talking about in its body copy recommendations.

First, user benefits should be easy to find with some research. If the object of your marketing efforts does not have true user benefits, then there's practically no reason to invest in marketing it. If you're promoting your own business, you already know what the user benefits are. If you're an agency, interview your clients. Here are the questions I usually ask:

- Why is your product or service a better choice than the competition and why do users in your targeted demographic segments care?

- What problems does your product solve?

- If you're talking to a potential customer on the phone, what are the three things you can say that would close the sale immediately?

- Why do customers love your product?

Another terrific place we look to is competitors' sales pitches by way of historic search PPC (pay-per-click) competitive intelligence. We want to know what messages our competitors have settled on enough to spend PPC dollars. Say we're marketing a hotel in South Beach, Miami. Figure 7.15 is a great example of using a competitor's PPC ad to clue us in to NewportBeachsideResort.com. The competitor pushes the oceanfront location and world-class service.

Figure 7.15 SpyFu competitive intelligence

There are countless examples of product benefits. Here are just a few:

- Largest selection
- Licensed practitioners
- Flexible fit
- Organic or natural
- Personalized customer service
- Taste great, less filling
- 38 miles per gallon

Anyway, you get the picture. Interview your client, poll customers, and/or conduct competitive intelligence to learn how similar products see their advantages. It's good for ads to contain some element that highlights user benefits and inspires users toward proceeding on to a click.

So far as the calls to action go, there are hundreds of common variations. Here are some classic action calls:

- Contact us today
- Start [keyword]ing now

- Learn how to
- Talk to an expert
- Get a free
- Enroll in
- Act now
- Call us today for
- Subscribe now for
- Read how to get
- Reserve a
- Watch this video for
- See how we help
- Listen to
- Only [number] [hours, days, or months] remain
- What are the first five questions to ask your
- What are the classic signs of
- Find out how we've helped other businesses [verb]
- See examples of our [adjective] [noun]
- Join
- See how
- Download
- Use our online [tool] to
- Live chat ordering

Just keep in mind that Facebook's advice about action calls is all about getting users to click because that's how FB makes money. Of *course* Facebook recommends calls to action. Just remember that there are cases, as we've discussed surrounding branding KPIs, where getting the click is not always the main objective.

Here are some examples of non-calls to action, for branding ads:

- Thanking customers
- Celebrating *XX* years in the community
- Acknowledging awards
- New hires
- We care
- Working for you

Next, offers are the easiest part to think about because most promotion-based advertising comes to the marketer predefined. Here are some classic offers:

- 25 percent off
- XYZ Savings
- Web-only special
- Free shipping
- Once a year
- Deals
- Money-back guarantee
- Free returns

Great! Now that we've discussed benefits, calls to action, non-calls to action, and offers, let's talk about various ways to use body copy to make headlines pay. There is a real art to complementing headlines and images with just enough body copy.

If the headline is sideways, try being more literal with the body copy because sideways headlines often require clarification. If the headline and image are more literal, as in the jumbo prawns examples later in this chapter, expand the copy enough to impart what is needed to drive the conversion.

For headlines that are questions, consider using the copy to actually answer the question. Body copy for "Will Grandma Groove NYC?" could be, "Yes, if she stays at [Hotel Name] for 50% off in June." Make a caped-hero image with the headline "Why Pilates Rules" pay big with "Because you too can be built like a mega-superhero" as the body copy.

For headlines touting product benefits, expand the body copy to explain sufficiently enough to clinch the deal. For the B2B headline "Be A Welding Rock Star," the body copy might be "Rhino Auto Darkening Welding Helmets feature radical styles, designs, and colors. Creativity lives! Rock the job site dude."

If the headline leverages the power of clichés or memorable phonetics, then get superliteral to make sure the user understands. "Go To The Zoo You Too" may be best served by copy such as "Just Off 35E in Eagan, Sundays Families Pay Only $18." It's also pretty cute to follow tongue-twisted headlines with body that starts with "Wow that's a mouthful" or otherwise makes fun of the ad itself before providing elucidatory information.

To close our discussion of body copy, here are some examples targeted to me, in my personal FB account, which show various combinations of a product's defining qualities, offers, and action calls.

The ad in Figure 7.16 is a cool example of clarifying the headline and image with body copy and using a call to action. The headline states the name of the company, Acxiom. The first line of body copy explains who Acxiom is and why I, as a marketer, should care. Then comes the classic call to action, "Download now!" This ad, though not colorful, is complete.

Figure 7.16 Facebook ad with headline clarified by body copy and call to action

The American Express ad in Figure 7.17 is really well written. The headline serves up the benefit (grow my business) in tandem with the image (picture of the card), which makes who the advertiser is clear. The body copy calls out to my demographic, asking me if I am a small business owner. That's really compelling because I am a small business owner. The call to action is also right up front; get a response within a minute. Well done.

Figure 7.17 American Express Facebook ad with compelling copy and call to action

The Adgooroo ad in Figure 7.18 is cool, also. Since I happen to be a search marketer, I really care to know if EDU (.edu) links are smart or not. The image is of a cap and diploma, which plays on the smartness of building links from educational websites. The body copy reinforces things by stating the benefit, which I (as the ad recipient) will understand as how link building can help drive traffic and keep my site safe from Google reprisals. The call to action is "See how," which will help drive the click. Good ad!

Figure 7.18 Adgooroo Facebook ad with reinforcing ad copy and an inviting call to action

The Pearle Vision Ad in Figure 7.19 is, to my mind, rather sloppy, but it works. The benefit is 50 percent off and is framed in a cute explanation that the sale is to celebrate 50 years in business. There's no mistaking that the image is touting the benefit,

50 percent off. What I dig about this ad is that there is no online call to action. The advertisers did not provide additional details, store locations, local phone numbers, and so on. Only the most interested glasses wearers will click, which should keep the media spend down and the traffic well focused. I also like how the logo/50%/50 years approach leaves users remembering the name of the company and that there is a half-off sale.

Figure 7.19 Compelling Pearle Vision Facebook ad without a strong call to action

Not every ad needs to have every element. A general rule of thumb is that body copy should always be viewed as a semantic utility to complete whatever context is put forward in the unified statements of headline and image. I suggest that you start looking at ads in your FB account, over and over, and evaluating which elements are included and which are not. Test various approaches until you find the perfect combination to accomplish your KPI.

Body Copy Length

Another consideration is how long the body copy should be. We've done lots of testing, and there is a definite correlation between sparse body copy and higher CTR. Given the firefly-like attention span of many Facebook users, there is a case to be made that the best ads don't need much body copy at all. The more verbose an ad is, the more we're asking users to read, so say what you need to say and get out of there.

Figure 7.20 shows just how many concepts can be stuffed into a Facebook ad's body copy. Follow this line of thinking. First, the headline, "16 Jumbo Prawns, 12 Bucks," pretty much tells the whole story in conjunction with the picture of a succulent shrimp on the barbeque. I chose a single shrimp, as opposed to 16, because the zoomed-in single shrimp, in all its redness, has a better chance of attracting the gaze of the local seafood lovers this ad is targeted to.

Figure 7.20 Austerity works. This ad uses only 77 characters.

The copy in Figure 7.20 is short, sweet, and to the beat. The KPI here is a phone call, without spending money on the click if possible—so why clutter up the ad with unnecessary verbiage? As with any kind of copywriting, the fewer words presented, the greater value each word has proportionally. The phone number looks huge with so few words in the body text.

Figure 7.21 introduces another concept: That special Shrimpfest deal is limited by the number of seats available in the restaurant. This is reasonable because many consumers are somehow compelled by the notion that if they don't act quickly enough, the special offer may disappear. That's not the only thing starting to disappear. Notice the phone number, ostensibly the KPI, starting to blend into the ad. Still, it's present. Even with this slightly longer copy, we've only used 95 characters of the 135 available, and there's a lot of contextual density to the ad already. Consider testing this version against the prior one; move on to more ad production (shown in Figures 7.21 and 7.23) if the ads did not work or the client forced more detail in the ads.

16 Jumbo Prawns, 12 Bucks

Sandy's Seafood Shack Friday Shrimpfest, Call 218-234-5678 for reservations. Seats are limited.

Figure 7.21 Facebook ads can be effective in 100 characters or less.

© iStockphoto.com/grandriver

Let's introduce yet another layer to the information imparted by the ad (Figure 7.22). The advertiser wants users to know that there are two sittings, which I would argue is extraneous and should be explained to the user during the phone call to make the reservation. Still, some clients are pushy and want to include the entire sales proposition in a single ad. Now, the phone number is getting buried. That's a problem since it's the phone call we're after.

16 Jumbo Prawns, 12 Bucks

Sandy's Seafood Shack Friday Shrimpfest, Call 218-234-5678 for reservations. 2 sittings, seats are limited.

Figure 7.22 Adding more detail to the ad still leaves us with 28 characters on the table.

© iStockphoto.com/grandriver

That being the case, I would move the phone number to either the beginning or the end of the ad, as shown in Figure 7.23, to once again feature it and keep emphasis on the fulfillment mechanism. The good news is that if we get users to read this entire ad, it's more likely that they will convert if they're our perfect customers because they have all the information. The bad news is that it's asking a lot of users to read all this.

16 Jumbo Prawns, 12 Bucks

Sandy's Seafood Shack Friday Shrimpfest, 2 sittings, seats are limited. For reservations call 218-234-5678.

Figure 7.23 If a phone call is your KPI, consider moving the phone number to the beginning or end of the copy for more emphasis.

© iSTOCKPHOTO.COM/GRANDRIVER

Creating the killer ad for your FB Ads campaign is a true art form. Start with an awareness of the five levels of brand clarity, which can matter a lot in social PPC space. Keep in mind how headlines, images, and the target demographic segment work together in unison to attract users and incent them to read the body copy. Use the body copy, just enough, to make the headline and images pay. Test, test, and then test some more. Rock on, killer Facebook ad writer!

Deploying Your Facebook Ads Campaign

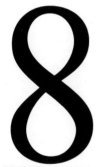

So, your ducks are in a row and you're ready to rock. KPIs are set, targets researched, ads written, and campaign structure defined. Now, it's time to pull the trigger. This chapter deals with payment options, budgeting, bidding, landing pages, tracking, and dialing in optimization tweaks—in other words, making sure things are set up, copacetic, and ready to rumble. Some of this stuff is fairly dry; let's face it, listing currency types or account structure isn't that sexy. However, the information is vital. Let's dig in. I'll make some music suggestions along the way to keep things groovy.

Chapter Contents

Facebook Ads Finances

Landing Page Considerations

Final Prelaunch Checklist

Facebook Ads Finances

Giddyup! Now that the groundwork is laid, it's finally time to deploy your Facebook Ads campaign. But first, there are a few more factors to consider. The bids need to be in a range that is high enough to get the ads displayed—the higher the ad ranking (where it appears on the page), the better the click-through ratio (CTR). Facebook is a bit idiosyncratic in how advertisers are and are not allowed to manage their budgets.

Payment Options

Advertisers can pay for ads using Visa, MasterCard, American Express, Discover, some cobranded debit cards, and JCB for certain currencies. Facebook offers monthly invoicing for qualified customers spending a minimum of $10,000 a month. If you plan on spending $10K or more, contact Facebook's sales team via the Help Center form. For more detail, search Facebook Ads Help Center for "What are my payment options?" Personally, I'd rather use American Express and have Facebook pay for my free airlines tickets. See, I told you I'd make this fun!

Currently, Facebook accepts the following currencies: Australian dollar (AUD), British pound (GBP), Canadian dollar (CAD), Chilean peso (CLP), Colombian peso (COP), euro (EUR), Danish krone (DKK), Hong Kong dollar (HKD), Japanese yen (JPY), Norwegian krone (NOK), Swedish krona (SEK), Swiss franc (CHF), Turkish lira (TRY), U.S. dollar (USD), and the Venezuelan bolivar (VEB). Since this may change over time, search the FB Ads help pages for "Which currencies are accepted for Facebook Ads?" To run campaigns with multiple currencies, it's necessary to create a second account. Within your one Facebook login, you can keep two accounts: one for each currency.

Budgeting and Spend Limits

There is a daily budget for each campaign, which can be arrived at by two different methods (see Figure 8.1).

- The Per Day budget is hardwired, use-it-or-lose-it. Unused funds don't roll over.
- The Lifetime Budget option is dynamic. Unused funds do roll over, with Facebook setting each new day's daily budget based on a formula that takes into account lifetime budget, how many days are in the schedule, and if there are any unused funds rolled forward from previous days.

There are four basic financial constructs to understand:

- Daily spend limit, imposed by Facebook
- Lifetime account cap, set by advertisers
- Daily budget, set for campaigns
- Bids, set for ads

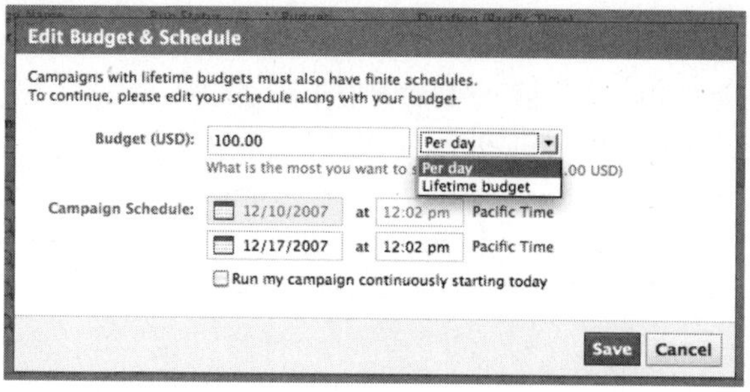

Figure 8.1a Creating your campaign budget in Facebook Web UI

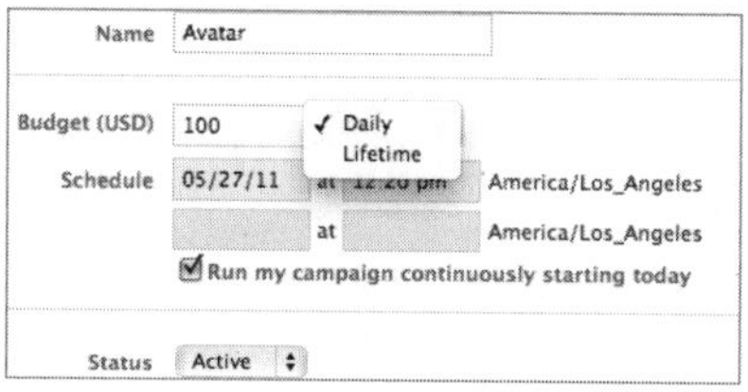

Figure 8.1b Creating your campaign
budget in Facebook Power Editor

If they seem a little complicated at first, don't worry. Hang in there and it will all make sense. At a few points, I'll italicize a sentence. Please read that sentence over and over until you understand it. I suggest that you turn on "Gloria's Step (Take 2)" by Bill Evans, from the *Live at The Vanguard* record. Dude, this chapter requires music.

Daily Spend Limit and Lifetime Budget

Every account comes wired with an overall daily spend limit, which is imposed by Facebook. Facebook sets the daily spend limit when you set up the account. The bad news is that new accounts default to a paltry $50 per day, per account. "New" means the first implementation of Facebook Ads deployed from an account. The daily spend limit will routinely increase after a few days because Facebook is successful at charging your credit card at each proceeding level. When the daily limit reaches $1,000, you'll need to contact Facebook to request further increases. To be clear, you can't raise the account-wide daily budget past what Facebook allows. You have to earn their trust first. This can be frustrating. In 2008, aimClear was running a large holiday campaign for Martha Stewart Omni, and for days, we could not convince Facebook that it was cool to raise our limit over $50. Go figure.

If you're lucky enough to have a Facebook representative, these higher-ups can log in to their administrative tools and change the daily limit, which will take effect the next billing day. This is not the case for most advertisers; it's not that easy to get a dedicated representative unless you spend big bucks.

You can contact Facebook's technical support via a web form to request an increased limit. Don't count on a fast response time, but it will get done—eventually. Adding another currency type does not increase the daily limit. Rather, the aggregate limit is allocated across both currency accounts.

Lifetime Spend Cap

One way to avoid overspending in a Facebook Ads account is to set a lifetime *spend cap*, which designates the absolute total sum the entire account is authorized to expend. All ads will be paused within 15 minutes of when your account reaches the cap. Advertisers can reset this cap at any time, but keep in mind that the lifetime spend limit has nothing to do with the pace of ads served. Facebook simply pauses everything when the desired expenditure restriction has been reached. Check out Figure 8.2 for a look at the Facebook interface for setting a lifetime spending cap. Here's how you go about doing it:

1. Head over to the Billing Manager by clicking Billing in the left-hand column.

2. Click Edit next to your current account spend cap amount. You'll find it immediately below Account Spend, which defaults to Unlimited.

3. Enter your new account spend limit.

4. Click Save. OK, your lifetime budget is safe now, and you won't go over.

Figure 8.2 Setting your Facebook account lifetime spend cap

First, be careful when setting a lifetime spend cap, and if you do, check it every day. Here's where things get slightly technical. Take a deep breath. Each Facebook Ads *account* holds campaigns. Understanding the nuances of configuring each campaign's daily budget is crucial, though a bit confusing. Per Day, also known as Daily budget, and Run My Campaign Continuously Starting Today are the defaults for Facebook campaigns. *Advertisers are given options to start and stop the campaign date with a per-day budget or to set a lifetime budget. Setting a lifetime budget requires a fixed time schedule.*

First, let's explore Per Day, the simplest option, because each day, the campaign's budget is use-it-or-lose-it. If the per-day budget is $100 and only $80 is spent on Monday, Tuesday's budget is still $100. The unused $20 does not roll over to increase any future day's budget. Until you're experienced with Facebook Ads, Per Day is the suggested setting because it's very easy to conceptualize.

Setting a campaign's lifetime budget and its associated time schedule authorizes Facebook to determine the campaign's daily budget by dividing the lifetime budget by the number of days in the schedule. For experienced users, this can be a super-cool option because if the campaign does not spend to its expected daily limit on Monday, Facebook will attempt to make use of the remaining daily ad spend on Tuesday, and so on. In other words, unused portions of daily budgets roll forward. It should be noted, however, that regardless of this formula, the *account's* daily limit and the lifetime spending cap (that is, the limits imposed by Facebook, not you) won't be exceeded in any situation.

Whew, that was some pretty dry stuff, albeit essential constructs to understand. Take a short break and listen to some U2 for a few minutes before moving on. I suggest the song "Vertigo."

Daily Campaign Budget

Feel better? Now that we understand the two methods that determine how each campaign's daily budget is established, we need to examine how the total of all campaigns' daily budgets works against Facebook's daily spend limit.

Remember what that means. Each campaign has a daily spend budget, set by you. Facebook also sets an account-wide daily spend limit. Stated most simply, *while it's possible to create campaigns that have daily budgets adding up to more than Facebook's daily spend limit, the whole campaign will be shut off at the daily spend limit regardless of how much daily budget is left in any campaign.* Got that? Read that sentence again a couple of times.

Assume there are two campaigns, each set at a daily limit of $50. Each campaign's daily limits will spend down at whatever rates the ads within are clicked on. It's not likely that this will occur evenly between campaigns. Using round numbers to easily illustrate, if Campaign 1 spends $30 and Campaign 2 spends $20, then the default $50-per-day limit will shut the account down until the next calendar day. This is a double-edged sword because the account-wide daily limit does a nice job regulating spend on the campaigns. Reciprocally, it's a bummer having a default limit because we usually want to spend more than 50 bucks in a single day.

Another problem is that if one campaign charges out of the gate and the campaign limit is set too high, the other campaigns (which by their very nature will move slower because they're smaller segments) might not get an airing. The workaround is to launch with lower daily campaign amounts by dividing the media spend more evenly to discover which campaigns are going to spend faster. Then, once you've been running the account for a few days, start making adjustments based on knowledge of how each campaign is performing. Some campaigns should spend faster because the segments are bigger, while other campaigns with smaller segments will move more slowly.

Interestingly enough, Facebook defaults each campaign's daily budget to $50 even though the entire account daily spend is limited to $50. As a result, accidents can occur. For instance, if Campaigns 1, 2, 3, and 4 are left at the $50 default daily budget and the account-wide limit is set to $1,000, the account may spend $200 before you wake up. If you have a Facebook representative, be careful that they do not increase the daily spend too much because there is then a risk that the whole account will spend to the level of the campaigns.

The bottom line of setting the budget is as follows:

- If Facebook won't increase the spend limit and you don't have enough cash to test all your campaigns, then consider rolling out the campaigns one at a time to test how fast each will spend. Ultimately, testing each campaign is the only way to know for sure how much a campaign will spend each day. Once you understand each campaign, it's easier to budget holistically across all campaigns.

- Regardless of how big the daily limit is, regulate the account's growth at the campaign level. Use the lifetime spend setting to make sure no accidents occur.

- Be aware that campaigns spend at different rates, slower or faster, for various reasons. These include segment size, how good your ads are, and how much you bid.

- Beware of the $50 default campaign limits. They don't matter when the account restriction is low, but if Facebook increases the daily spend constraints when you're not watching, like on a weekend (which happens), and there are many campaigns, you need to expect unexpected spending.

OK, we're through the nitty-gritty, but there's still more to go. Choose whatever music you enjoy for this next section. It will make a difference.

Setting Bids

To review, *campaigns* hold one or more *ads*, and each campaign has a daily budget. Every ad within a campaign holds copy, an image, targeting, and a bid. Bids are set at the ad level and can be manipulated either within the creation/editing process for each ad and/or at the campaign overview level.

Facebook Ads is an auction model, meaning that advertisers bid against other advertisers who are vying for the same onscreen real estate. Facebook is willing to bill your credit card by two methods, from which you can choose at the individual ad level: CPC (cost per click) or CPM (cost per one thousand impressions). There is also a "quality score" for each ad comprising several signals FB monitors, including CTR, users who click the little "X" saying they don't like the ad, and other factors. The ad's position on the page, higher or lower on the right-hand sidebar, is most likely determined as follows: bid + quality score (qScore) = ad position. To you AdWords PPC jockeys, this is familiar turf.

Facebook seems to calculate the quality score inclusive of effectual CPC (eCPC) whether the ad is bid on a CPC or CPM basis. We'll get into quality score and eCPM a bit more in Chapter 9, under the "Optimizing for CTR" subheading. What you need to know at this point is that the FB algorithm pushes away from continually displaying ads on which nobody clicks, regardless of the billing model. Bummer.

A standard method of testing is to run identical ads, CPM versus CPC alternating. Such tests are the only real way to tell what's what as applies to your campaign, ads, bids, competitiveness of the social segment, and other factors.

The most important takeaway is that it is not the bid alone that establishes where your ad will be placed in relation to the other ads. It's the combination of bid and qScore. Bid + quality score (qScore) = ad position. As for the bidding strategy, Facebook suggests bids at two different points in the ad UI (that don't entirely sync up). After an ad is made, the bid is set automatically, right below the targeting information and next to where you decide what campaign the ad will be in. You can edit this preset bid, of course. The initial bid is typically about the middle of the bid range that will be suggested later in the campaign interface. Experience has shown us that bidding to the highest suggested level gets premium placement, as evidenced by CTR. The ads are low-cost enough that there is no reason to be cheap on initial launch. In fact, a poor CTR seems to affect your quality score, which will impact the cost in the future for that ad. Later in this chapter, we'll look at various methods to sharpen bidding to be more efficient.

There is no official way to correlate the bid to the position at which the ad will appear on the page (rank), or if the ad will appear at all. That's not to say that it's impossible to figure out where your ad will be placed in relation to your bid. There is an easy workaround. Go to your own Facebook profile and add in the interests you're marketing to. Though it's a far-from-perfect solution, the ranking of the ads that appear will give some indication of the competition for that social segment as well as the ranking of your ad in relation to the bid.

Change the bid and watch the effect. If it seems other, more dominant interests in your Facebook profile are impacting the ads too much, simply remove the other interests, at least temporarily. Try adjusting the bids, taking note of any change in placement. As a word of caution, there were some rogue tools out there for a while that scraped inside of Facebook to reveal ad ranking for social segments. Facebook has shown a proclivity to sue people for such activity. If you're a gray-hat marketer and data extraction is your tactic of choice, be advised.

Another classic method to figure out what bid is actually required is to start high and gradually back the bids down, all the while noting the traffic changes. It's vital not to do this in the other direction. Facebook does not say exactly what its qScore is, but certainly, there is a component that recognizes which ads do not receive clicks. It is probable the qScore takes the ad's position into account. However, the platform is too young for us to trust this algorithm, which was designed to make Facebook more money. We'd always rather start by giving Facebook money to "like" our ad (pun intended) and then gradually scale back the bids. Our experience tells us that if we start low and move higher, the results are not as good as starting high. It's always better to give Facebook money first. Consider it "buying your way into the auction."

As mentioned above, there are two basic models of bidding in Facebook Ads: cost per click (CPC) and cost per thousand impressions (CPM), shown in Figures 8.3a and 8.3b. Some advertisers swear by one of the two models, but conventional wisdom seems to skew toward CPC these days. In both bidding models, the ad's ranking is contingent on the bid and quality score. The minimum CPC at this time is $.01. The current minimum CPM is set at $.02. The minimum daily budget for CPC and CPM is $1.00. In addition, your budget must be at least two times the CPC or CPM you have specified. So, if you designate an $8.00 CPC, then the daily budget must be at least $16.00.

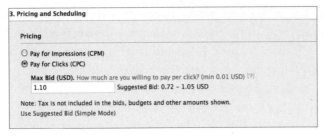

Figure 8.3a Choosing your pricing model: CPM vs. CPC Web UI

Figure 8.3b Choosing your pricing model: CPM vs. CPC, Power Editor

Cost-per-Click (CPC) Model

In the cost-per-click model, advertisers are never charged anything more than the maximum bid entered, but usually, the amount charged per click (CPC) is less. For instance, if you bid $1.10 CPC for an ad, you're telling FB that you're willing to spend up to $1.10 for a click. However, if the system determines that your ad can "win the auction" to claim the next highest position by bidding only $.80, you'll only be charged $.80 for that click. One reason we love cost per click is because all impressions that are *not* clicked on are not charged for. The other way of thinking about cost per click is no cost for no clicks! In a paradigm where hundreds of millions of impressions are common in a campaign, I really don't want to pay for impressions that don't result in traffic. Consider these extra impressions not clicked on as free branding that dilutes the CPM within the CPC model.

Your maximum CPC has to be less than the daily budget. Your daily budget has to be at least double the CPC you've stipulated. The total cost of clicks each day won't ever exceed your daily budget.

Cost-per-Impression (CPM) Model

The other bidding model, CPM, is where advertisers are charged for every thousand impressions shown regardless of whether or not users click. Facebook preaches, "As a CPM advertiser you are indicating that it is more important to you that many people see your ad, not that they actually take action after seeing your ad. CPM advertising is usually more effective for advertisers who want to raise awareness of their brand or company, while CPC advertising is more effective for advertisers who are hoping for a certain response from users (such as sales or registrations)." It has not always been our experience that CPM is less expensive for branding assignments, as opposed to clever use of CPC. Only testing will tell. CPM bottom line is that you're invoiced for impressions.

Brand advertisers should also test the CPC model, undertaking tactics whereby the CTR is limited by the ad copy. Then, all the non-clicked impressions are free. For more context, refer to the section "The Five Levels of Brand Clarity" in the previous chapter. CPC bidding and ad copy modeling are the crafty marketer's method to pay for only a few clicks while keeping the CPM extremely low.

Your maximum CPC or CPM has to be less than the daily budget. Your daily budget has to be at least double the CPC or CPM you've stipulated. The total cost of clicks or impressions each day won't ever exceed your daily budget.

Finally, Facebook also offers another option: Use Suggested Bid (Simple Mode). Selecting this option simply places your bid in the middle of the range of suggested bids in Set a Different Bid (Advanced Mode), which is how the UI defaults. Facebook does not document whether Simple Mode automatically scales the bid up or down in the pack as other advertisers bid higher or lower.

Bids can be changed at any time. We'll illustrate where in the web UI you can do this, as well as bid adjustment tactics, in Chapter 9, which deals with optimizing live campaigns.

Note: For advanced users, the really big issue with deciding between CPC and CPM is your eCPM (effective cost per thousand impressions) or eCPC (effective cost per click) across both CPC and CPM. One will be more economical based on what the advertiser wants to optimize for.

Landing Page Considerations

Targeting defines the user. The ad's creative, copy, and picture make a promise. The landing page needs to sincerely *welcome* the user, reinforce their decision to click, and funnel toward conversion. This triumvirate, when executed properly, is the magical sequence great marketers leverage in holistically herding users to KPI conversions.

The *landing page* is the web destination users are routed to by clicking on an ad (and, therefore, its underlying URL). The decisions as to where users are sent are based on two crucial factors. First, landing pages need to be based on the marketing objectives at hand. Second, there are a number of persnickety rules in the Facebook Ad Guidelines. Search FB Help section for "Advertising Guidelines" to find them. Some landing pages have forms in them for lead generation, and others have a product's detail with a Buy Now button. There are landing pages that feature white-paper downloads and event signups. The landing page is the conversion mechanism for the traffic driven from FB ads.

Experienced advertisers understand how important the quality of the landing page is to conversion. I can't tell you how many times I've heard from people that Facebook ads don't work…yet their landing page is terrible. If you care about conversion, landing pages can make Facebook ads look either really effective or really terrible. Marketers good at targeting and ad writing can drive clicks until the cows come home, dump traffic en masse on an audience all day, but whether or not those users convert probably has more to do with the landing page than anything else.

It's much the same in the real world, if you think about it. Say you're hungrily walking in the mall's food court but undecided as to what to eat. You're a fertile target for all the food-court vendors because you're a hungry human looking for food in the mall. A colorful sign for beefy, succulent Coney Island hot dogs catches your attention, but as you approach the stand, the only wieners offered on the menu are made of pinkish braised tofu. The actual destination did not keep the promise of the advertising. There's a pretty good possibility you'll turn away to find some real beef, so obviously, the conversion rate for the tofu dog vendor will suffer for the lack of promise keeping. Landing pages are the same way.

Your landing page does not exist in a vacuum. It works hand in hand with the demographic targeting and an ads creative. That's why any discussion of landing pages includes targeting and creative, the magic mustard that drove the click in the first place. Search PPC professionals have served pages contextually customized for keywords since the '90s to lift landing page conversion. Now that Facebook facilitates überfocused targeting based on personal interests, shrewd advertisers understand that users' predilections can be leveraged even further with the right socially sensitive landing page.

Let's study how the ad's creative can influence landing page elements. For Facebook users who clicked because they are interested in "Nikon hunting official," it only makes sense to route users to a gorgeous Nikon Buckmasters product page. If the ad's headline stated, "Take the Big Buck," then it may work to have the landing page's headline be, "Bag the Big Buck! Nikon Buckmasters." Subtle differences also matter. Users who clicked because of a "university" interest may respond more enthusiastically to pictures of students walking outside ivy-covered campus buildings than those interested in "music college," who may react to tight shots of undergraduates in the student-union building playing guitars. Only testing such theories will definitively tell.

It's generally accepted as best practice to reinforce the targeting criteria that incented the click as text and/or salient images on the landing page. Also, the copy, look, and feel on the landing page should be congruent in concept, message, and vernacular to the ad's headline and body copy. It's essential to undertake multivariate landing page testing, which means experimenting with different social segments, ad copy, and landing page combinations, until KPI conversion is optimized. We call this multivariate targeting/ad message/landing page testing.

Landing pages for Facebook Ads can easily be crafted to resonate on a much deeper and personal level. That's because, in addition to basic targeting elements (geographic location, ad copy concept, and time of day), other elements in the targeting grid can be amplified for landing page leverage. Just think of the groovy possibilities embodied in landing page customization contingent on gender, age, interests, education, workplace, age, sexuality, relationship status, and other social graph elements.

The extent to which landing pages can be customized is dependent on how radically the marketer divides segments into smaller, more-focused buckets. Let's say we manufacture super-stylized iPad protection cases and want to sell to everyone in the United States as well as English speakers in other countries. As opposed to lumping all the iPad users into one huge bucket, let's separate these users by age, gender, and geographic locations. A great landing page starts with segmented targeting. Let's take a look at how segmented targeting buckets would look. Figure 8.4 shows the basic United States demographic, without very much segmentation. Ads and landing pages for this segment need to be extremely general.

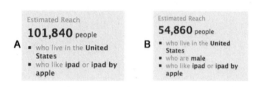

Figure 8.4 Segmenting iPad fans by qualifying "likes," age, gender, and location can help ensure that users see ads that truly speak to them.

In version B of the Estimated Reach box, we've got a bit more segmentation now. Knowing that we're targeting males means we can customize things a little more. Perhaps the landing page should show a hot lady or a dude's big muscles. Consider the effect of various background colors, font decisions, and copy density based on targeting variables and the simplicity or complexity of the ad's copy. Understanding that we're dealing with men should help focus the entire look, feel, and substance of landing pages to test.

Version C shows the same considerations as B, only for females.

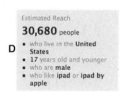

In version D, things are getting more specific. This demographic segment is targeted to males 17 and younger. The youngest Facebook user is 13 years old. Make fun of Justin Bieber and Hannah Montana, show a cute 15-year-old girl with an iPad, or otherwise invoke teenage-boy things. Keep vernacular in mind; use words such as *like, dude, OMG,* and *LMAO* in your ads. Facebook editorial usually lets us get away with colloquialisms in body copy, though perhaps not headlines. Tightly integrate the landing page by amplifying the colloquial nature of the ad's verbiage on the landing page.

Estimated Reach

5,660 people
- who live in the **United States**
- between the ages of **48** and **64** inclusive
- who are **male**
- who like **ipad** or **ipad by apple**

E

Version E is pretty interesting, because these are all the old guys (like me) who are into iPads. If you're going to sell with sex, maybe make it a mature-looking 35-year-old lady. Show an iPad in the hands of a man in that age group. Grown-ups, on average, tend to be more responsible than kids, so try pushing the "protect your coveted iPad investment" buttons in ad copy.

1,460 people
- who live in one of the countries: **United States** or **Canada**
- who are **female**
- who like **ipad** or **ipad by apple**
- who are interested in **women**

F

Version F shows that Facebook identifies 1,460 gay women in Canada or the United States. Be bold. Show women holding hands or kissing with an iPad in the picture. As mentioned earlier in the book, homosexual market segments tend to have more disposable cash, so even though this group is smaller, you might have a good amount of luck. Evaluate gay websites such as Advocate.com and OutTraveler.com for image themes, copy vernacular, color patterns, and other creative variables as insight into to how your landing page targeted to gays fits in.

Estimated Reach

4,400 people
- who live in the **United States**
- who live in **Minnesota, Wisconsin, Illinois, Michigan, New Hampshire, Massachusetts, Connecticut, New York, Vermont, Maine, Rhode Island** or **New Jersey**
- between the ages of **24** and **38** inclusive
- who are **female**
- who like **ipad** or **ipad by apple**

G

The segment shown in version G targets women between 24 and 38 living in the northern United States from the Midwest to the East Coast. During winter months, perhaps set the scene at the ski hill. Show a very cold lady dreaming of a hot guy with an iPad in Cancun. Find buttons emotional to this demographic. Push them.

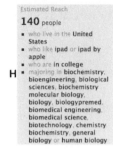

Version H is a microsegment targeting intensely scientific college students. Maybe this means technical language in the ads and pictures of lab coats on the landing page. Try quirky permutations of classic formula syntax in headlines and body copy. You know who these people are. Leverage that information.

Finally, version I shows all married guys who speak English and live in countries *other* than the United States. From Hong Kong to Austria, draw a bead on these users. Joke about whether or not they share the iPad with their wives. Maybe sell them on the protection, "If you're going to share it with the wife…." Perhaps it would be useful to portray couples so the users feel acclimated.

Dynamic Landing Pages, Tagging, and Conversion Tracking

There are two elements that are essential to good return on investment (ROI):

- The ability to build landing pages with creative elements that automatically configure based on what ad was clicked

- Conversion tracking to ascertain whether or not certain ad/landing page combinations are yielding sweet KPI fruit

This speaks to techniques that advanced marketers have using for years to sharpen campaigns in paid channels from Google AdWords to email.

The technology for both dynamic external landing pages and external page conversion tracking relies on the same technique, which involves tagging the destination URL with variables. These tags are used to "tell" the landing page's content management system how to configure the page. They're also used by web analytics to create reports that detail whether or not the landing pages are converting to KPIs or not.

When marketing to more than a few targeting segments, creating gazillions of customized landing page permutations is just not feasible with static HTML. Also, we're going to need to track conversion for pages outside of Facebook by some method. Tagging each ad with a unique set of URL variables easily facilitates these two critical needs. URL variables are the string of text after the ? in many page URLs. Most marketers are familiar with URL variables, also known as *tracking tags* or *URL parameters*, and have been using them in search PPC, email, and other online campaigns for years. Many third-party marketing programs that track metrics do the same thing.

Let's break down this example:

```
http://www.aimclearblog.com?campaign=nikon-buckmaster&headline=
Bag%20The%20Big%20Buck&ad-id=243
```

- The question mark introduces the variables. The ampersands concatenate one variable to the end of the previous one. Variables are stated as [variable name]=[variable value].

- %20 is the American Standard Code for Information Interchange (ASCII) text character to express a space (spaces are forbidden in URLs).

- campaign, headline, and ad-id are the names of the three variables.

- nikon-buckmaster is the value for the campaign variable.

- Bag%20The%20Big%20Buck is the value for the headline variable. Note that we've capitalized the words in this variable's value because this text is going to appear as the headline on our landing page.

- 243 is the value for the ad-id variable.

Start by tagging every ad with these three URL variables, where campaign is the campaign name, headline is the desired landing page copy headline, and ad-id is a unique identifier for every ad in the entire account. Keep track of the tagging in a spreadsheet, with a simple format akin to that shown in Figure 8.5. It's fine to use the same headline in various accounts. If you're ready, go ahead and include the headline, body copy, and image from each ad in the spreadsheet as well.

1	ad-id	campaign	headline
2	243	nikon-buckmaster	Bag%20The%20Big%20Buck
3	244	nikon-buckmaster	Best%20Hunters%20Use%20Nikon
4	245	nikon-scopes	Bag%20The%20Big%20Buck
5	246	nikon-scopes	Scope%20Bigger%20Bucks
6	247	nikon-scopes	Bag%20The%20Big%20One

Figure 8.5 Document your ad tagging structure in a spreadsheet for later referral.

For dynamic landing pages that autoconfigure contextually based on URL variables, ask your friendly web developer to code a request for the `headline` variable from the inbound URL and display it as text on the page. Also, ask that the main image on the landing page be swapped out (dynamic), contingent on either `headline` or `ad-id`. If this does not make sense to you, sit down with your web developer and ask them to explain. A deeper explanation is outside this book's scope, but you'll find the concepts very easy to digest. Pretty much every web developer has this basic maneuver in their bag of tricks, no matter what dynamic language your landing page is coded in—.ASP, .PHP, .JSP, .CFM, and so on.

The system of URL variables serves double-duty for use as conversion tracking tags to keep track of conversion (or not) at the `campaign`, `headline`, and/or unique `ad-id` level. Ask your analytics person to create reports that correlate traffic containing these URL variables to a completed conversion. It's really simple. If a user comes in with any [variable value] and also makes it to the dedicated "Thank You For [Converting]" page, then a conversion has occurred.

Here are some other considerations, many of which could be considered best practices:

- The variable names I used can be changed. Speak with your analytics team to ask if there are standardized variable names to serve these purposes, names that jive with the analytics platform or conversion-tagging schema in place.

- The tagging schema is by no means limited to just three variables.

- The headline concept behind using %20 is to get around using a database and to keep the dynamic landing page, actually a small application, simple. Another common method is to use only the unique `ad-id` to call a database record, which can contain any number of page elements.

- Users might link to these pages from blogs or sites. To avoid duplicate content, as pertains to search engine optimization (SEO), it is strongly suggested that these landing pages be dedicated for PPC. Keep them from being indexed organically by search engines by using `meta noindex nofollow` on the page, which is a `robots.txt` entry excluding bots from indexing the pages, and by making any links within the site to these landing pages `noindex no follow` as well. If you want to get your PPC landing pages indexed for organic search, it's usually better to create different versions.

Socializing External Landing Pages

Should direct marketers place Facebook, Twitter, YouTube, and/or other social buttons as part of the template for every PPC landing page? On first thought, the answer seems an easy yes. "Of course," you shout, "socialize everything! After all, isn't the Net all about social media these days?" How could it be right even to consider omitting the all-powerful and ubiquitous social media like-me-now buttons?

But consider the outcomes. Providing options on a landing page, other than those leading users down the conversion funnel, can bleed and spray traffic away from the conversion. We've studied many outbound-click maps for landing pages that offered users various options in addition to the conversion path. Some users, who might have converted otherwise, will absolutely forsake the commercial funnel for the social click.

If a direct-response action is the KPI, we often advise that clients relegate "being social" as the secondary KPI, minimized in graphic weight so long as testing proves it does not distract from the primary conversion. In such circumstances, I'd rather put the socialization features on the thank-you page. Sure, sometimes it makes sense to sacrifice conversions for happy social pals, but make that decision intentional, data-driven, and based on real business priorities.

For external landing pages, test enough to make sure that socialization features are not cannibalizing the primary KPI. One thing's for sure: There's no one-size-fits-all policy. Test and push the social envelope. Always remember to place customers in a well-laid funnel, herd them toward conversion, and be careful where you fragment the objectives, for any reason, even to make a friend.

"Buying Fans" with Ads and Social Landing Pages

As discussed previously in this book, you can target your own Facebook page with ads. Many organizations use Facebook Ads to build out their fan count and effectively "buy fans." The cost can be very low and the results impressive. We've seen hundreds of thousands or even millions of fans purchased for less than pennies each. Facebook Ads can be very effective in promoting social KPIs both inside and outside of Facebook. Ruminate on the possibilities. Promoting an event organized using Facebook's events tool? Consider routing clicks from ads to the event's page. The URL is easy to get by simply copying it from your browser and placing it in your ad. Facebook ads are great at supporting other Facebook social KPIs, such as getting users to like a company page, download a Facebook app, view videos, join groups, and even jump into a provocative dialog. Social landing pages inside of Facebook are the latest rage in an environment where "Ls" matter and user engagement is the new black.

Often referred to as "buying friends," sending users who click on ads to fan pages, or other in-Facebook profile pages, is probably the most ubiquitous practice. We've seen hot guerilla marketers incent users to like pages for as little as pennies per like, signing up thousands or even hundreds of thousands of users. I personally love the measurement "cost per fan" acquired (CPF). The classic play is to make desirable content available to Facebook users, but only if they've liked your page. Try posting fan-only special offers, premium content, the inside track foreshadowing an upcoming product development, or personal access to a celebrity's inside information.

Offer users anticipated white papers prior to releasing them to the general public, again, only if they like the page. There is literally a cottage industry sprouting up where third-party Facebook Ads production companies offer friend acquisition packages charging by the friend. As with most third-party lead-generation services, it may well be less expensive to do it on your own. Be the most creative kid on the block in crafting the pitch and don't be spammy. About buying friends: It's been our experience that sometimes, purchased friends are not authentic in that they don't participate much or stay around after the initial incentive has worn off. That said, other times, buying friends is a great tactic for helping people find pages they should be connected to. It depends on the pitch and the quality of the marketer's thinking. Getting users to like a page with an offer is quite different from being a good friend back and retaining your new peeps over the longer haul.

Facebook applications are another natural fit for Facebook Ads marketers. It's a no-brainer to promote an organic food authenticity calculator app to moms and dads interested in organic food, sustainable farming, children's nutrition, and other related affinities. Selling game app downloads is super-easy when marketing to Facebook users fanatically interested in Farmville and other extremely popular games. Try marketing a human memory development application to users interested in Mensa, Rubik's Cube, or the popular board game Mastermind. As with all Facebook Ads campaigns, the Tao lies in the relationships between targeting, ad creative, and how effectively you welcome users on the landing page.

Sending users to landing pages inside of Facebook has some really hot viral possibilities. Upon achieving a social KPI, the newly converted user essentially becomes a rebroadcast engine for the marketer's cause. The user's friends can usually see their pal's activities in their news feed. Since the users are in Facebook, a crucible where sharing is a main focus, your promoted content is easily trafficked from user to user, which is a common outcome. Of course, this ultimately dilutes the CPA because you pay only for the click bringing the original converted user, while the user's friends cost nothing. We've seen viral waves ripple outward from in-Facebook landing pages, as communities of users engage surrounding great content. In fact, if that does not happen, it's sometimes a reliable sign that the content is not worthy. For this reason, we often use Facebook Ads to judge the potential virility of content. Remember, we're sending users, prequalified by what we already know interests them.

Social landing pages *outside* of Facebook can be truly effective. In fact, when we're hired to promote YouTube videos organically, we'll usually test the videos' viral proclivity by sending super-focused, paid Facebook traffic to the YouTube video. Sometimes, it seems like magic. After turning on the FB ads, users thumbs up/down the video in YouTube, comment, and share the link with others...or not. Promote blog posts, Twitter feeds, Flickr photos, and socialized commerce sites with Facebook Ads.

Of course, it's nearly always a defensible choice to use your own company's website as the host domain for Facebook Ads campaign landing pages. That's where marketers have the most control. If the campaign is for a large corporation that does not cede access to the mothership website to marketers, consider marketing to a subdomain that you can control. As we'll cover in more detail in the next chapter, there are definite conversion-tracking issues when using landing pages inside Facebook, YouTube, and other sites outside your technical control. Oftentimes, it's worth the conversion tracking compromise because of potential viral implications. It's always a trade-off.

Final Prelaunch Checklist

Now, we're ready to rock. Let's make sure everything's in place:

❑ Review your payment options to confirm that the billing source is set up as you wish it to be.

❑ Facebook will constrain you with a $50 daily spend limit. Contact Facebook if you need to spend more from the get-go.

❑ Set a lifetime spend cap, if you so choose.

❑ Set each campaign's daily budget or make sure its lifetime budget and schedule are set up as you wish.

❑ Go through every ad, confirm it is set up as CPC or CPM, and make sure the bid is in range and comfortably within your budget.

❑ Determine each ad's landing page according to market segment. If marketing to an external landing page, double-check that the tracking tags are in place, according to your spreadsheet's syntax, and that the landing pages configure dynamically as expected.

❑ Adjust your campaign's budgets so there's room for ads to spend. If the Facebook-imposed daily limit is too little and Facebook won't change it, consider running fewer campaigns to start.

❑ Make sure the analytics team has actually tested your tracking tag syntax to prove conversion tracking is in place.

❑ Un-pause at every level: account, campaigns, and ads.

Great! You've worked your butt off and the Facebook Ads marketing game is on! The next chapter deals with optimizing for maximum conversion and financial efficiency.

Field Guide to Optimization and Reporting

Marketing with Facebook Ads is far from a set-it-and-forget-it affair. Once ads are running, the entire account requires constant scrutiny because plenty can go wrong, or, at the very least, your ads could not run at optimal effectiveness. Monitoring ads, campaigns, and the overall account performance is fundamental, both for tweaking efficiency and reporting results to stakeholders.

This chapter details essential Facebook Ads metrics, including how to glean actionable insights, take action to optimize the account, and report progress to team members.

Chapter Contents

Introducing Ads Manager
Navigating Facebook Ads Manager
Optimization
Facebook Reports
Wrapping Up and Looking Forward

Introducing Ads Manager

There are many nuances to the collection of administrative screens and reports made available to Facebook Ads users. Knowing which ones to call upon in order to find insight and take action can be daunting at first. Fear not, noble Facebook Ads warrior! At the end of the day, Facebook is not all that different from other online advertising platforms when it comes to optimizing campaigns.

Yes, we look at classic metrics like click-through ratio (CTR), cost per click (CPC), cost per thousand impressions (CPM), and overall cost. However, there are other measurements that are idiosyncratic to social space, and Facebook does an interesting job of parsing them for our pure social KPI optimization pleasure.

Like most ad platforms, there is a cornucopia of available data—just enough to keep advertisers from seeing the forest for the trees. Don't get caught up in the information-overload avalanche. While this chapter handles plenty of extremely granular details pertaining to nearly all the Facebook Ads reporting features, think of it more as a guerilla guide to street-level optimization. Nearly all of the really great optimization feats that can be accomplished surround the basics I just mentioned: CTR, CPC, CPM, cost, and a couple of groundbreaking social insights.

Best practice is to optimize Facebook Ads accounts, as associated with KPIs, at three levels:

- Compare ads within campaigns to all other ads within the same campaign.
- Compare ads to all other ads account-wide (including those in other campaigns).
- Compare campaigns to all other campaigns. This requires exporting reports to spreadsheets, for evaluation outside of Facebook Ads Manager.

If you're already familiar with the screens that the Ads Manager user interface (UI) comprises, feel free to skim the next section, "Navigating Facebook Ads Manager," or skip all the way down to "Optimization."

Navigating Facebook Ads Manager

OK, so you're interested in an overview of the Ads Manager UI, either as an introduction or to freshen up. Great! I have to warn you that the subject matter is pretty dry, albeit essential. As in Chapter 8, music may help. This is the hors d'oeuvres part, before the section on optimization. As I write, I'm listening to the classic Elton John, *Goodbye Yellow Brick Road* album. Let's get on with it, shall we?

Being able to easily navigate the campaign management screens in Facebook's live reporting UI, also known as Ads Manager, is the first step to learning how to optimize your Ads account. You can access the UI at any time by clicking the Campaigns & Ads option on the left-hand navigation bar after entering Facebook Ads. In the upper-left corner, all campaigns are listed and there's a handy search box to locate ads, shown in Figure 9.1.

Figure 9.1 Search, monitor, and manage all ads and campaigns in Facebook.

Ads Manager comes in two top-level flavors: All Campaigns and All Ads. At these two main levels of Ads Manager, certain properties are editable and the data can be sorted by column. The sorting is key. These two screens are where much of the optimization activity takes place, especially in All Ads. There are other reports that yield more insight, particularly at the campaign level, but sadly, the data is not editable.

In addition to the two main-level pages, there is another page with editable attributes crucial to optimization. Clicking on any campaign from the "Campaigns & Ads" screen brings you to that campaign's detail page, which shows top-level campaign data, along with one line for each ad in the campaign. Yeah, I know that this sort of nitty-gritty is rather laborious, but keep your head in the game. If you want to be a rock 'n' roll optimization soldier of love, these are the indispensable boot camp items. Metrics available directly within Ads Manager pages are updated within an hour, according to Facebook.

All Campaigns Screen

First, we'll focus on understanding the Campaigns & Ads screen. This is the default in Ads Manager and accessible at any time by clicking Campaigns & Ads in the upper left or, after you've already drilled into a campaign, by clicking on the Campaigns & Ads link on the left sidebar. Most screens in Ads Manager maintain the left-hand menu for easy access to Campaigns & Ads.

Across the top of the All Campaigns UI, recent notifications show status messages from Facebook for matters such as spending limit increases and ad approval. Daily Spend, which means how much money was spent that day, in the upper right of the screen, shows the last five days of ad spend across all campaigns.

Below Notifications, the first drop-down menu lets you toggle the time frame of visible data between viewing lifetime campaign stats, today, yesterday, last week, and a custom time frame. Figure 9.2 shows the upper part of the All Campaigns UI in all its glory.

Figure 9.2 All Campaigns main-level UI

The next drop-down box to the right lets you filter the campaigns you're looking at by status; the default filter option is All Except Deleted. Choose to view either Active (campaigns that are running), Scheduled (campaigns that are not ongoing and subject to future start and stop dates), Paused (campaigns that are currently not running), and Completed or Deleted (scheduled campaigns that have run their course or any deleted campaign). Let's stay with the default, All Except Deleted. From left to right, the columns in the Ads Manager campaign view are as follows (* denotes editable attributes):

Campaign* Editable by clicking the pencil icon as you roll the curser over the name.

Status* Sort campaigns by those running, those paused, when they are scheduled, those that have run their course, and those completed or deleted. This attribute is editable by clicking the downward-facing triangle. Use this editable field to pause an ad, make it active, or delete it.

Start Date Sort campaigns by their start date and whether they are running continuously (ongoing), paused, completed, or deleted.

End Date Sort by the end date for scheduled campaigns or by those running continuously (ongoing).

Budget* The designated maximum budget per day or the allocated for campaign lifetime budget. This field is editable by clicking the pencil icon as you roll the curser over. Remember, the entire account will be paused when your daily spend limit is reached, regardless of whether each individual campaign's budget is reached or not.

Remaining The funds remaining in today's daily budget or lifetime budget.

Spent The total amount spent on the campaign for the selected time period.

Click any column head to sort the entire report by the attribute it represents, high to low or vice versa. This view has limited actionable value because you can't see or sort all campaigns by CPC, CTR, clicks, or social attributes. Yes, Facebook removed the ability to see CPC, CTR, clicks, and social data at this level. Count that as a big, huge bummer, dude. As a result, in order to truly compare the performance of campaigns, you need to access an Ad Performance report, which details the CPC, CTR, clicks, and social data at the campaign level but does not allow you to edit anything. Later in this chapter, as we practice optimization techniques, I'll show a workaround.

Practice clicking the column heads to sort the data by each column, both descending and ascending. This is an important skill you'll need later on. Try sorting CPC from low to high and high to low, or figure out which campaign has the highest budget. Become fluent in sorting data by column because the act of optimization is all about harvesting insight from sorted data and making changes.

The check boxes on the left side of each row allow you to operate on more than one line at a time. The Select Rows To Edit button becomes active when boxes are checked, enabling batch edits to the selected rows. After clicking that button, change an attribute (Status, for example), and then click the little down arrow that appears to the right; doing so makes the same change to all selected rows.

Now, clicking on any campaign navigates to that campaign's detail page. We'll discuss that next.

(Individual) Campaign Screen's List of Ads

After clicking on a campaign from the All Campaigns screen, you arrive at the Campaign screen (Figure 9.3). This corner of the Ads Manager UI provides basic controls, metrics for all the ads within a single campaign, and some editable attributes for both the campaign and its ads. Across the top, you can edit the campaign name and change the campaign status to active or paused, or you can delete it. Budget and Duration are different links to the same pop-up to modify the daily budget (for continuously running campaigns) or lifetime budget and schedule (for campaigns that are not set to continuous). It's possible to change between continuous or scheduled here. The circular Audience graph provides relative visual representations of the following metrics:

- How many users the campaign targets (Targeted)
- How many unique users saw your ads (Reach)
- How many users' friends engaged with FB assets you're marketing with Facebook Ads (Social Reach)

Social Reach is a proprietary FB metric that shows "people who saw your campaign's Sponsored Stories or ads with the names of their friends who liked your Page, RSVP'd to your event, or used your app." If you're not using Sponsored stories or advertising a page, event, or app, you won't have social reach.

Roll your mouse pointer over the Targeted, Reach, or Social Reach circles in the Audience graph to see the exact count of users that make up the circle.

The Response graph is a line graph with the following information about the last 28 days:

- How many total clicks your ads garnered (Clicks)
- How many users liked your Facebook page, RSVPed to your event, or installed your app within 24 hours of seeing this sponsored story or ad (Connections)

If you're not promoting a page, event, or app, you won't see Connections data.

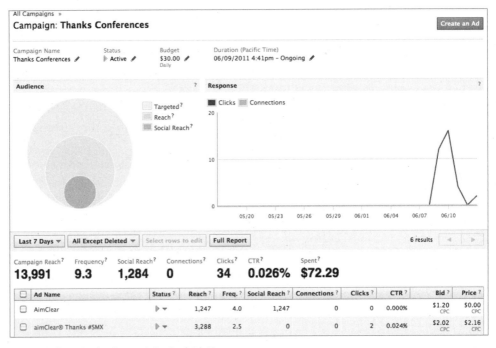

Figure 9.3 Campaign detail screen in Facebook Ads Manager

Next, moving from top to bottom, come high-level campaign metrics and controls. You can choose the time frame for the data you're looking at. The options are Last 7 Days (the default), Today, Yesterday, Last 28 Days, and Custom. The next dropdown to the right lets you choose to view ads in the following categories: All Except Deleted (the default), Active, Pending (review), Paused, Disapproved (by FB editorial), and Completed Or Deleted.

Clicking Full Report brings you to the View Advertising Report page. The report is not full at all. It's an abbreviated version of the Ad Performance Report. Though abridged, the Full Report is still useful for exporting basic data or automating email reports. I'll cover the Ad Performance report and exporting and automating reports in the section "Facebook Reports" later in this chapter.

Next on the Campaign screen, the following high-level campaign metrics are displayed:

- Campaign Reach is a numeric representation of the green Reach circle in the Audience graph. Remember, the Audience graph defaults to 28 days, so you'll have to view 28 days of data for the numeric version to get the two numbers to match.

- Frequency is a cool metric that measures the average number of times each targeted user saw your ad. I love this statistic because it gives us another way to quantify branding impact. Frequency was rolled out in May 2011 and is a sweet contribution to brand marketers. Out of the entire Ads Manager UI makeover in May, this was one of the one few substantial enhancements past cosmetics.

- Social Reach and Connections are numeric representations of the same metrics from the Audience and Response graphs. Again, you'll have to view 28 days numerically to match the two graphs' numbers.

As we explore the Campaign screen UI, take note of which attributes are editable.

One of the important methods to optimize an account is to compare ads within campaigns to other ads within the same campaign. Therefore, the Campaign screen is where that intra-campaign ad optimization takes place. We'll discuss optimization techniques shortly. For now, the columns, moving from left to right across the UI just above the list of ads within the campaign, are as follows:

Ad Name* Sort the data you're looking at alphanumerically by ad name. Each ad's name in this column is editable by clicking on the pencil icon next to the ad's name.

Status* Sort the current view by ads' status:

- Active: Ads that are running
- Paused: Ads that are paused
- Deleted: Ads that have been deleted

Each ad's status is editable by clicking the little blue triangle.

Reach This is the number of unique users who saw the sponsored story or ad. In other words, if one user sees an ad 13 times (impressions), it counts as only 1 impression in the reach metrics. This is the same metric as Reach in the circular campaign Audience graph, only expressed at the individual ad level.

Frequency This metric is a cool rendering of what many marketers have been calculating for years using spreadsheets. Frequency is the average number of times each user in the targeted segment saw the ad. As an example, if there are 1,000 users in the targeted segments and there were 10,000 impressions, the Frequency would be 10, in that the average user saw the ad 10 times.

As cool as Frequency is, it's a major bummer that there is not a straight-up Impressions metric at this level anymore. Impressions are the *total* number of times the ad has appeared in Facebook. Oh, well. We used to count impressions and do the math to determine frequency. Now, we have to take frequency and do the math to figure out impressions when looking at individual ads with the Campaign screen.

Social Reach and Connections Social Reach and Connections are numeric representations of the same metrics from the Audience and Response graphs. Again, you'll have to view 28 days numerically to match the two graphs' numbers.

Clicks Sort the current view by clicks, that is, the total number of clicks the ad or sponsored story has received. However, if your landing page is a page, event, or app, this metric also includes page likes, event RSVPs, or app installs directly from the ad or sponsored story.

In this list of ads, it's sort of staggering that there's no way to see the total cash expenditure for each ad. This limits our ability to optimize. I'm very hopeful FB will add the clarity of showing total cash spent at the ad-list level of the Campaign screen.

CTR The click-through rate (CTR) for an ad is calculated as the number of clicks the ad received divided by the number of impressions (times the ad was shown on the site) in the given time period.

Many advertisers misread FB CTR statistics because they're not used to decimals followed by the percent sign (%). To most of the mathematical world, .01 means one percent. Placing a percentage sign after the decimal expression changes things a lot.

In FB Ads, 1.0% means one percent, .1% means one-tenth of one percent, .01% means one-hundredth of one percent, and so on. Recently, I was at a corporate presentation where a jubilant marketer bragged about her massive four-percent CTR, when, in fact, what she was looking at was .04%, or four-hundredths of a percent. I didn't have the heart to turn her in. That said, .04% is not all that bad a CTR in FB Ads, and often, FB seems to be willing to run ads sitting at .015%, or 15 thousandths of one percent. Even a CTR as low as .015%, over the course of 10 million impressions, will result in 1,500 visitors, 100 million impressions, 15,000 visitors, and so on.

The bottom line is that .04%—four-hundredths of one percent—expressed as a typical decimal percentage expression is .0004, which is a very tiny-looking number.

FB places the percentage sign in such a way that very infinitesimally small numbers look more substantial. In reality, not that many FB impressions result in clicks. It's just that the impressions count is so massive that even a very low CTR, as compared to search, can result droves of traffic (Figure 9.4).

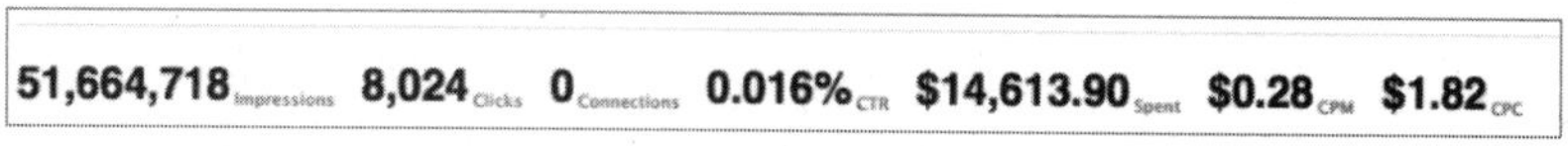

51,664,718 Impressions **8,024** Clicks **0** Connections **0.016%** CTR **$14,613.90** Spent **$0.28** CPM **$1.82** CPC

Figure 9.4 Even a CTR as low as 0.016% (16 thousandths of one percent) results in significant traffic given over 50 million impressions. There are zero connections because this campaign marketed to an external landing page.

Bid* Sort the current view by how high your bids are per ad. *Bid* means the maximum amount you're willing to pay for clicks (CPC) or every 1,000 impressions (CPM). This attribute is editable by clicking the little pencil icon.

Price For CPC ads, *Price* is the average amount you paid per click. For CPM ads, it's the average price per thousand views.

Practice sorting the data in this report by column heads. Try clicking Campaign Reach to determine which ads have been displayed the most times to your Facebook user targets or CTR to see which ads get the most clicks in tandem with the impressions...or don't. All right then, are you saturated yet? No? That's great because we're only about halfway through the screens!

Inline Ad Preview, Targeting, and Performance

Click any ad's name in the Campaign screen and the ad's detail expands downward inline. This drop-down screen is a nice stop on the way to more intensive Facebook Ads editing, providing quick access to preview the ad and view it mocked up on the sidebar of your own FB profile so you can see what it looks like to other people, as shown in Figure 9.5. The graph on the right provides quick access to that ad's performance. Toggle the drop-down menu to switch between impressions, clicks, or CTR.

Clicking on either of the pencil icons, next to Ad Preview and Targeting, takes you to the same Edit Facebook Ad screen, shown in Figure 9.5. The ad's creative, targeting, scheduling, and payments fields are prepopulated with your existing ad settings. Any changes you make here will overwrite your existing ad, and once the changes are submitted, it will stop running until reapproved by FB editorial. Once edited, the ad can be saved to only the campaign from which it originated.

The Create A Similar Ad button opens an ad creation screen that's prepopulated with attributes cloned from that very ad. This creates a totally new ad, which can be assigned to any campaign, including the campaign currently holding the original ad.

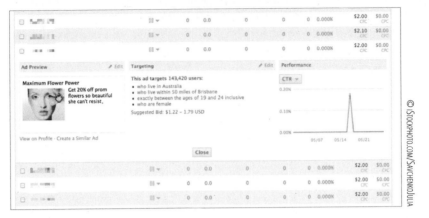

Figure 9.5 Inline ad preview, targeting, and performance screen

OK, turn up the music and let's rock on, dude! We're almost done cranking through the screens that make up Facebook's Ads Manager on our way to optimization and reporting.

All Ads Screen's List of Ads

Onward and upward, optimization ninjas! The All Ads UI is accessible by clicking the blue All Ads link, which is located just below the Campaigns & Ads link in the left column, as seen on most screens in the UI.

The difference between this screen and the previous (Campaign) is that this UI shows all ads in *every* campaign as opposed to ads for a single campaign (see Figure 9.6). The columns and editable attributes for the ads are almost exactly the same as those for ads within each Campaign screen: Ad Name*, Status*, Reach, Frequency, Social Reach, Connections, Clicks, CTR, Bid*, and Price. The only difference, since we're now looking at ads from *every* campaign, is that there is a Campaign column to show what campaign the ad is from. The ads on the All Ads screen are sortable alphanumerically by the name of the campaign that holds the ad (* denotes an editable attribute in the All Ads screen).

Clicking any ad's name opens exactly the same inline ad preview, targeting, and performance screen that's accessible via the Campaign screen. Again, take time to practice clicking the column heads to sort the data by each column, both descending and ascending. This is an essential skill you'll need later on. Try sorting bids from low to high and high to low. Sorting this view by Campaign groups ads from the same campaign. Checking multiple check boxes enables the Select Rows To Edit button for making batch edits to all rows checked. To be clear, this does allow you to limit the view to only the checked boxes. The multiline editing operation affects rows within the whole of all rows.

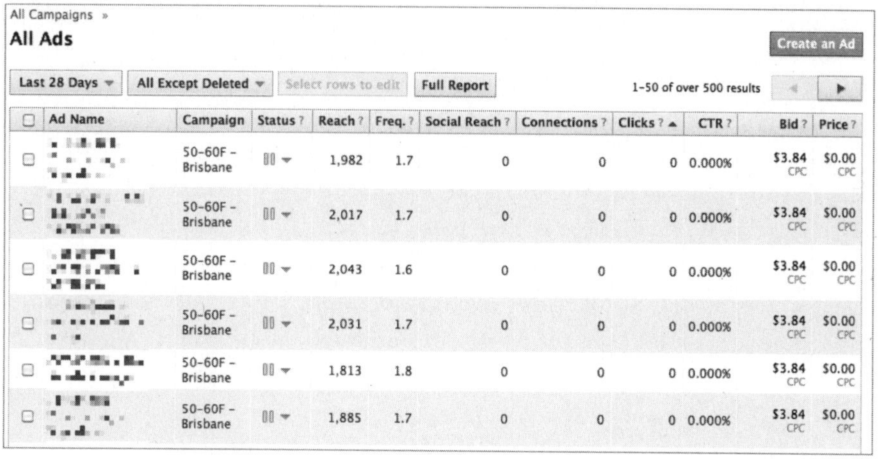

Figure 9.6 All Ads view in Facebook Ads UI

Is it starting to come together for you? Here's a quick summary:

All Campaigns screen Accessible via the Campaigns & Ads link. This UI page lists all campaigns in the account. Use this screen as follows:

- Sort campaigns.
- Edit basic campaign attributes.
- Click through to individual campaigns.

Campaign screen Accessible by clicking any campaign from the All Campaigns screen, this UI page lists all the ads within the campaign you've selected. Use this screen as follows:

- Edit campaign attributes.
- Sort ads.
- Edit ads.
- View an individual ad's detail inline, with pathways to preview the ad in your FB account, edit, and clone to any campaign.

All Ads screen Accessible by clicking on the All Ads link, this UI page lists all the ads within the entire account. Use this screen as follows:

- Sort ads, including by campaign.
- Edit ads.
- View an individual ad's detail inline, with pathways to preview the ad in your FB account, edit, and clone to any campaign.

Optimization

Now that you've had the wow-that's-dry-stuck-in-your-throat hors d'oeuvres, it's time for the caviar, baby. (I don't know about you, but I'm rocking out to "Black Cat" by Janet Jackson for this section.) To *optimize* a Facebook Ads account means to increase the efficiency of ads that remain running. *Efficiency* can mean different things to different marketers, depending on objectives and priorities.

In the simplest terms, optimizing sometimes is as easy as pausing campaigns and ads that have too high a CPC or CPM. Advertisers optimize for any metric FB gives them. Optimizing for Connections means you're working to attain conversion using a FB asset as a landing page. This might include page likes, event RSVPs, and so on. Optimizing for CTR can be about proving messages, driving a lot of traffic, or boosting quality score to keep the account healthy. It's common to optimize ads keyed on any metric FB provides—and even external analytics for external landing page KPIs. It all depends on what you're after.

An elementary expression of optimization is to pause ads or campaigns that have too low a CTR. Changing bids, thus raising or lowering an ad's rank on users' pages, is also a fundamental component of optimization. Changing out creative elements, including pictures, headlines, and body copy, is another tactic commonly employed in the optimization process, as is cloning successful ads to create derivatives. Whenever possible, conversion data should be taken into account as an account optimization variable.

There's more than one way to skin a cat, and the same goes for optimizing Facebook Ads accounts. Consider the variables at hand. Such decisions are, of course, dependent on out-of-FB variables such as KPIs, budgets, costs per lead, time frame, and other thresholds that vary from account to account, campaign to campaign, ad to ad, and advertiser to advertiser.

One marketer's bloated, overpriced lead is another's bargain-basement find. Smart brand marketers know they can purposely discourage clicks with no call to action to keep the effective cost per thousand impressions (eCPM) low while paying for only enough clicks to maintain maximum visibility. Public relations ninjas measure a social segment's penchant for various messages by how *high* a CTR they can attain, at whatever bid necessary, to rank atop the pack of ads. Direct response marketers with tight ROI margins seek the intersection of high clicks, low cost, and good conversion. Some arbitrage warriors are after cheap traffic volume against how a landing page is monetized using AdSense or other revenue-sharing affiliate networks. Just understand that whatever *you* consider optimized is relative in the eyes of the beholder.

Another important decision is whether you plan on optimizing for averages across the entire account versus strict success criteria at the individual ad or campaign levels. I usually take the former approach; if my averages are where they need to be across a whole account, I usually don't care if there are individual ads or campaigns that don't meet my criteria but are close. Others take a different approach and never let any campaign or ad be out of range at all.

There is a pallete of actions one can apply to accounts, campaigns, ads, and landing pages toward the end result of having a more efficient program, however one defines efficiency. Some optimization tactics that are not possible in the Facebook Web UI, such as cloning campaigns, *are* possible using third-party API tools. We'll work with actions one can take online in the Web UI.

Optimizing for CTR

The physical act of optimizing an account is all about the Tao of sorting data and making modifications based on insights attained by various views of the data. Let's get our hands dirty straight away and practice sorting by CTR. Know that the sorting process itself is similar for any metric we'd choose to optimize for.

Navigate to the All Ads screen by clicking the All Ads link in the upper part of the left column. Have a look at the CTR column and let's practice sorting the list of ads by CTR. The All Ads screen view defaults to CTR *ascending*, which means ads with the lowest CTR are at the top of the list. The lowest CTR may well be zero percent if you have ads that have not received any clicks. Now, let's reverse the sort. Click CTR at the top of the column. The list of ads is now ordered by ads that received the *highest* CTR. Each next click toggles between high to low and low to high.

In Figure 9.7, the descending CTR ranges downward from just over two-tenths of one percent, which isn't bad for Facebook Ads. For the record, the highest CTR we've seen for FB ads is just over 2.5%, but such a CTR is extremely rare. For perspective, usually we are very happy to attain a 1.0% CTR.

CTR ?

0.211%

0.084%

0.083%

0.077% **Figure 9.7** CTR descending

No matter what the optimization priority is, it's important to run ads for a long enough time period and deliver enough impressions to obtain sufficient data for optimization, hence referred to as a *large enough sampling*. How much data is needed? For CTR, since I look for a minimum CTR of .015%, I like the minimum number of 7,500 impressions per ad before I decide it's shown enough to judge the CTR. At 7,500 impressions, the ad should have received a minimum of one click to make my minimum

CTR of .015%. For hard-core pros who create a lot of ads and use automation, 7,500 impressions may be way too many impressions. FB uses predictive technology and may make decisions as to the "quality" of an individual ad in as soon a time as several hundred impressions. This much is not revealed. If you are in a position to make hundreds or even thousands of ads ahead of time and automate, then it can be prudent to automatically pause ads that do not attain any clicks within 300 to 500 impressions. My personal CTR minimum may be lower or higher than the next marketer. In reality, I'd much rather see CTR that approaches .04%, but sometimes that's just not realistic. In FB Ads, 7,500 impressions is a low number. The larger the sampling, the more reliable the data is. At only 7,500 impressions, one click, or lack thereof, could be a fluke. Be careful not to give up on ads and campaigns too soon, before the sampling is large enough to really tell.

Got the tunes cranking? Great! Now, we're going to use our understanding of Ads Manager screens and experience sorting reports by different values to optimize based on various real-world criteria.

In both CPC and CPM campaigns, a front line of Facebook Ads optimization is getting clicks, at least some. Whether bidding CPC or CPM, quality score (essential to any ad's ability to rank for a reasonable cost) is probably inclusive of CTR. Why does Facebook care about CTR, even for CPM bidding? Because, in the interest of serving users with ads that are compelling, Facebook is not interested in continuing to display high-ranking ads that nobody clicks because it means the ads don't serve users' needs. It's essential that you don't keep ads with terrible CTR running, even when bidding on a CPM basis, because it ultimately hurts the quality score. Just keep in mind that it takes a minimum sampling of impressions to prove CTR.

As a general rule, we don't accept CTR lower than .015%. Your clicks divided by Reach (how many unique users saw your ad) should be .1%. We'll show you how to access the unique CTR in the section "Facebook Reports" later in this chapter.

There are two main screens in Ads Manager to optimize for CTR. The first is within individual campaigns, accessible by choosing any campaign from the All Campaigns screen. Choose this option to optimize the ads within a single campaign compared to each other. The other place to optimize ads is the All Ads screen, accessible by clicking All Ads from the menu in the left sidebar. Choose this option to optimize all the ads in the entire campaign, compared to each other.

Whether you choose to optimize ads next to other ads in the same campaign or to optimize ads account-wide is a matter of personal preference. Some optimizers start with the All Ads view to get a general idea of the best and worst of each campaign's ads, and compare them to each other. With that information in hand, they dive into individual campaigns. My preferred method is to work in the All Ads screen. I tend to pause ads at the bottom of the CTR totem pole and, if any campaign has no ads left standing, deal with that later. I just don't want to leave any ads running with terrible CTR.

Here are the steps for optimizing ads for a target CTR, whether within a single campaign or the entire account by way of All Ads:

1. Run a minimum number of impressions for a large enough sampling. I like to wait for at least 7,500 impressions. As referenced above, this number may be much lower if you are in a position to create many ads and automate.

2. Navigate to either the All Ads screen or any individual campaign.

3. Sort by CTR, descending. Scroll down until you find ads that have at least 7,500 impressions and no clicks.

4. If there is not even a single click after 7,500 impressions, it's time to pause the ad. I need to see at least one click per 7,500 impressions to make my minimum CTR of .015%. Once again, this number may be much lower if you are in a position to create many ads and automate.

5. Decide what to do with newly paused ads that are below the desired CTR. If you have similar ads running with an acceptable CTR, pause ads with horrible CTR and be done with them. If you don't have any similar ads with decent CTR, then you've got some options:

Option 1: Raise the CPC or CPM bids to 20 to 30 percent above the higher end of the suggested range and keep a close eye on them. Some messages resonate better from higher positions. Keep in mind the two bid models: CPC and CPM. A bid in Facebook is the most you'll pay, not always the actual amount. Usually, the CPC bid for each ad will be at or below the bid. Actual CPMs are the same way, at or below the bid. If you took my advice and overbid in the first place, don't choose this option. Most likely, the ads just don't work well for the targeting.

Option 2: You can always run the ads a little longer, but be careful—there is probably an account-wide quality score, so we don't like to run ads with low CTRs for long.

Option 3: Pause these ads forever and make new ads. Test new ad copy or pictures in the replacements. The idea is to learn what compels users, and the best way to discover what works is to make new ads. To make new ads, choose the ever-present green Create An Ad button and assign the new ad to the appropriate campaign.

Option 4: Another great option is to clone successful ads from other campaigns and creative derivatives. Though undocumented, cloned ads retain the quality score of the source, it's better to clone a successful ad with a higher quality score than to try to improve the one that performed poorly out of the gate. Sometimes, CPC branding advertisers optimize for a lower CTR to keep the CPM down. Regulating CPM by restricting CTR (fewer clicks, less cost) while bidding on a CPC model can be more effective than CPM bidding in the hands of an expert. To optimize for lower CTR, follow the same steps but lower the bid to reduce high CTRs. Don't take CTR below the .015% threshold.

Optimizing for CPC

There are a number of reasons to optimize based on cost per click. Many external landing pages have a long-established history of user behavior, including monetization, from various channels, including Facebook Ads. In other words, site owners know that for every 500 visitors (arbitrary number) who arrive on the site via a Facebook Ads click, a certain percentage will consistently convert to a given KPI. Once an external site owner has this sort of empirical data, the assignment sometimes becomes more about the cost per click to keep the return on ad spend (ROAS) down. There are other reasons a site owner might want traffic limited to a specific cost. Perhaps, they're not sophisticated enough to handle conversion tracking or the mission is branding. Advertisers marketing to FB assets may also have a set cost per like, event signup, or application download. These are all great reasons to optimize for CPC.

CPC optimization is all about keeping the cost per action (CPA) within a set amount. When traffic at a maximum cost per click is the objective, optimize for CPC. Please understand that some social segments are more competitive than others. You might not be able to achieve the target CPC in every space.

Here's the CPC optimization technique, assuming the ads have run long enough to gather some data. Navigate to the All Ads screen, and then follow these steps:

Round One

1. Sort either the (individual) Campaign or All Ads screen by CPC, descending. That is with the highest CPC at the top.

2. For each ad that realized a CPC that's too high, calculate the percentage of the overage.

3. Reduce the bid by the same percentage of the overage.

Round Two (after running another minimum set of impressions)

1. Sort the report by CPC, descending.

2. For any ads where the impressions dropped off radically or the CTR plummeted to below the minimum .015% target CTR, pause the ads. You probably won't be able to squeeze the target CPC out of this ad without making changes other than bidding. The creative could be wrong or the bid is just too low for the ad to attain a high enough ranking to attract clicks.

3. For any ads that are still receiving decent impressions and CTR but are still over the target CPC, repeat round one.

4. Run another minimum set of impressions. Repeat round two until all ads are in range or paused and/or you decide that the desired CPC is unattainable.

Optimizing for CPM

The motivations to optimize for CPM are similar to those that drive CPC optimization. Brand marketers may purposely seek a low CTR and are after inexpensive impressions, as measured by CPM. Still, as already discussed, you have to maintain something of a CTR to keep the ads running. Here's the technique to optimize for a lower CPM, assuming the ads have run long enough to gather some data. Navigate to the All Ads screen, and then follow these steps:

Round One

1. Sort either the (individual) Campaign or All Ads screen by CPM, descending. That is with the highest CPM at the top.

2. For each ad that realized a CPM that's too high, calculate the percentage of the overage.

3. Reduce the bid by the same percentage of the overage.

Round Two (after running another minimum set of impressions)

1. Sort the report by CPM, descending.

2. Pause any ads where the impressions dropped off radically or the CTR dropped to below the minimum .015% target CTR. You probably won't be able to squeeze the target CPM out of this ad, to this social segment, without making changes other than bidding.

3. For any ads that are still receiving decent impressions and CTR but are still over the target CPM, repeat round one.

4. Run another minimum set of impressions. Repeat round two until all ads are in range or paused and/or you decide that the desired CPC is unattainable.

Optimizing for Conversion

Whenever the conversion is something *other* than impressions or clicks, optimizing for KPI conversion is almost always a great way to go.

In the case of impression KPIs (branding/exposure), optimizing means keeping the CPM low. That can be handled just fine within Facebook Ads Manager by running only ads that have low CPM and high enough CTR. If there are no ads that meet those criteria, the answer is to modify the creative. If the KPI is CPC (traffic cost), we're looking for clicks at a cost. CPC KPIs can also be handled within Ads Manager.

Other types of conversion are interesting beasts because the conversions happen *after* successfully enticing users to click. When optimizing for conversions that involve landing pages, both in and outside of Facebook, things get a little trickier. Let's look at both scenarios.

External Landing Pages

Tracking external landing pages involves external analytics software, like Google Analytics, because FB no longer offers technology to track external conversions in Ads Manager. Tracking the external "Thank You" page is a common technique; however, any *trigger* page can be used. It's important to make sure the trigger page is not accessible by any links other than at the end of the conversion funnel. Most modern analytics packages, including Google Analytics, can easily handle such conversion-tracking techniques. In Google Analytics, the easiest method is to create advanced segments that employ the following logic for each level of desired granularity. This is based on the tagging syntax suggested in Chapter 8, but you can substitute whatever tagging variable names you use:

- Conversion from any Facebook ad: `source=facebook AND page=[conversion trigger page]`
- Conversion by headline: `(source=facebook AND headline=[value]) AND page=[conversion trigger page]`
- Conversion by ad: `(source=facebook AND ad-id=[value]) AND page=[conversion trigger page]`
- Conversion by campaign: `source=facebook AND campaign=[value]) AND page=[conversion trigger page]`
- Conversion by headline within a specific campaign: `(source=facebook AND campaign=[value]) AND headline=[value]) AND page=[conversion trigger page]`

Don't be put off by how intense this looks. All we're really saying is that we want our analytics package to track any time a user shows up on the site with the URL variables and ends up on the trigger page. It's outside the scope of this book to delve deeply into handling Google Analytics or other such software, but I strongly suggest following "Occam's Razor," a fantastic blog by Avinash Kaushik, in tandem with his book *Web Analytics 2.0* (Sybex, 2010).

Analytics segments are not the only way to track Facebook conversions on external pages. Third-party products like Acquisio, ClickEquations, and others offer the ability to place their proprietary conversion technology on the trigger page, which is received and tracked as a conversion within those products. This approach is particularly useful when running hybrid-marketing programs that use other platforms, such as search PPC. Because Facebook does not offer a JavaScript–trigger page conversion code solution anymore (it tested one and withdrew it), Google Analytics is the best free solution absent a third-party tool you have to buy. We also like Wooopra, which carries a small monthly cost but is easier to handle and more visual than other tools.

Entire books have been written regarding conversion technology and the intrinsic relationship between ad copy and landing page messaging and design. I highly recommend Tim Ash's *Landing Page Optimization: The Definitive Guide to Testing and Tuning for Conversions* (Sybex, 2008).

Here are the steps for conversion tuning on the landing page:

1. If you're not using a dynamic headline (Chapter 8) on the landing page to really keep the ad's promise, consider doing so.

2. Test variations of the landing page, rotating key elements like copy, images, form fields, and color schemes with different design weight on the page. You're dealing with visitors who already clicked an ad that made a promise. Ask yourself why the promise is not paying off with conversions. Be brutal in the assessment. Ask if the KPI is actually possible.

3. Consider adjusting the KPI and/or the approach of the ad messaging.

4. Check for traffic bleed using a feature such as Google Analytics overlays. Are there way too many options on the page for users to take, moving them away from the conversion funnel? If so, limit the options by reducing link choices on the page except for those pointing to the conversion path.

5. Does the conversion require less information than is offered on the page? Is page copy too dense? Replace the excess with bullet points that summarize. Use bigger fonts.

6. Does the conversion require more information? Make the landing page a *microsite landing page*. In other words, create several interlinked pages with the conversion funnel entry in the same place on every page. Make the interlinked pages the only options on every page. This way, there will be no bleed because the only destinations have the conversion funnel.

7. Pull Responder Demographics and Responder Profiles reports for insight as to the age, gender, and other interests of the users you're driving to the page. Mine that insight and make changes to the page. We'll discuss those reports later in this chapter.

Here are the steps to help conversion tuning in Facebook Ads creative:

1. Pause ads that drive traffic, even at a good CTR. Clone them and test variations that align more closely with the substance and form of the landing page.

2. Test more congruent images.

3. Foreshadow the landing page content concept in a more tightly aligned manner.

4. Change the dynamic headline to form a better one-two punch between ad and landing page.

Facebook Internal Landing Pages

Tracking conversion within Facebook is possible with Facebook's Conversion and newly minted Connections metrics. Connections are reasonable measurements of internal Facebook conversion. They replace the recently retired Actions metric. If you're not marketing to an internal FB asset (page, event, or app), you won't see Connections data. Sadly, even when exporting reports to CSVs, there is no Connections percentage—only a hard count.

FB describes Connections as "the number of users who liked your Facebook Page, RSVPed to your event, or installed your app within 24 hours of seeing this Sponsored Story or ad." Connections can be considered a conversion metric if the KPI is about likes, events, or app installation.

The Conversions metric is essentially the same as Connections, except that Conversions includes users who liked your Facebook page, RSVPed to your event, or installed your app within 28 days of clicking on (not viewing) your Sponsored Story or ad, as opposed to 24 hours.

 Tip: To facilitate conversion tracking for FB assets, segment your campaigns by the type of FB asset. In other words, keep event, app, and page ads separated by campaigns dedicated to each KPI. FB lumps together the three internal conversion types in the Connections and Conversions metrics, and you'll want to be able to track them separately.

Of course, there is less you can do to optimize the landing page for some internal FB assets because we're talking about Facebook here, so design options are fairly limited. Still, you can redesign the page, rejig the app, or run an event users care about more. The key is looking at the demographic segment and ad copy that incented the click and asking if the FB asset's landing page keeps the promise made by the ad's creative.

Here are some steps for optimizing ads for KPIs measuring page/app likes and event RSVPs, at either the All Ads or Campaign level:

- Run a minimum number of impressions until you're satisfied that there is a large enough sampling.

- Consider optimizing for CTR first and running another sampling so you're operating on ads that users actually click while keeping the quality score up.

- From either the All Ads or All Campaigns screen, sort the data by Connections, descending. The ads at the top, with the highest connection numbers, are the best converting ads or campaigns. Since there is only the Connections count, you'll have to calculate the conversion ratio. To do so, divide the total clicks by total connections.

- Decide what percentage of conversion is acceptable.

- Pause the ads on which you're spending money and not achieving any conversion. If you have ads that convert at a high enough ratio, consider running just those ads.

- Clone the ads that convert sufficiently and make subtle changes—just enough so that users don't get sick of them over time.

- Change the verbiage, pictures, and any other elements of the page, event, or application that are within your control. If users are not converting after clicking, then it's critical to determine where the disconnect is.
- Double-check the targeting to make sure the crowd you're getting to click is really the best audience for the page.
- Pull Responder Demographics and Responder Profiles reports for insight into the age, gender, and other interests of the users you're driving to the page. Mine that insight and make changes to the page.

If the Connections metric suffers from the same lack of consistency as Actions did, then Connections won't work all the time. This is not to criticize FB because we love what they're bringing to market. Know that you might be doing everything right, marketing to an internal FB asset, and the Connections stat might act wonky.

Keep *Social reach* in mind when optimizing for conversion for internal FB assets. As mentioned earlier, Social Reach is a proprietary FB metric that shows "people who saw your campaign's Sponsored Stories or ads with the names of their friends who liked your Page, RSVP'd to your event, or used your app." Here's how it works: FB user #1 converts in a way that is measured in the Connections metric. When their friends see the ad or sponsored story, the impression is bolstered by an additional caption highlighting user #1's conversion by saying user #1's name. If you're not using sponsored stories or advertising a page, event, or app, you won't have Social Reach.

The main method to optimize for greater social reach is to create apps, events, and pages that truly resonate with the users you're targeting. With no connections, there is no social reach. Sort your data by social reach and note ads and targeting segments that have both connections *and* social reach.

Ad Fatigue, Rotation, and Variants

A final note about optimization: Facebook users tend to get sick of ads that are in their faces for too long. When users click the little *X* to signify they don't like the ad, it affects quality score and can hurt advertisers—that is, if you believe Facebook. One surefire sign of so-called ad fatigue is when the CTR begins to decline for ads that have been consistently successful. Ads left on for too long almost always show signs of fatigue at some point.

The antidote is to constantly create variants of ads by cloning successful ones and altering them enough to change the feel without hurting whatever intrinsic qualities make them successful. Once you have three or four derivatives of successful ads that work, plan a schedule of rotating them to the social segment to which you're marketing.

It's best practice to give users a break sometimes. We've all had ads that made us sick because they've been crammed in our snoot for weeks at a time. Don't be that guy (or girl). Best practice for beating ad fatigue is to create variants of successful ads, rotate them, and take breaks.

Facebook Reports

The good news is that after working with Ads Manager, you'll find that using Facebook reports is a piece of cake because there are only a few additional metrics to think about, which we'll highlight in the following sections.

The Facebook Reports module has really matured over the last year, but keep in mind that Facebook is famous for trotting out new reports that don't completely work or are inconsistent. There's sometimes little rhyme or reason as to why some reports produce results and not others. Little documentation exists, and saying it like it is, things can add up to a great big OMG! Bottom line: If something is not working, there's at least some chance it's not your fault. These reports have changed without notification over the years, so expect them to change overnight. Visit KillerFBAds.com for updates on current changes to the reporting module.

There are four types of FB Ads reports: "Advertiser Performance," "Responder Demographics," "Responder Profiles," and "Conversion By Impression Time." We'll tackle them each in order.

Advertiser Performance Reports

Advertiser Performance reports are by far the most commonly used reports in FB Ads. They provide insight regarding the entire account, campaigns, ads within any individual campaigns, and ads compared to others across the entire account. In fact, the FB Ads Manager UI data screens are, in a sense, preset versions of Advertisers Performance reports, with the ability to edit some attributes and extra goodies (like graphs and other controls) on the side. There are three levels of preset Advertising Performance reports by way of the Ads Manager UI screens. We'll start there before heading into the designated Reports module directly for more granular custom reports.

Via Ads Manager UI Screens

First, the Ads Manager HTML UI screens—All Campaigns, (Individual) Campaign, and All Ads—are essentially preset "light" versions of Advertiser Performance reports with key editable attributes. What makes these UI screens unique is that they're the only place that attributes essential to live optimization are editable. The other three levels of reporting provide insight, but you must return to the Ads Manager UI screens to actually make the edits. This is a huge difficulty. We hope that in the future, FB brings the ability to view and sort by additional metrics in the Ads Manager UI screens so the feedback provided by advanced metrics is more actionable for optimization.

At the next level of Advertising Performance reports by way of the Ads Manager UI, the full report provides another HTML view of the UI screen. The full report is accessible as presets in each of the UI screens mentioned earlier in the chapter. Full reports are not full at all. Sure, additional metrics are added to, but others are removed from, those proffered in the stock Ads Manager UI. The columns are sortable as HTML, but no attributes are editable at this level, except for the date range of the full report you're viewing. Once you select any full report, you are no longer in the Campaigns or Ads sections of Ads Manager. If you look at the left sidebar, you'll see that Reports is now highlighted.

At the third level of Advertising Performance reports via the Ads Manager UI, CSV exports come to us by exporting full reports. Again, they are preset Advertising Performance reports, traceable to the root Ads Manager UI that resulted in the Full report. Compared to the Full report, no metrics are lost and several are gained. CSV exports provide the fullest rendering of FB Ads metrics. You view them in spreadsheet software, like Microsoft Excel. Be aware that reports via CSV export may take up to 48 hours to fully populate.

Table 9.1 shows preset metrics available for All Campaigns, (Individual) Campaign, and All Ads at the UI, full report, and CSV export levels. Take a look at how All Campaigns, (Individual) Campaign, and All Ads screens offer pathways to levels of Advertising Performance reports.

Via Reports Link

Click Reports to access the screen to create custom reports (Table 9.1). Advertising Performance reports are functionally the same as full reports and CSV exports. However, they are not presets.

Here, you can choose from many additional options for more or less granularity in reporting. Spawn reports at the account, campaign, or ad level. Preset time ranges are monthly, weekly, daily, and a custom option, which makes it extremely easy to report for any time period, like three-day or two-week intervals.

The filters control is the bomb because it was long awaited. Facebook has finally given us tools to pull reports that include only the campaigns or ads we actually *want* in reports. (Read this next part slowly!) When you're pulling reports segmented by campaign, filtering by campaign brings up a system of check boxes that, when checked, create a report that includes only the selected campaigns. Filtering by ads gives you the option to include individual ads.

Any report that can be created by hand can be scheduled by email, which means automating reports is a snap. Just look for the Schedule This Report button, and follow along with the processes shown in Figure 9.8 and Figure 9.9. Choose weekly or daily and then active, paused, or deleted. Enter the recipients' email addresses and there you go.

▶ **Table 9.1** Preset Advertising Performance reports attributes for Ads Manager UI screens, Full reports, and CSV exports. (An asterisk denotes editable attributes.)

	All Campaigns UI HTML	All Campaigns Full Report HTML	All Campaigns Full Report Exported to .csv	(Individual) Campaign UI HTML	All Ads UI HTML	All Ads UI Full Report HTML	(Individual) Campaign Full Report HTML	All Ads UI Full Reports Exported to .csv	(Individual) Campaign UI & All Ads UI Full Reports Exported to .csv
Metrics									
Campaign (Name)	X*	X	X	X* (Campaign Only)	X	X	X	X	X
Notifications & 5-Day Spend	X								
Audience & Response Graphs				X (Campaign Only)					
Campaign ID			X						
Ad Name				X* (Ads Only)	X*	X	X	X	X
Ad Id						X		X	X
Status	X*			X* (Campaign & Ads)	X*				
Start Date	X								
End Date	X								
Date or Date Range (Current View)	X*	X*	X	X* (Ads' view)	X*	X*	X*	X	X
Duration (Start Date & End Date)	X			X* (Campaign only)					
Budget	X*			X* (Campaign Only)					
Remaining	X								
Spent	X	X (Account & Individual Campaign)	X	X (Campaign only)	X	X (Account & Ads)	X (Campaign & Ads)	X	X
Bid				X* (Ads Only)	X*				
Price				X (Ads Only)	X				

	All Campaigns UI HTML	All Campaigns Full Report HTML	All Campaigns Full Report Exported to .csv	(Individual) Campaign UI HTML	All Ads UI HTML	All Ads UI Full Report HTML	(Individual) Campaign Full Report HTML	All Ads UI Full Reports Exported to .csv	(Individual) Campaign UI & All Ads UI Full Reports Exported to .csv
Impressions		X (Account & Individual Campaign)	X			X (Account & Ads)	X (Campaign & Ads)	X	X
Social Impressions		X	X					X	X
Clicks		X (Account & Individual Campaign)	X	X (Campaign & Ads)	X	X (Account & Ads)	X (Campaign & Ads)	X	X
Unique Clicks			X					X	X
Social Clicks			X					X	X
CTR		X (Account & Individual Campaign)	X	X (Campaign & Ads)	X	X (Account & Ads)	X (Campaign & Ads)	X	X
Unique CTR			X					X	X
Social CTR			X					X	X
CPC		X (Account & Individual Campaign)	X			X (Account & Ads)	X (Campaign & Ads)	X	X
CPM		X (Account & Individual Campaign)	X			X (Account & Ads)	X (Campaign & Ads)	X	X
Reach			X	X (Campaign & Ads)	X			X	X
Social Reach			X	X (Campaign & Ads)	X			X	X
Social %			X					X	X
Frequency			X	X (Campaign & Ads)	X			X	X
Connections		X (Account Only)	X	X (Campaign Only)		X (Account Only)	X (Campaign Only)		

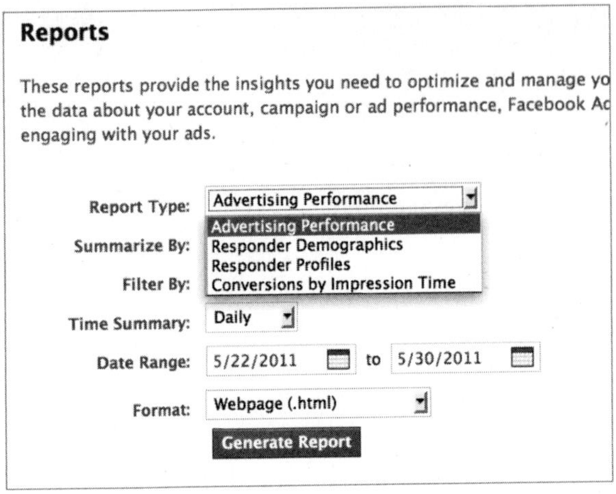

Figure 9.8 The Reports screen, accessible by clicking the link of the same name on the left sidebar

Figure 9.9 Create recurring reports for Facebook Ads campaigns.

Advertiser Performance Metrics

Previously, we've detailed the following metrics that appear in Table 9.1. These metrics represent nearly all the metrics FB offers by way of the Ads Manager UI and Reports:

Audience & Response Graphs

Reach

Social Reach

Frequency

Connections

Ad Name

Status

Clicks

CTR

Bid

Price

CPM

Spent

Campaign Name

Start Date, End Date, and Date Range

Remaining

Impressions

Budget

A few additional metrics appear in full reports and their CSV exports:

Campaign ID and Ad ID Facebook assigns unique identification number to campaigns and ads, thus the Campaign ID and Ad ID metrics.

Unique Clicks, Unique CTR The *unique* statistics take into consideration that a single person may click an ad multiple times and that person is counted as only one click in the unique metrics.

Social Impressions Facebook has described this metric as "how many times your ad was displayed along with social context surrounding the viewer's friends who have connected with your page, event, or application." While this metric still appears on some reports as of this writing, FB appears to be renaming it Social Reach.

Social % Facebook has described this metric as "percentage of overall impressions that included social impressions." Keeping in mind that Social Reach means how *many* users saw your ad with friends' names, Social % is the percentage of users who saw the ad in a social context.

Social Clicks How many clicks resulted from Social Impressions (Social Reach). I love this metric because it clearly demonstrates if there is any value to serving ads in a social context.

Social CTR The social click-through rate is the percentage of Social Impressions (Reach) that result in social clicks.

Responder Demographics

The Responder Demographics report offers fascinating data about users who are viewing and clicking ads. This can be incredibly useful for tweaking campaign attributes from the targeting grid to landing page copy and images. Each row is different, which can be a little confusing at first. The Demographic column is the key to each row, meaning it explains the rest of the data in the row. For instance, if it reads region, then this row will tell you how a certain region and its states (subregions) responded to your ad. Other possibilities include gender, age, and country.

Have a look at the report shown in Figure 9.10. It tells us that over 5 percent of the target segment Gamer - YoVille hails from New Hampshire. That segment made up 7.2 percent of clickers and, as one would assume, had over .8 percent CTR. Our Car Town targets responded in an even more impressive way. From South Carolina, these users made up 1.21 percent of overall impressions and 7.46 percent of clickers and also had more than .8 percent CTR. Restaurant City gamers, comprising 3.43 percent of our impressions and a whopping 17.52 percent of clickers, are male and between the ages of 35 and 44.

Report Type Responder Demographics	Summarize By Campaign	Time Summary Monthly	Date Range 2/1/2011 - 4/6/2011				
Date ?	Campaign ?		Demographic	Bucket 1	Bucket 2	% of Impressions	% of Clickers	CTR ↑
Apr 2011	*Gamer - YoVille		region	us	New Hampshire	0.502%	7.205%	0.866%
Apr 2011	*Gamer – Car Town		region	us	South Carolina	1.215%	7.463%	0.842%
Apr 2011	*Gamer – Restaurant City		gender_age	M	35-44	3.436%	17.528%	0.568%

Figure 9.10 Responder Demographics report

Use the extra insight available in this report to optimize Facebook accounts. I'd craft landing pages for YoVille users that feature pictures of New Hampshire landmarks and ones for Restaurant City users with pictures of 32-year-old ladies with a fork in their hand. Sure, it takes a lot of time to plod through Responder Demographics reports, but they can yield a particularly powerful perspective on who the users are within certain social segments. Don't eat it all at once.

Responder Profiles

When it works, and it often does not, the Responder Profiles report is completely awesome. For campaigns or ads, Facebook tells us more about the users who view or click the ads. Excerpts from the users include books, movies, TV shows, and other interests. The report is rather intense, radical, and bordering on experimental. In my mind, it's freakin' miraculous.

According to Facebook, "the 'Responder Profiles' report will give you more information about the types of users who see or click on your ads based on interests they have listed in their personal Facebook profiles." Facebook doesn't tell us much at all about how to read the sucker. Here's some advice on how to think about it.

The Responder Profiles report looks for characteristics that users of the same interest have in common. In the demonstration report shown in Figure 9.11, users who like Buddhism (line 2) tend to read the Bible, like the movie *Lord of the Rings*, listen to classical music, and watch *Family Guy* on TV. Whew! What does this mean? Well, quite a lot—now I know that I may get a good result targeting users who like *Lord of the Rings*.

Campaign Name	Interest	# Clickers (Interests)	Rank by Estimated CTR (Interests)	Book	# Clickers (Books)	Rank by Estimated CTR (Books)	Movie	# Clickers (Movies)	Rank by Estimated CTR (Movies)	Music	# Clickers (Music)	Rank by Estimated CTR (Music)	TV Show	# Clickers (TV Shows)	Rank by Estimated CTR (TV Shows)
Spiritual - Buddhism															
	reading	252	1	harry potter	51	1	lord rings	75	1	beatles	174	1	house	183	1
	buddhism	221	2	bible	41	2	star wars	67	2	classical	167	2	family guy	154	2
	art	190	3	catcher in rye	34	3	matrix	64	3	jazz	159	3	lost	130	3
	photography	140	4	new earth	34	4	notebook	64	4	blues	108	4	office	101	4
	music	352	5	power now	30	5	fight club	57	5	rock	106	5	dexter	99	5
	meditation	113	6	siddhartha	< 30	6	pulp fiction	57	6	pink floyd	100	6	weeds	95	6
	yoga	111	7	kill mockingbird	< 30	7	casablanca	48	7	classic rock	84	7	heroes	82	7
	writing	105	8	alchemist	< 30	8	shawshank redemption	48	8	bob marley	83	8	greys anatomy	77	8
	movies	104	9	four agreements	< 30	9	amelie	47	9	radiohead	74	9	simpsons	77	9
	cooking	100	10	tao te ching	< 30	10	princess bride	47	10	reggae	66	10	csi	73	10

Figure 9.11 Responder Profile report

Responder profiles don't always work, so don't be surprised if you're doing everything right and the report returns all goose eggs. Again, FB's platform is young, and it brings new features to market quickly and then troubleshoots.

Conversions by Impression Time

The Conversions by Impression Time "shows the number of conversions organized by the impression time of the Facebook Ad a conversion is attributed to, categorized by the length of time between a user's view or click on the ad and the conversion (i.e., 0–24 hours, 1–7 days, 8–28 days)."

Well, we've done it. We've spent some solid time looking at account optimization and reports. Good for you, loyal reader, for hanging in there through some pretty granulose hyperbole.

Wrapping Up and Looking Forward

We are living in a golden age of contextual targeting. As exciting as it is, experienced online marketers know that just about the only thing that truly stays the same is that practically nothing ever stays the same. Just look at formerly monolithic Internet icons such as Netscape, AOL, Yahoo! Search, and Myspace. During the height of their successes, it seemed as if things would go on forever as users adopted the channels and flocked in massive droves. Time has taught us that even the mightiest Internet Goliaths are not impervious to technology's relentless march and whims of flighty users. Sure, Facebook seems strong, really strong. But is it realistic to think that it will remain the dominant social platform in perpetuity? Will Facebook be the daily destination for the bulk of our planet's online users in 30 years? Maybe, but probably not...

What's really important about Facebook is that it was first to market with a forward-thinking advertising product based on social-graph data points—which, it turns out, do an awesome job of profiling people. The targeting capabilities rolled out in 2007 incinerated the day's paradigm. They still do. Never before were advertisers able to serve ads targeted to such an extraordinarily focused grid of tangible human behaviors, as advised by the undertakings of physical humans. The accomplishment is nothing short of anthropological in nature. For this magical moment in time, Facebook's reach and targeting muscle represent the uncontested gold standard for new-world contextual targeting.

What's important to marketers is that we seize the opportunity and learn to market in contextual space. Many people I run into at online marketing conferences have never heard of AltaVista or Lycos, nor do they remember the early days of Netscape, GoTo, or Overture. In the '90s, many of us cut our teeth on those channels. Those channels are long gone from the public eye. Dude, they were absolutely essential to early-adopter marketers as we learned to navigate an incredible new paradigm known as search!

Facebook is of the same magnitude and, to be frank, much more important than just Facebook. As an industry, we're preparing for what's next, mastering targeting theory that will last forever. Facebook and whatever channels bubble to the surface next will most likely bring fully functional contextual targeting to fruition to take its rightful place next to search.

One thing's for sure. Getting good at Facebook Ads now prepares you for what's next. There are already other emergent contenders in the contextual-targeting universe. International B2B powerhouse LinkedIn has amassed over 100 million users, as of this writing, and is expanding quickly. Having recently added the ability for advertisers to take aim at individuals' occupations in a grid of other attributes, including workplace and seniority (Figure 9.12), LinkedIn Ads just got a whole lot more serious. One would think LinkedIn has the data points to refine and deepen targeting even further, should it rise to the occasion. Still, the community is one-sixth the size of Facebook, and advertising can cost more than four times what Facebook ads cost on either a CPC or CPM basis. LinkedIn is all about professional behavior, so no matter what, it's not likely we'll ever be able to target the "whole user" to the same extent we can on Facebook.

Google-owned YouTube, in tandem with Google itself, has fascinating possibilities. To market to a "social graph," a large sampling of users must undertake social and information-seeking activities, fill out their profiles, interact with each other, and share. Certainly, the voluminous nature of users searching Google and YouTube—and interacting with each other on YouTube—has given Google the critical mass of data required to create a true socio-contextual targeting platform. We'll have to wait and see. For now, in the world of social-graph marketing, Facebook's dominance is uncontested.

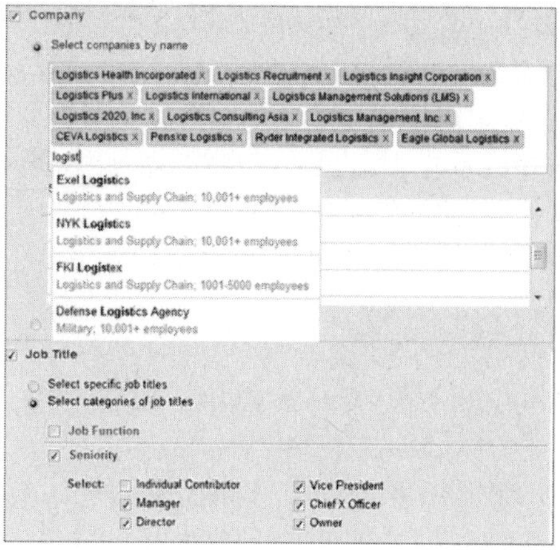

Figure 9.12 Targeting by job title and company in LinkedIn

What will be next? For physical world businesses, whose locations matter, geographical context will have something to do with it. As smartphones such as BlackBerry, iPhone, and Droid continue to evolve into "the norm," online communities accessed by mobile handsets will mash up whole-person social-graph targeting with physical location and surely offer next-gen' social-graph targeting. Mash in community platforms like foursquare (Figure 9.13) and discount websites like Groupon or review sites like Yelp and the possibilities are fascinating.

Figure 9.13 Geo-tagging social platform foursquare

Perhaps social platforms will be integrated into other devices like cars and refrigerators. Whatever the evolution, Facebook is poised to succeed, if for no other reasons than the critical mass of users and a guerilla throw-it-at-the-wall philosophy. One thing's for sure, the seeds for what's next probably already exist technologically and socially, just waiting to be brought online as a reflection of real life.

The future may well be both embodied in the combination of services like those just mentioned and in partnerships formed by mergers and acquisitions and mashed up with modern mobile. No matter what's next, Facebook was the first real target practice any of us have ever had in shooting at the social graph.

Facebook could emphasize search behind its walled garden. Or, it'll continue in partnership to integrate more deeply with Bing. To many, the holy grail of demographic targeting is to assign social attributes to keyword queries. For instance, what if marketers reliably understood that 47-year-old single men from New York who like the New York Rangers searched for "Rubbish removal service," while college girls in Boston who like Lady Gaga search for "Trash removal company"? Microsoft adCenter Labs has long had early tools along such lines, though it did not have the sampling to make the data reliable. Facebook has the means to make this future possible.

In the future, there will be new platforms, Facebook and/or others, that mash up search, social graph, and physical location to offer extreme benefits to users who will migrate toward those benefits, to or away from Facebook. As that happens, futuristic ad platforms will be built, affording advertisers more insight than ever to identify and target market segments. However, there's no reason whatsoever to wait. My friends, the future is here. Rock on, killer Facebook Ads!

Facebook Ads Preflight Pocket Checklist

A This checklist includes everything from determining strategic direction to setting up account infrastructure to creating great ads, targeting, bidding, and optimizing. It's a great document to consult to make sure all the suggested steps, core tasks, and crucial things to remember are in place before you launch any campaign.

Set KPIs.

- ❏ Verify objective fits within Facebook's terms of service.
- ❏ Take feedback from team and/or client.
- ❏ Achieve team buy-in.
- ❏ Render KPIs in writing.

Designate Facebook account.

- ❏ If using client's account, gain administrative access to the ad account.
- ❏ If not using client's account, create business (Ads Only) account.
- ❏ Share access to the account with client or other managers as appropriate.

Designate payment method.

- ❏ Credit card (agency's or client's).
- ❏ PayPal account.
- ❏ Facebook credit.
- ❏ Contact Facebook for $10K+ media spends, to request a direct account.

Choose landing page according to KPI.

- ❏ External URL: Optimize landing page variants for testing and code dynamic page attributes contingent on URL tags, or
- ❏ Internal Facebook asset: Ad account must have administrative access to the Facebook page for this.

Set targeting attributes.

- ❏ Location
- ❏ Likes/interests
- ❏ Advanced demographics
- ❏ Education/work
- ❏ Connections on Facebook
- ❏ Literal, competitive, and/or inferred targeting

Design ads.

- ❏ Choose from five levels of brand clarity to test.
- ❏ Choose ad images, double-check licenses.
- ❏ Treat images.
- ❏ Create headlines and body copy.
- ❏ Have enough images to support rotation and reduce ad fatigue.
- ❏ Legally, determine what you can say (consider TOS).
- ❏ Choose from five tiers of brand transparency, headline, and body copy.

Determine budgets and bids.

- ❏ Choose CPC vs. CPM.
- ❏ Decide between ongoing or fixed schedule.
- ❏ Set schedule if fixed schedule.
- ❏ Set daily campaign limits if ongoing.
- ❏ Check bids.
- ❏ Set account lifetime cap.
- ❏ Contact Facebook to raise daily limit if necessary.

Confirm analytics sufficient to verify KPIs.

- ❏ Confirm campaigns are segmented sufficiently to delimit conversions using the "Connections" metric.
- ❏ Confirm analytics installation and confirm conversion trigger for out-of-Facebook landing pages.

Launch!

- ❏ Make sure all ads and campaigns are not paused.

The Great Big
Search & Social Media
Marketing Twitter
Follow List

B

At conferences, I'm commonly asked which marketers I personally follow. This appendix formalizes the answer. While Facebook ads are vastly underrepresented in social media sharing, my friends still tweet about them. These connected tweeps also chatter about important marketing stuff that's crucial to Facebook Ads marketers. Since Killer Facebook Ads *is primarily a marketing book that deals with KPIs, ad writing, and so on. Those I've included are important social media and search marketing resources to follow, not necessarily specific to Facebook Ads, but still packing crucial information.*

One thing I totally love about the online marketing community is how completely willing so many talented professionals are to share their tricks, resources, and very lives in public for free. Straight up: To follow these marketers means to be in the know. Some of them are famous in the industry, others fly under the radar. This is not intended to be any kind of complete list, just some of the twitterpies that matter to me the most. Yep, these folks are among the tops on my personal follow list and I owe each a debt of gratitude for teaching me every day.

@aaronwall Aaron Wall, founder of the famed SEO Book, offers unique insights on search engine optimization (SEO) and world and industry news. If you don't read SEOBook, you should.

@AirDisa Disa Johnson is owner of SearchReturn and creator of Mobile Sidecar. Disa has a passionate flair for marketing and a penchant for sharing her finds on Twitter.

@aknecht Alan K'necht, President of K'nechtology and founding partner at Digital Always Media, blogs at TheLastOriginalIdea.com and tweets really useful nuggets.

@AmyVernon Amy Vernon: bacon queen, Tumblr lover. This freelance writer and new media strategist injects humor into her tweets without fail. Check out her posts on AmyVernon.net.

@Andrew_Beckman Andrew Beckman, CEO of Location3 Media, shares his passion for SEO by blogging on Location3.com and sharing news, advice, and insights via Twitter.

@andrew_goodman Andrew Goodman is author of *Winning Results with Google AdWords* (McGraw-Hill/Osborne, 2005), blogger at Traffick.com, and columnist with ClickZ.com. He's also the president of Page Zero Media (agency) and cofounder of HomeStars.com.

@andyatkinskruge Andy Atkins-Krüger is CEO of WebCertain and your go-to Twitter resource for international SEO, search, and PPC information.

@AnnieCushing Annie Cushing is director of analytics for BlueGlass. She makes data sexy, ninja-tweets technical tidbits, and blogs for the company.

@aschottmuller Angie Schottmuller is founder of Interactive Artisan and an active tweeter focused on conversion, e-commerce, SEO, social media, mobile, design, analytics, and more.

@audette Adam Audette is CEO of AudetteMedia and an SEO specialist who offers real Twitter conversation. Check out AudetteMedia.com for a slew of insightful posts.

@avinash Avinash Kaushik authored *Web Analytics 2.0* (Sybex, 2010) and *Web Analytics: An Hour A Day* (Sybex, 2007) and is cofounder and CEO for Market Motive, analytics evangelist for Google, and blogger for Kaushik.net.

@beebow Lauren Litwinka, online marketer and publications manager at aimClear, tweets 'round the clock on the latest in search and social. A nice blend of snark, sweet, and smart.

@beussery Google Webmaster Help Top Contributor, Search Engine Watch moderator, Flash SEO expert, UGA official artist, director of SEO technology for Search Discovery, Inc., and blogger for BEUssery.com and SearchEngineWatch.com.

@bgtheory Brad Geddes is a PPC geek, official AdWords seminar leader, and author of *Advanced Google AdWords* (Sybex, 2010), which you can find at AdvancedAdWordsBook.com. Brad's totally one of our go-to dudes for everything AdWords.

@billhunt Bill Hunt is a global marketing consultant, author, and blogger behind WHunt.com. Bill tweets expert tips on international SEO and tells it like it is.

@BrentDPayne Brent Payne, SEO and social media director of 435 Digital (consulting arm of Tribune), has an addiction to Twitter that benefits us by providing thoughtful posts and links.

@brian_hancock Brian Hancock is manager of web visibility services at MedNet Technologies and blogger at Brian-Hancock.com. Brian's 14 years of marketing experience is obvious from his straightforward and informative Twitter account.

@briancarter Brian Carter is your go-to SEO, PPC, and social media guy. He's CEO of FanReach, speaker, and blogger for BrianCarterYeah.com, not to mention a stand-up comedian.

@brianchappell Brian Chappell: senior social search strategist for Ignite Social Media, owner of Adapt Marketing, and blogger on BrianChappell.com.

@btabke Brett Tabke: CEO of WebmasterWorld and PubCon founder/chairman. Brett's often first to the Twitter table with the most important developments of the day and compelling conversation.

@CarriBugbee Carri Bugbee is an award-winning tweeter. This social media marketing strategist, educator, speaker, and PR/ad pro is also a social TV/music devotee and jazz gal. President/founder of Big Deal PR and an instructor at Portland State University, Carri's a pretty big deal herself.

@chiropractic Michael Dorausch is owner at PlanetChiropractic.com and blogger on MichaelDorausch.com. A tweeter of all things awesome.

@ctreada Founder and CEO of Notice Technologies and coauthor (with Mari Smith) of the bestseller *Facebook Marketing: An Hour a Day* (Sybex, 2010). Chris is the technical editor of this book and one smart guy about FB Ads.

@chriswinfield Chris Winfield is CMO and managing partner at BlueGlass. Chris's tweets focus on public relations, business, social media, and search marketing.

@dannysullivan Danny Sullivan, editor of SearchEngineLand.com, is all about Google, SEO, PPC, and every aspect of search engines and search marketing. Check out his personal blog, Daggle.com. Danny is one of the original SEO bloggers and my hero as a journalist.

@davesnyder David Snyder, SVP of product development for BlueGlass Interactive, also blogs for SearchEngineLand.com and DailySEOTip.

@davidmihm David Mihm, definitive authority in local SEO, is president/CEO for GetListed.org as well as a SearchEngineLand.com blogger.

@debramastaler Debra Mastaler is president of Alliance-Link and owner/blogger for LinkSpiel.com. She tweets about link building, online marketing, content promotion, and publicity.

@dennisyu Dennis Yu is director of Facebook marketing for WebTrends and cofounder/CEO of BlitzLocal.com. A Facebook marketing freak extraordinaire who tweets about Facebook advertising.

@dharmesh Dharmesh Shah, founder/CTO of HubSpot and blogger for OnStartups.com, focuses tweets on technical areas like coding as well as SEO and social.

@digitalalex Alex Cohen, senior marketing manager at ClickEquations and blogger responsible for AlexLCohen.com, tweets great PPC links, tips, and comments.

@DuaneForrester Duane Forrester manages Bing Webmaster Tools. Duane is a two-time author and blogger at TheOnlineMarketingGuy.com. He offers industry and tech-related news and resources.

@elisabethos Elisabeth Osmeloski, executive features editor/blogger for Search Engine Land, has a Twitter presence that focuses on travel and entertainment search topics.

@fantomaster Ralph Tegtmeier has been dominating the search engines since 1999. He's an industrial-strength cloaker, all about link building and SEO software development. Black, white, and gray hat geek, Ralph is a fabulous Twitter resource.

@Frank_Strong Frank Strong, director of PR for Vocus and blogger of SwordAndTheScript.com, tweets about marketing, PR, and social media.

@graywolf Michael Gray, owner/president of Atlas Web Service, moderator for Webmaster World & Sphinn, editor for ThreadWatch, and blogger for Wolf-Howl.com, mixes smarts with snark on a daily basis.

@GregBoser Greg Boser, president of BlueGlass Interactive, Inc., is an industry speaker with a concentration in organic search and a Twitter account that shares it. In fact, Greg coined the phrase "organic search."

@gregfinn CMO and blogger of CyprusNorth.com, Greg Finn offers great links and to-the-point posts.

@gregjarboe Greg Jarboe is president and cofounder of SEO-PR, author of *YouTube and Video Marketing: An Hour a Day* (Sybex, 2009), member of Rutgers CMD faculty, and Search Engine Watch correspondent. He's a good follow for the latest in top industry news.

@GrowMap Gail Gardner is the social media marketing and Internet strategist for GrowMap.com. GrowMap is all about helping you grow your business or blog.

@heatherlloyd Heather Lloyd, CEO of SuccessWorks and SEO copywriting pioneer, blogs at SEOCopywriting.com. She tweets useful tips and links related to SEO and copywriting.

@hollisthomases Hollis Thomases, CEO of WebAdvantage and author of *Twitter Marketing: An Hour A Day* (Sybex, 2010), wields a colorful Twitter stream and deep knowledge on all things social.

@JasonFalls Jason Falls is owner/operator/blogger for SocialMediaExplorer.com. He tells it like it is while providing relevant tweets and information on marketing, social media, and public relations.

@jc1000000 Director of SearchEngineWatch.com and regular blogger, Jonathan Allen's Twitter feed is packed with interesting links and great conversations.

@jengrappone Jennifer Grappone, coauthor of the book *Search Engine Optimization: An Hour a Day* (Sybex, 2006), is also the founding partner of Gravity Search Marketing. She tweets great SEO advice and fun musings.

@jennita Jennifer Sable Lopez is community manager and blogger at SEOmoz. Her tweets are bursting with social, community, and SEO tidbits.

@jillwhalen Jill Whalen is CEO of High Rankings. A pioneer in search engine optimization, beginning in the field in the early 1990s, Jill's awesome. If you get her retweet, your content is good.

@JoannaLord Joanna Lord, cofounder of YourJobStop.com and director of customer acquisition/blogger at SEOmoz, wields a rich Twitter stream always full of energy and social media tweets.

@johnandrews John Andrews is one of the smartest industry folks I've ever met. Based in Seattle, John does web consulting and SEO. His tech and programming skills add invaluable information to Twitter and his blog, Johnon.com.

@JordanKasteler Jordan Kasteler, SVP of content development/marketing partner/blogger at BlueGlass, is also a blogger for JordanKasteler.com. Jordan's really adept at measuring social media and a clever all-around marketer.

@kalena Kalena Jordan, SEO/PPC ninja and founder of SearchEngineCollege.com, is also director at Jordan Consulting Group and columnist on Ask-Kalena.com.

@kategamble Kate Gamble, search manager at Bruce Clay, Inc. Australia, and owner of the KateGamble.com blog, serves up choice tweets on SEO, SMO, CRO, and many other Internet acronyms.

@KeriMorgret Keri Morgret, president of Strike Models and freelance SEO/live blogger, is arguably one of the smartest people in online marketing.

@kevgibbo Kevin Gibbons, founder and director at SEOptimise, a UK search marketing agency, answers questions on Twitter and writes for the SEOptimise.com blog.

@kim_cre8pc Kim Krause Berg is a seasoned columnist, speaker, and usability/IA tutor with Search Engine College.

@lauralippay Laura Lippay is a partner at Nine By Blue and industry speaker. Laura's Twitter feed focuses on future tech, marketing, and their intersection.

@LaurieSullivan Laurie Sullivan, MediaPost.com reporter, combines marketing and tech for a unique and useful Twitter feed.

@leeodden Lee Odden, CEO of TopRank Online Marketing, is also executive editor for and contributor to Online Marketing Blog. He shares online marketing insights flavored with SEO, content, social media, and PR topics.

@LisaBarone Lisa Barone, cofounder, chief branding officer, PITA, and blogger for OutspokenMedia, is one of the most respected bloggers in the industry. Count on her tweets for informed snark and crucial information.

@lisabuyer Lisa Buyer is president and CEO of The Buyer Group and writer for ClickZ .com. She tweets about social media strategy, online branding, and SEO. Lisa is an established SES speaker and ClickZ writer.

@localseoguide Andrew Shotland, SEO expert, strategy consultant, and blogger for LocalSEOGuide.com, is one of the best and a go-to guy for all things SEO…and deeper.

@lorenbaker Loren Baker is SVP of social media strategies and managing partner of BlueGlass Interactive. His Twitter feed is filled with check-ins and compelling news.

@marcpoirier Marc Poirier is founder/CMO and blogger at Acquisio. Check out Marc's feed for cutting-edge PPC news and tips.

@MarshaCollier Marsha is a master eBay/e-commerce writer and author of *The Ultimate Online Customer Service Guide* (Wiley, 2011). She harnesses Twitter to connect and advise.

@Matt_Siltala Matt Siltala, cofounder/president/blogger at Dream Systems Media, broadcasts all things digital mixed in with marketing and SEO.

@mblumenthal Mike Blumenthal is all about Google Maps and Local Search. The owner of and blogger at Blumenthals.com, Mike's stream offers up expert tips, links, and humor with a focus on local search.

@Mel66 Melissa Mackey is Fluency Media's online marketing manager and blogger for BeyondThePaid. Melissa writes for SearchEngineWatch.com and is a consummate veteran marketing pro.

@MerryMorud Merry Morud is a killer online marketer at aimClear, specializing in all things Facebook advertising. She tweets about search, social, paid, contextual, and the occasional sporting event to boot.

@MichelleRobbins Michelle Robbins is director of technology for Sphinn, Search Engine Land, Search Marketing Expo, and Search Marketing Now at Third Door Media. Michelle is one smart cookie and her tweets show it.

@mikegrehan Mike Grehan is the VP, Global Content Director for SearchEngineWatch, ClickZ, NS SearchEngineStrategies. Mike's SEO musings can be found at MikeGrehan.com.

@monicawright Monica Wright is director of search marketing at Hall Internet Marketing and owner/blogger for MonicaWright.com. Monica is a terrific tweeter on all things online marketing.

@msaleem Muhammad Saleem is CEO of Consumer Media Network and director of social media strategy at Chicago Tribune Media Group. Muhammad spends his time on Twitter posting news and social marketing nuggets. His content tweets are golden.

@NetMeg Meg Geddes, owner of Netmeg and president at Michigan Integrated Solutions, tweets deep, thoughtful, and seriously relevant nuggets.

@oilman Todd Friesen is VP of search at Position Technologies and blogger of Oilman.ca. Todd combines industry news and advice with humor and snark in his tweets.

@PapaSlingshot Jeremy Dearringer, cofounder and CRO of SlingshotSEO.com, blogs for the company, tweets about all things SEO, and recommends other Twitter thought leaders to follow.

@portentint Ian Lurie, owner of Portent Interactive and writer behind ConversationMarketing.com, consistently tweets insightful questions and great tips—a real engager.

@problogger Darren Rowse is a professional blogger who offers insights about life in the blogosphere. His posts on ProBlogger.net are top-shelf.

@Randfish The one and only Rand Fishkin, founder of SEOmoz and blogger at SEOmoz.org. Rand's one of my muses, a brilliant kid, grown-up now, who found the way and shares it straight up.

@Rhea Rhea Drysdale is cofounder of OutspokenMedia.com. Her blog posts and tweets focus on ORM, SEO, and link development.

@rustybrick Barry Schwartz is widely regarded as a foundational SEO blogger. Founder of SEORoundtable.com, executive news editor for SearchEngineLand, and CEO for RustyBrick.com, Barry is a must-read Tweeter and blogger.

@RuudHein Ruud Hein is a web publisher, programmer, developer, and blogger on RuudHein.com, moderator for Cre8asite Forums, and senior SEO/editor for Search Engine People.

@schachin Founder of SitesWithoutWalls.com, Kristine Schachinger is always up for great Twitter conversations. Kristine also has a monthly column at SearchEngineWatch.com.

@scottclark Scott Clark has spent 13+ years growing web businesses. Senior SEO, SEM, lead gen, UI design, and blogger for BuzzMaven, Scott's a great marketer. His tweets are sparse but thoughtful.

@SebastianX Sebastian is an IT consultant and blogger for Sebastians-Pamphlets.com. He tweets SEO gems and web development tips as well as a daily roundup.

@semlady Helen Overland is vice president and blogger at SearchEnginePeople.com. She combines news and daily Twitter roundups valuable to any marketer.

@SEOmom Gillian Muessig, president and cofounder SEOmoz, is a seasoned industry pro with lots to share. She's also CEO coach on WebmasterRadio.fm, Mondays at 10 a.m. Pacific time.

@seosmarty Ann Smarty, owner of SeoSmarty.com and MyBlogGuest.com, is a respected Search Engine Journal editor/blogger who never fails to tweet interesting posts and relevant information.

@si1very Chris "Silver" Smith, Internet marketing and technology expert, tweets about local search, Google Maps, social media marketing, analytics, image SEO, and shopping search. Director of optimization strategies for KeyRelevance, Chris also blogs for SearchEngineLand.com and Silvery.com.

@SimonHeseltine Simon Heseltine, director at AOL and columnist for SearchEngineWatch.com, rebroadcasts important industry news while adding his own ideas and tips.

@steveplunkett Steve Plunkett, senior manager of content strategy for Rockfish Interactive, offers up advice and news relating to design, coding, SEO, ORM, and more.

@storyspinner Liana "Li" Evans is an online marketing geek genius and internationally respected conference speaker. Author of *Social Media Marketing* Que Publishing, (2010), Li tweets all things social and is an ever-popular conference speaker.

@streko Michael Streko is cofounder of KnowEm LLC. He's on a different level. Michael introduced me to Facebook Ads in 2007. He's also one of the best fishermen I personally know.

@SusanEsparza Susan Esparza, managing editor at Bruce Clay, Inc., offers SEO tweets and posts that are in-depth without being over the top.

@Suzzicks Cindy Krum, CEO of MobileMoxie, is a globally known author, speaker, and marketing extraordinaire. She shares her expertise on mobile marketing and SEO via Twitter.

@sweena Serena Obhrai is a community manager for PokerStars.com and freelance writer for Zath. This lady's a tweet-card you just don't want to miss.

@Szetela David Szetela is the owner of Clix Marketing, a search and social PPC advertising agency. David tweets about AdWords, adCenter, Facebook, LinkedIn, and Twitter advertising. He's one of my best friends in the industry and a pioneer in the PPC space.

@tamar Tamar Weinberg is the community manager for NameCheap, social media marketing manager for M80, community support and advertising for Mashable.com, and social media marketing consultant/blogger at Techipedia. Tamar is one of my most important influences.

@TheGrok Bryan Eisenberg is a best-selling author, professional speaker, and cofounder of Web Analytics Association. His tweets focus on links, conversations, and marketing.

@theGypsy David Harry, SEO consultant and IR geek, heads up an online community, The SEO Dojo. It's a killer one-stop shop for outstanding online marketing advice.

@tim_ash Tim Ash, CEO of SiteTuners, author of *Landing Page Optimization* (Sybex, 2010) and chair of ConversionConference.com, is a seasoned keynote speaker and SearchEngineWatch.com columnist. He keeps his Twitter account fresh with recommendations and news posts.

@toddmintz Todd Mintz, senior account manager at PPC Associates, editor/blogger at Sphinn, president at Tough Love SEM, and blogger on ToddMintz.com, is a very serious marketer. Follow him.

@tonyadam Tony Adam is a top-shelf startup advisor, entrepreneur, and previously of BillShrink, Yahoo!, and PayPal. Tony is the director of online marketing for MySpace, founder of Visible Factors, and an avid blogger on TonyAdam.com.

@w2scott CEO of Search Influence, Will Scott tweets about marketing, Facebook, and life in general.

@webmona Mona Elesseily is all about PPC and online marketing strategy. Speaker, author, and columnist; VP of online marketing strategy at Page Zero Media; and Search Engine Land columnist, Mona tweets great resource articles and insight.

@yoast Joost de Valk builds and tweaks websites for performance, SEO, and conversion, often using his WordPress plug-ins. Web developer and SEO blogger on Yoast.com, Joost also runs a weekly WordPress podcast and boasts a Twitter feed filled with WordPress tweaks, news, and the occasional update in Norwegian.

Facebook Targeting Segments

At aimClear, we've built a massive catalog of Facebook demographic segments, which we look to often. After all, there's no need to reinvent the wheel. When first thinking about this book, I pictured the whole shooting match as a giant catalog of segments clustered around themes and real-world topical clusters. My wonderful publishers (thankfully) convinced me that we had a lot more value to offer than simply a catalog of pre-researched targeting inventory.

That said, this is one part of the book that our team members will return to over and over. If you use Facebook Power Editor or Acquisio, you can simply copy and paste this data from the "Segments" pages on www.KillerFBAds.com *and paste it in to your editor. The site also includes tutorials. Even without Power Editor or Acquisio, the segments are still incredibly useful in the Facebook Ads Web UI. Knowing what they are, simply type the ones you want into the Interests bucket.*

From job titles to outdoor activities, we've included some of our favorite go-to segments for your marketing pleasure. Enjoy. Don't eat them all at once! As a reminder, the estimated reach is likely to change over time, but it is included to give readers a ballpark measurement of how big each segment is. As FB penetration increases, the segments should stay roughly proportional in size.

 Note: aimClear offers thousands of other pre-researched interest bucket segments for sale and immediate download at www.KillerFBAds.com.

Fortune 500 Companies

Matriculate these with Interests Bucket occupations such as corporate accountant, marketing director, C-titles, etc....

Estimated Reach: 2,132,780 people who live in the United States and who work at Wal-Mart, Chevron Corp., ConocoPhillips Company, Fannie Mae, General Electric, Berkshire Hathaway, General Motors, General Motors, Bank of America, Ford Motor Company, Hewlett-Packard, AT&T, Citigroup, McKesson Corporation, Verizon, AIG, IBM, Cardinal Health, Inc, Freddie Mac, UnitedHealth Group, Wells Fargo, Valero, Kroger, Procter & Gamble, AmerisourceBergen Corporation, Costco, Marathon Oil, Home Depot, Pfizer, Walgreens, Target, Medco Health Solutions, Apple, Boeing Company, State Farm Insurance, Microsoft, Archer Daniels Midland Company, Johnson & Johnson, Dell, WellPoint, Pepsico, United Technologies, Dow Chemical, MetLife, Best Buy, UPS, Kraft Foods, Lowe's Home Improvement, Lockheed Martin, Merck & Co., Goldman Sachs, Express Scripts, Intel, Sears Holdings, Caterpillar Inc., Safeway, SUPERVALU, Cisco Systems, Morgan Stanley, Prudential, The Walt Disney Company CIS, Comcast, SYSCO, Sunoco, Abbott Laboratories, Coca-Cola, Coca-Cola Bottling, New York Life, Northrop Grumman, FedEx, Hess Corporation, Ingram Micro, Johnson Controls or Aetna, Amazon, Humana, Enterprise Products Partners, Honeywell, Liberty Mutual Group, News Corporation, DuPont, Sprint, General Dynamics, TIAA-CREF, Delta Air Lines, Allstate, HCA, American Express, Google, Google, Tyson Foods, Philip Morris International, Time Warner, Oracle, 3M, John Deere, John Deere, Plains All American Pipeline, Rite Aid, Mass. Mutual Life Ins., Publix, CHS, Raytheon, International Paper, Travelers, Macys, Staples, Tech Data, DIRECTV, Inc., McDonalds, Northwestern Mutual Financial Network, Murphy Oil Corp., Eli Lilly, Motorola, Hartford Financial Services, AMR Research, TJX Companies, Emerson, Xerox, CIGNA, Alcoa Inc., Alcoa, Fluor Corporation, Aflac, Bancorp, Nationwide Insurance, Tesoro, Occidental Petroleum Corp., Kimberly-Clark, Bristol-Myers Squibb Company, Avnet, World Fuel Services, Capital One, Nike, Freeport-McMoRan, Time Warner Cable, Manpower, Goodyear Tire & Rubber, Arrow Electronics, Exelon, Kohl's, Whirlpool, Halliburton, USAA, JCPenney,

Southern Company, US Steel, AES Organization, PNC Financial Services, EMC, Union Pacific Railroad, Altria Group, Computer Sciences Corporation, Nucor, Medtronic, L-3 Communications, Colgate-Palmolive Company, Dominion Resources, Amgen, Progressive, The Bank of New York Mellon, General Mills, Gap, Loews Hotels, American Electric Power, Baker Hughes, Inc., TRW Automotive, Constellation Energy, Duke Energy, CBS, Texas Instruments, Toys R Us, Eaton Corporation, Health Net, Viacom 18 Media Pvt. Ltd., PPG Industries, Jabil Circuit, FirstEnergy, Chubb Group of Insurance Companies, Cummins, Danaher, Dollar General, Oneok, Inc., Sara Lee, Baxter Healthcare Corporation, ARAMARK, Omnicom Group, Waste Management, Kellogg's, Conagra Foods, Public Service Enterprise Group, National Oilwell Varco, Dean Foods, Navistar, Southwest Airlines, Apache Corporation, Lear Financial, US Airways Group, Qwest Communications, Marriott International, Office Depot, Coventry Health Care, Entergy Services, Inc., Yum Brands, Smithfield Foods, ITT Industries, SAIC, BB&T, BJ's Wholesale Club, QUALCOMM, Anadarko Petroleum, Liberty Media, Marsh & McLennan, Avon Products, Inc.,Thermo Fisher Scientific, Penske, Starbucks, CSX Corporation, Devon Energy, H J Heinz, Textron, Monsanto, First Data, Xcel Energy, PACCAR, Unum, Progress Energy, Praxair, Inc., KBR, Genworth Financial, SunTrust Bank, Guardian Life Insurance, Ameriprise Financial, RR Donnelley & Sons, Parker Hannifin, Peter Kiewit Sons', Jacobs Engineering, Western Digital, Oshkosh Truck Corporation, State Street, Nordstrom, Liberty Global, Williams Companies, Limited Brands, Applied Materials, Norfolk Southern, GameStop, Chesapeake Energy, Huntsman International, Tenet Healthcare, URS, Principal Financial Group, eBay, Air Products, Ashland, Whole Foods Market, Sempra Energy Solutions, ADP, NRG Energy, Caesars Entertainment, PPL Corporation, Synnex, BlackRock, DTE Energy, Reynolds American, Assurant, Inc., Aon, Micron Technology, Black & Decker, Holly Corporation, Reinsurance Group of America or Discover Financial, Owens & Minor, Republic Services, Visa, Western Refining, Gilead Sciences, Ball, Family Dollar, Ross Stores, Bed Bath & Beyond, Boston Scientific, Estee Lauder, Sherwin-Williams, VF, CarMax, Campbell Soup, Ameren, Masco, Hertz, Becton, Dickinson and Company, Henry Schein, Thrivent Financial for Lutherans, Visteon, Quest Diagnostics, Cablevision Systems, AutoZone, Stryker, Winn-Dixie Stores, Hormel Foods, Fifth Third Bank, Eastman Kodak Company, Grainger, Autoliv, OfficeMax, Dover Corporation, Darden Restaurants, Inc., Charter Communications Holding Company, Centurylink, Pepco, Shaw Group, Goodrich, Sonic Automotive, AGCO, Dole Food Company, Inc., Broadcom, SLM Software Company, Mosaic, Eastman Chemical Company, Calpine, Corning, Energy Transfer Partners, Fortune Brands, AECOM, Weyerhaeuser, Interpublic Group, Avery Dennison, AMD, American Family Mutual Insurance Co, DaVita, Commercial Metals Co., Nisource, CIT Group, Yahoo!, Sanmina-SCI, Reliance Steel & Aluminum, Steel Dynamics, Smurfit-Stonentainer, Dillard's, Omnicare, McGraw-Hill, MeadWestvaco,

Virgin Media, Cameron, EOG Resources, Ecolab, Inc., Jarden, MGM Resorts International, Spectrum Medical Group, Symantec, Expeditors International, TravelCenters of America, Tenneco, Advance Auto Parts, Celanese, Mattel, Franklin Resources, Domtar, Barnes & Noble, AMERIGROUP, Newell Rubbermaid, Fidelity Investments, Mutual of Omaha Ins., PetSmart, Hershey's, BorgWarner, Dr Pepper Snapple Group, Pacific Life, UGI, Universal Health Services, Precision Castparts Corp., MasterCard, Clorox, Group 1 Automotive, Anixter Inc., Gannett, KeyCorp, Mylan, Mylan, Agilent Technologies, WellCare Health Plans, Pitney Bowes, CH2M Hill, Lubrizol, O'Reilly Auto Parts, Auto-Owners Insurance, Fidelity National Info Services, Mohawk Industries, Consol Energy, Inc., Harris Corporation, Integrys Energy, Western Union, Avis Budget Group, SunGard, Health Management Associates, St. Jude Medical, Ryder System, CB Richard Ellis, Starwood Hotels and Resorts, Spectra Energy, Wesco International, Live Nation, Avaya, Foot Locker, Owens Corning, Telephone & Data Sys., Ralph Lauren, Apollo Group, Inc., Big Lots, Con-Way, Kelly Services, Western & Southern Financial, Allergan, Harley-Davidson, Northeast Utilities, SPX, Erie Insurance Group, Bemis Company, Dick's Sporting Goods, Rockwell Automation, United Stationers, SanDisk, NCR, The Washington Post, Insight Enterprises, Alliant Techsystems, AbitibiBowater, W.R. Berkley, Biogen Idec, Rockwell Collins, Graybar Electric, El Paso Corporation, J.M. Smucker, SCANA, Cognizant, TEREX, Genzyme, YRC Worldwide, American Financial Group Inc., Sealed Air, Charles Schwab & Co., Inc., RadioShack, Centene, NYSE - Euronext, Levi Strauss & Co., Ruddick Corporation, D.R. Horton, Inc. or Seaboard Credit Union

Job Titles

Coaches/Personal Trainers Estimated Reach: 537,120 people who live in the United States and like:

american volleyball coaches association avca, assistant baseball coach, assistant basketball coach, assistant coach, assistant football coach, assistant softball coach, assistant swim coach, assistant volleyball coach, asst coach, baldo alberti personal trainer, baseball coach, basketball coach, basketball coaching, body design personal training, certified personal trainer, cheer coach advisor, coach baseball, coach football, coach soccer, coaches, coaches vs cancer, coaches vs cancer spokane, coaching, coaching baseball, coaching basketball, coaching cheerleading, coaching football, coaching football baseball, coaching gymnastics, coaching hockey, coaching lacrosse, coaching playing soccer, coaching rugby, coaching soccer, coaching softball, coaching sports, coaching swimming, coaching track, coaching volleyball, coaching wrestling, figure skating coach, football coach, getright personal training, gymnastics coach, head coach, hockey coach, im personal training, jon personal trainer, lift personal training, max fitness personal training, monika kovacs professional personal training, o2 fitness personal training, personal fitness professional, personal fitness trainer, personal trainer, personal trainer dlf fitness, personal trainer licni trener, personal trainer studio, personal trainers forum powered by nasm, personal training, playing coaching soccer, ricky personal trainer, soccer coach, swimming coach, taekwondo coaches, teaching coaching, tennis coach, tony cress personal training, volleyball coach, wrestling coach, yiorgos chadimoglou personal trainer

Teachers Estimated Reach: 2,473,000 people who live in the United States, are age 18 and older, and like:

4th grade teacher, 5th grade teacher, 6th grade math teacher, 6th grade teacher, 7th grade math teacher, 8th grade language arts teacher, 8th grade math teacher, art teacher, biology teacher, business education teacher, business teacher, chemistry teacher, cornerstone for teachers, drama teacher, elementary school teacher, elementary teacher, english language teacher, english teacher, fifth grade teacher, fourth grade teacher, french teacher, high school art teacher, high school english teacher, high school math teacher, high school science teacher, high school spanish teacher, high school teacher, history teacher, i am teacher, instrumental music teacher, kindergarten teacher, language arts teacher, language teacher, math teacher, mathematics teacher, maths teacher, middle school teacher, music teacher, pe teacher, physical education teacher, reading teacher, retired teacher, science teacher, spanish teacher, special ed teacher, special education teacher, substitute teacher, teacher, teacher aide, teacher education, teacher english, teacher mathematics, teacher retired, teacher science, teachercoach, teachers, teaching, teaching assistant, teaching english, teaching resources, teaching sunday school, third grade teacher, violin teacher, vocal music teacher

MultiLevel Marketers Estimated Reach: 71,300 people who live in the United States, are age 28 and older, and like:

Avon Products, Inc., Primerica, Mary Kay, The Longaberger Company, Arbonne International, Forever Living Products, Tupperware Brands, Mannatech, Watkins, Herbalife, Passion Parties, Inc., ACN, AdvoCare International, Agel Enterprises, Discovery Toys, Inc., Amway, Shaklee, Sunrider International, MonaVie, Tahitian Noni International, Freelife International, Neways, Nu Skin Enterprises, XanGo, LLC., Pampered Chef, Partylite, ACN, Avon, Oriflame

Accountants Estimated Reach: 271,260 people who live in the United States and like:

accountant, accountantbookkeeper, accounting, accounting auditing, accounting books, accounting clerk, accounting coach, accounting community, accounting finance, accounting financial tax, accounting office, accounting principles, accounting tech, accountingfinance, beckers cpa exam review, become cpa, book keeping, bookkeeper, bookkeeperoffice manager, bookkeeping, branch accountant, business accounting, certified public accountant, chartered accountant, chief accountant, childress accounting llc, company accountant, corporate accountant, cost accountant, cost accounting, cpa, cpaexcel cpa review, diploma business accounting, director accounting, etax accountants pty ltd, finance accounting manager, financial accountant, financial accounting, forte accounting, front accounting, fund accountant, general accountant, georgia society cpas, group accountant, i will be cpa, management accountant, manager accounting, map cpa group, member accounting club meba, national association black accountants, national institute accountants, office manager bookkeeper, on point accounting, payroll accountant, professional accountants, project accountant, property accountant, robert half finance accounting, roger cpa review, senior accountant, senior staff accountant, senior tax accountant, sr accountant, staf accounting, staff accounting, studying for cpa exam, tax accountant, tax accounting, thomson reuters tax accounting, young cpa network

Restaurant/Bar/Club/Hotel Managers Estimated Reach: 18,160 people who live in the United States, are age 22 and older, and like:

assistant restaurant manager, bar manager, bartender manager, club manager, hotel management, hotel manager, hotel managers forum, hotel restaurant management, life bar owner, manager bartender, mgs restaurant, restaurant general manager, restaurant management, restaurant manager, restaurant owner

Professors Estimated Reach: 74,140 people who live in the United States, are age 18 and older, and like:

adjunct professor, assistant professor, assistant professor english, associate professor, associate professor english, asst professor, clinical assistant professor, college professor, english professor, professor english, professor music, research assistant professor, visiting assistant professor, visiting professor

Logistics Estimated Reach: 33,620 people who live in the United States, are age 22 and older, and like:

logistic, logistic manager, logistics, logistics analyst, logistics assistant, logistics coordinator, logistics management, logistics manager, logistics officer, logistics specialist, logistics supervisor, usn logistics specialist

Operations Manager Estimated Reach: 64,280 people who live in the United States, are exactly between the ages of 18 and 64 inclusive, and like:

assistant manager operations, assistant operations manager, branch operations manager, manager operations, operations coordinator, operations director, operations management, operations manager, operations mgr, operations supervisor, regional operations manager

Sales Reps Estimated Reach: 108,560 people who live in the United States, are age 22 and older, and like:

customer sales representative, independent sales rep, independent sales representative, inside sales rep, inside sales representative, outside sales representative, pharmaceutical sales rep, pharmaceutical sales representative, retail sales representative, sales marketing representative, sales represenative, sales representative, sales representitive, sales representive, sales service representative, senior sales representative

Real Estate Agents Estimated Reach: 116,920 people who live in the United States, are age 25 and older, and like:

dependable real estate agents, essential new york real estate, georgia real estate investors, hamptons real estate, nj estates real estate group, official real estate referral group, real estate agent alliance, real estate agent hub, real estate agent insider, real estate agent society, real estate appraiser, real estate assistant, real estate associate, real estate board new york, real estate book, real estate books, real estate broker, real estate brokeragent, real estate brokerowner, real estate consultant, real estate friends magazine, real estate inner circle, real estate investors forum, real estate manager, real estate news, real estate paralegal, real estate professional, real estate pros, real estate rockstars, real estate sales agent, real estate sales associate, real estate salesperson, real estate specialist, realestatecom, strategic real estate coach, young real estate pros

Weapons

Call-of-Duty Guns Estimated Reach: 424,700 people who live in the United States or Canada, are age 25 and older, and like:

357, 357 magnum, 44 magnum, ak47, ak47 kalashnikov, ar15, as50 sniper rifle, barret 50 cal sniper rifle, barrett 50 cal sniper rifle, claymore, colt m16a4, colt python 357 magnum, desert eagle, desert eagle 50, dragunov, fn fal, glock, grenade grenade launcher, grenade launcher, gun shooting, guns, hunting rifles shotguns, love grenades, m16, m16 assault rifle, m16 rifle, m4, m4 carbine, m4a1, m60, magnum sniper rifle, mossberg shotguns, mp5, mp5 submachine gun, pistol shooting, pistols, remington 870 shotguns, remington shotguns, rpg7, shooting guns, shooting people, skorpion, smith wesson 357 magnum ssr, sniper rifles, svd dragunov, thompson submachine gun, uzi mini uzi micro uzi submachine gun

Weapons Estimated Reach: 10,800 people who live in the United States, are age 25 and older, and like:

9mm, 9mm parabellum bullet, ak47, ak47 калашњиков, ak47 keleş, ak47budburnerz, as50 sniper rifle, automatics, barret 50 cal sniper rifle, bayonets, beretta, beretta 92 fs 9mm, beretta 92fs, beretta 9mm, beretta ar 7090, beretta international, beretta px4 storm, beretta usa, brass knuckles, brass knux, colt 45, desert eagle, desert eagle 50, forty five 51, glock, glock 17, glock gmbh, guns, handguns, heckler, heckler koch, heckler koch inc, hunting rifles shotguns, katana, katanas, knifes, knives, mossberg shotguns, mossberg sons firearms, orange 9mm, pistol, pistol shooting, pistols, remington arms company, remington shotguns, revolvers, rifle, rifle shooting, rifleman, shotguns, smith wesson, smith wesson 357 magnum ssr, smith wesson corp, smith wesson j frames, sniper rifles, taser x26, taser x3, winchester repeating arms

Infantry (Micro Military) Estimated Reach: 297,220 people who live in the United States, are age 18 and older, and like:

1116th infantry battalion, 114 infantry battalion, 198 squadron amory, 1st infantry division, 1st lieutenant, 256th infantry brigade, 25th infantry division, 2nd lieutenant, 36th infantry division, 3rd infantry division, 4th brigade 2nd infantry division stryker, 633 squadron, amphibious squadron eight, bravo company usa, canadian infantry, charlie company bstb 86th ibct, first lieutenant, infantry, infantry officer, infantry soldier, infantryman, lieutenant colonel, lieutenant commander, m1 platoon, officer cadet, official 1st infantry division page, parachute regiment, platoon leader, platoon sergeant, regimental combat team 7, second lieutenant, squad 51 johnny roy, us army signal regiment, us naval sea cadet corps

Notorious Drug Lords Estimated Reach: 10,220 people who live in the United States, and like:

american drug war last white hope, bloods, chambers brothers, cocaine cowboys, crips, crips bloods made in america, el capo, escobar pablo, freeway ricky ross, gotti, griselda blanco, john gotti, killing pablo, nino brown, pablo emilio escobar, pablo escobar, pablo escobar el rey de la cocaina, ricky ross, soñar no cuesta nada, street stars, superfly

Tech and Gaming

Torrent/Gamers Estimated Reach: 1,407,380 people who live in the United States, are age 18 and older, and like:

bit torrent, bittorrent, counterstrike, counterstrikecom, gaming online, i love online gaming, isohuntcom, kick ass torrents, kickass torrents, lan gaming, lan parties, lan party, lanparty, mininova, mmo gamer, mmorpg, mmorpgs, movie torrentz, online gamer, online gamers, online games download games, online games with friends, online gaming, online gaming community, pacifica online mmorpg, pirate bay, quake live, runescape, save piratebay, secondlife, secondlife friends, starcraft, starcraft 2, starcraft 2 guide, starcraft 2i love it, starcraft ii, starcraft two, thepiratebay, torrenting, torrentreactor, torrents, torrentscancom, torrentz, utorrent, warcraft iii, warcraft iii reign chaos, warcraft iiifrozen throne, world warcraft, world warcraft ampm, world warcraft burning crusade, world warcraft cataclysm, world warcraft feeds, world warcraft horde side, world warcraft strategies, world warcraftwarcraft, worldofwarcraft, worldofwarcraftstrategy, wow, wow world warcraft

Skype/Video Chat Estimated Reach: 412,160 people who live in the United States, are age 18 and older, and like:

3 skype friend finder, 360mate video chat, camfrog video chat, face book video chat, facebook audio video chat, facebook video chat activation, friendcam video chat, friendcameo video chat, grouperz video chat, i love skype, instant video chat, onconference video chat, peep video chat, skype, skype 3, skype fans, skype for business, skype fun, skype go, skype me, skype online status, skyping, tinychat video chat, video chat, video chat chatarazzi, video chat rooms, video chat rounds, video chat vchatter, video chatter, video chatting, videochat, whats your skype, who got skype

Nintendo Estimated Reach: 1,359,740 people who live in the United States, are age 18 and older, and like:

battletoads, bomberman, bubble bobble, capcom, castlevania, chrono trigger, donkey kong country, double dragon, duck hunt, duke nukem, earthbound, earthworm jim, legend zelda, legend zelda link past, megaman, mortal kombat, punchout, samurai shodown, sega genesis, sega master system, sega megadrive, street fighter 2, super mario bros, super mario world, super metroid, super nintendo, zelda

SIMS Estimated Reach: 132,700 people who live in the United States, and like:

all sims games, game sims 3, jugar los sims, jugar los sims 2, les sims 2, les sims 3, les sims three, los sims, los sims 3, los sims el mejor juego, los simson, my sims kingdom, my sims party, original sims games, playing sims, playing sims 2, purposely murdering your sims, sims 2 apartment life, sims 2 apartment pets, sims 2 bon voyage, sims 2 castaway, sims 2 double deluxe, sims 2 nightlife, sims 2 on faceboook, sims 2 online facebook, sims 3, sims 3 ambitions, sims 3 escapenet, sims 3 game, sims 3 hot new game, sims 3 late night, sims 3 nerd, sims 3 pc game, sims 3 website, sims 3 world adventures, sims 3 xbox 360, sims 4, sims city hot rods, sims disco bar gosselies, sims family farm corn maze, sims foundation, sims game, sims games, sims gifts, sims house party, sims house party 2, sims life stories, sims medieval, sims pet stories, sims quiz, sims reminds me my childhood, sims stories, sims three, sims two, sims3, simsocial

CityVille Estimated Reach: 1,089,280 people who live in the United States and like:

add cityville neighbors, city ville, city ville fast adds, cityville, cityville add neighbors, cityville bonus checker, cityville bonus collector, cityville cheats zone, cityville freak, cityville free bonus neighbors, cityville friend request, cityville friends exchange, cityville neighbors, cityville neighbours, cityville pro, cityville reference, cityville treasury, cityvilleadd me, trucos cityville

Video Editing Interests Estimated Reach: 110,120 people who live in the United States, are age 18 and older, and like:

adobe premiere, digital video, editing video, editing videos, film video editing, film video editor, filming, filming editing, filming movies, imovie, making videos, making youtube videos, sony vegas, video editing, video making, videography, windows movie maker

Interests Bucket Family Roles

My Family/Wife/Husband Estimated Reach: 1,724,940 people who live in the United States, are age 25 and older, and like:

amo mi familia, annoying my wife, anything do with my family, anything that involves my family, being around my family, being coolest member my family, being with my hubby, being with my wife, bonding with my family, camping with my family, chill with my family, chilling with my family, cooking for my family, cuddling with my hubby, dates with my hubby, dating my wife, doing anything with my family, doing stuff with my family, doing things with my family, enjoy spending time with my family, enjoying my family, enjoying my family friends, enjoying time with my family, going out with my family, hang out with my family friends, hangin out with my family, hangin with my family, hanging out with my family, hanging out with my wife, hanging with my hubby, hanging with my wife, having fun with my family, having fun with my family friends, i enjoy spending time with my family friends, i like spend time with my family, i like spending time with my family, i love being with my family, i love hanging out with my family, i love my family forever, i love my family friends, i love my hubby, i love my husband, i love my large family yes theyre all mine, i love my wife, i love spend time with my family, i my family, i my red family, just being with my family, looking after my family, love be with my family, love being with my family, love my family, love my family friends, love spend time with my family, love spending time with my family, loving my family, loving my husband, loving my wife, making my family happy, making my wife happy, mi familia, mi familia es lo mejor, mi familia y amigos, mi familia y mi trabajo, mi familia y mis amigos, my amazing family, my awesome family, my beautiful wife, my church family, my extended family, my fam friends, my familly, my family 3, my family always comes first, my family by familylinkcom, my family is crazy, my family is my life, my family other animals, my family tree, my familyfriends, my friends are my family, my husband, my husband family, my interests are my family, my lovely wife, my wife, my wife family, my wife is superwoman, my wonderful family, playing games with my family, playing with my family, playing with my wife, raising my family, reading spending time with my family, relaxing with my family, rest my family, saving my family money, seeing my family, spending quality time with my family friends, spending time with my amazing family, spending time with my beautiful family, spending time with my beautiful wife, spending time with my family, spending time with my husband family, spending time with my kids family, spending time with my wife family, spending time with my wonderful family, taking care my family, time with my family, traveling with my wife, vacationing with my family, watching movies with my hubby, working taking care my family, yo amo mi familia, yo amo mi familia

Sports Mom Estimated Reach: 66,980 people who live in the United States, are exactly between the ages of 24 and 50 inclusive, and like:

baseball mom, basketball mom, being soccer mom, busy hockey mom, confessions pagan soccer mom, football mom, going my kids sporting events, hockey mom, i am hockey mom, my kids activities, my kids gym, my kids sports, soccer mom, soccer moms, sports with my kids, watching my children play sports, watching my daughter dance, watching my daughter play soccer, watching my daughter play softball, watching my kids play sports, watching my kids sporting events, watching my kids sports, watching my son play baseball, watching my son play football, watching my son play hockey, watching my son play soccer, watching my son play sports

At-Home Mom Estimated Reach: 116,800 people who live in the United States, are between the ages of 25 and 45 inclusive, and like:

at home mom, busy homeschool mom, christian stay at home moms, homeschool buyers coop, homeschool mom, homeschooling, homeschooling my kids, stay at home mom, stay at home mommy, stay at home moms, stay at home mother, stay home mom, work at home moms

Retired Estimated Reach: 214,460 people who live in the United States, are between the ages of 30 and 64 inclusive, and like:

being retired, early retirement, enjoying retirement, now retired, retired, retired loving it, retired teacher, retirement, semi retired, teacher retired

Health

Aerobics Estimated Reach: 58,380 people who live in the United States and like:

aerobic kickboxing, aerobics, aerobics instructor, aqua aerobics, cardio aerobic, i love aerobic, power aerobic, sport aerobics, step aerobics, teaching aerobics, water aerobics

Bodybuilding Estimated Reach: 206,300 people who live in the United States and like:

african bodybuilding, american body building abb, body builder, body building, body building suppliments, body building trophies, bodybuilder, bodybuilder matt, bodybuilderz wars, bodybuilding, bodybuilding australia, bodybuilding lounge, bodybuilding pro, bodybuilding supplements, bodybuilding warehouse, bodybuilding women, bodybuildingcom, bodybuildinglt, flex bodybuilding magazine, gmv bodybuilding dvds, hardcore bodybuilding, i bodybuilding, martial arts weight lifting bodybuilding, natural bodybuilding, nicole acker ifbb figure pro bodybuilding, support womens bodybuilding, vegan bodybuilding book

Dieters Estimated Reach: 283,320 people who live in the United States and like:

black girls guide weight loss, diet, dieting, edietscom diet weight loss fitness community, i want lose weight, lose weight for our health, losing weight, my diet, weight loss resources, weight loss training tips, weight loss twins, weight watchers, weightwatchers

Youth Coaches Estimated Reach: 14,300 people who live in the United States and like: coaching kids, coaching kids sports, coaching little league, coaching little league baseball, coaching my kids, coaching my sons baseball team, coaching tball, coaching youth football, coaching youth soccer, coaching youth sports

Working Out Estimated Reach: 2,347,960 people who live in the United States and like: basketball working out, black women do workout, enjoy working out, going gym working out, good workout, gym workout, gym workouts, hourglass workout, i enjoy working out, i like work out, i love work out, i love workout, i work out, jari love my ripped workout, kimbo slice workout plan, like work out, love work out, love working out, love workout, lyoto machida workout plan, no excuses workouts, reading working out, roller derby workout, sports working out, swimming working out, top 10 workout songs, top 10 workouts, ttapp workout, work out, work out at gym, work outs, workin out, workin out at gym, working out, working out at curves, working out at y, working out at ymca, working out etc, working out gym, working out in general, working out in gym, working out reading, working out shopping, working out wwwelnutritioncom, workout, workout at gym, workout music, workoutbox, workoutcom

Yoga Estimated Reach: 914,800 people who live in the United States and like: 30 day yoga challenge, academia chilena de yoga, ananda ashram yoga society ny, asheville yoga center, ashtanga yoga, ashtanga yoga worldwide, astanga yoga, ayurveda yoga vedic astrology, back bay yoga studio, barefoot yoga co, beyond yoga, bhakti yoga, bharat thakurs artistic yoga, bikram hot yoga, bikram hot yoga houston, bikram yoga, bikram yoga college india, bikram yoga richmond, bikram yoga san antonio, brahma vidya vihangam yoga, bryan kests power yoga, cora wen yoga bloom, corepower yoga, dahn yoga, doing yoga, eclectic yoga, elinore cohen yoga, evolution asia yoga conference, faith hunter yoga, gaiam yoga club, global yoga journeys, golden bridge yoga, golden bridge yoga nyc, hacer yoga, hatha yoga, hot 8 yoga, hot bikram yoga, hot yoga, i love yoga, jennifer pastiloff yoga, kabalah yoga, kino yoga, kripalu center for yoga health, kriya yoga, kundalini yoga, kung fu tai chi magazine, la jolla yoga center, la yoga magazine, lake tahoe yoga retreat, laughing lotus yoga ny, laughter yoga, light on yoga, lotus palm thai yoga massage, love yoga, mark whitwell heart yoga, maui

Distance Runners Estimated Reach: 104,520 people who live in the United States and like: distance running, half marathons, ing philadelphia distance run, loneliness long distance runner, long distance running, longdistance running, marathon fla keys, marathon lovers unite, marathon maniacs, marathon running, marathon training, marathonjunkie, marathonman 365, marathons, marine corps marathon official page, middle distance runner, road runner akron marathon, running half marathons, running long distance, running long distances, running marathon, training for half marathon, training for marathon, training for marathons, womens half marathon

Outdoor Activities

Outdoors Estimated Reach: 4,479,640 people who live in the United States and like:

all outdoors, all things outdoors, anything active outdoors, anything outdoors, anything outdoors fishing, anything outdoors hunting, anything outdoorscamping, anything that involves outdoors, becoming outdoors woman, broken spoke western outdoors, charleston sc outdoors, doing stuff outdoors, doing things outdoors, enjoy outdoors, espn outdoors saltwater, exploring great outdoors, exploring outdoors, extreme outdoors, fishing anything outdoors, flw outdoors, flw outdoors magazine, fly cast america espn outdoors, georgia outdoors info, getting outdoors, go outdoors, going outdoors, great out doors, great outdoors, hiking anything outdoors, hiking outdoors, honey creek outdoors llc, hoosier outdoor experience, i enjoy being outdoors, i enjoy outdoors, i like be outdoors, i love anything outdoors, i love be outdoors, i love out doors, i love outdoor activities, i love outdoors camping, i love outdoors hiking, leave no trace center for outdoor ethics, like outdoors, loon outdoors, love anything outdoors, love be outdoors, love being outdoors, love out doors, most things outdoors, new outdoorsmen outdoor network, northern outdoors, out door, out door stuff, outdoor activities, outdoor activities hiking, outdoor activitiestrekking, outdoor adventure, outdoor adventure team, outdoor adventures, outdoor alabama, outdoor alliance, outdoor anything, outdoor channel, outdoor club, outdoor divas, outdoor education, outdoor fun, outdoor idaho, outdoor indiana, outdoor life, outdoor life magazine, outdoor nation, outdoor photographer magazine, outdoor photography, outdoor pursuits, outdoor swimming society, outdoor yoga, outdoors, outdoors anything, outdoors club, outdoors fishing, outdoors hunting, outdoors nature, outdoors sports, outdoorsman, outdoorsnature, playing outdoors, playing outside, really anything outdoors, thing out doors, thing outdoors, thrifty outdoorsman, unlimited outdoors with wesley jones, walking outdoors or working outdoor

Canoeing and Kayaking Estimated Reach: 674,220 people who live in the United States and like:

camping canoeing, canoëkayak, canoe, canoe africa, canoe beach bar, canoe trips, canoeing, canoeing kayaking, canoeist, canoes, grupo kayakofficial web site, kayak fishing, kayak is life, kayak session magazine, kayak yapmak, kayakillasound, kayaking, kayaking canoeing, kayakingcanoeing, kayaks, liquidlogic kayaks, ocean kayak, ocean kayaking, old town canoes kayaks, paddlespin kayaking network, pyranha kayaks, sea kayaking, whitewater kayaking

Mountain Bikers/Cyclists Estimated Reach: 386,060 people who live in the United States and like:

adventure cycling association, angel fire mountain bike park, bicycle bmx mountain bike, bicycle times, big mountain bike adventures, biking road mountain, borovets mountain bike park, brown county mountain biking, cedric gracia mountain bike school, crosscountry mountain biking, cube mountain bike fan club, extreme mountain biking, freeride mountain biking, fruita mountain biking, gary fisher mountain bikes, gravity assisted mountain biking, haro mountain bikes, highland mountain bike park, hiking mountain biking, inside line mountain bike club, montana mountain bike alliance, mountain bike, mountain bike adventure, mountain bike magazine, mountain bike mtb, mountain bike oregon, mountain bike racing, mountain bike slopestyle, mountain bike specialists, mountain bike trials, mountain bike world, mountain biken, mountain biker, mountain biking, mountainroad biking, orange mountain bikes, riding mountain bikes, riding my mountain bike, road cycling mountain biking bikeradar, singletrack mountain bike magazine, singletrackscom mountain bike trails reviews, swamp mountain bike club, turbolince mountain bike, whistler mountain bike park, woodhill mountain bike park

Camping Estimated Reach: 5,397,900 people who live in the United States and like:

alps outdoorz browning camping, backcountry camping, backpacking camping, bayleys camping resort, big bear camping, big timber lake camping resort, boating camping, california camping, california rving camping, camping, camping at beach, camping backpacking, camping being outdoors, camping bella terra, camping boating, camping canoeing, camping caravanning club, camping cooking, camping equipment company, camping gardening, camping in colorado, camping in maine, camping in montana, camping in mountains, camping in our rv, camping in rv, camping in summer, camping kikopark, camping life magazine, camping on beach, camping paradis, camping reading, camping rotterdam, camping shopping, camping shower world, camping survival, camping swimming, camping travel, camping traveling, camping travelling, camping with family, camping with family friends, camping with friends family, camping with my family, camping with my family friends, camping world, campingfishing, campinginfo, campingninja, campingoutdoors, campingrocksbg, canoeing camping, carry on camping, coleman camping trailers, cool camping, country camping, danforth bay camping rv resort, deepdale backpackers camping, enjoy camping, fishing camping shows, going camping fishing, going camping with raoul moat, hunting camping, hunting fishing camping, hunting fishing camping deals, i like camping fishing, i like go camping fishing, i love camping hiking, i love campinglets go now, i love fishing camping, i love go camping fishing, i love going camping, i love outdoors camping, lake allatoona camping, lakewood camping resort, lets go camping, like camping, like go camping, love camping fishing, love go camping, love going camping, love outdoors camping, magazine camping caravaning, marval family camping resort, outdoor activities camping, outpacker camping backpacking network, pipe dream camping tubing, running bear camping area, rv camping, rv outfitter camping, sawmill camping resort, settebello camping village, solo campings, sunseabeach camping, survival camping world, swimming camping, tent camping, traveling camping, walking camping, wild camping, wilderness camping, winter camping, woodalls camping rving more, world camping, zeta camping, zmar eco camping resort

Fishing Estimated Reach: 4,507,000 people who live in the United States and like:

alabama fishing buddy, alaska fishing expeditions, albright fly fishing, american fly fishing co, anything about fishing, arkansas tournament fishing, art fishing guide service, bass fishing, bass fishing favorites, bc fly fishing charters, big bite baits fishing lures, biggame fishing, boating fishing, bow hunting fishing, branson fishing guide service, buckroe beach fishing pier, carolina fishing tv, carp fishing, cascade fishing adventures inc, coarse fishing, commercial fishing, crappie fishing, cypremort point fishing, dave mercers facts fishing, deep sea fishing, deer hunting fishing, dpond cebu fishing, drinking fishing, duckett fishing, eat sleep go fishing, ekotrofej fishing club, faculty fishing, fins fishing, fintech fishing tackle, fishing, fishing anything outdoors, fishing at remote lakes, fishing boating, fishing bonefish macabi, fishing books, fishing buddies, fishing camping shows, fishing channel, fishing cooking, fishing crabbing, fishing drinking, fishing fishing, fishing football, fishing for kids, fishing for living, fishing for monster walleye, fishing gardening, fishing golf, fishing golfing, fishing guide, fishing guides home page, fishing hard, fishing headquarters, fishing hiking, fishing hook, fishing hot spots maps, fishing hq, fishing hunting, fishing hunting shows, fishing in bc, fishing in dark, fishing in florida keys, fishing life, fishing lots more, fishing magazines, fishing mags, fishing more fishing, fishing music, fishing outdoors, fishing party, fishing patch, fishing proshops, fishing reading, fishing rights alliance, fishing shooting, fishing shop, fishing show, fishing shows, fishing sports, fishing strip, fishing swimming, fishing traveling, fishing tv, fishing when i can, fishing with bill dance, fishing with joe bucher, fishing with john, fishing with my boys, fishing with my dad, fishing with my husband, fishing with my son, fishing with rod, fishingboating, fishingcamping, fishingcross, fishingflamingocom, fishingguycom, fishinghunting, fishinglakesdotcom, fishingnccom, fishingpike bass, fishingtonpost, fly fishing, fly fishing block on yardsellr, fly fishing colorado, fly fishing in salt waters, georgia hunting fishing federation, get kayak fishing, glenn van hoesen fishingcom, going fishing, going hunting fishing, gold fishing, golf fishing, gone fishing, hawaii goes fishing, high standards fishing, hobie fishing, hong pekan fishing sports, hook line sinker australian fishing show, hunting fishing, hunting fishing magazines, hunting fishing shows, i like go hunting fishing, i love fishing, i love go camping fishing, i love hunting fishing, ice fishing, id rather be fishing, ilusiones sport fishing, kristinas fishing blog, lake fishing game, latest catch fishing, love camping fishing, love fishing, love go fishing, love hunting fishing, matador sport fishing charters, milf man i love fishing, mr trigger sport fishing, navarre beach fishing pier, night fishing is not crime, norcal fishing news, offshore fishing, okuma fishing usa, pike fishing, pompano beach fishing rodeo, port oconnor texas fishing, recreational fishing, reel dreams fishing charters, reel job fishing, robson green extreme fishing, salt water fishing, saltwater fishing, sea fishing, simms fishing products, simply fishing tackle, snags fishing tackle, sport fishing magazine, steves custom fishing rods, still water fishing, strategic fishing systems, surf fishing, tica fishing rods reels, total sea fishing magazine, tournament fishing radio, trout fishing, trout fishing in america, walleye fishing, wave fishing

Hunting Estimated Reach: 2,962,440 people who live in the United States and like:

1000000 hunters united, alabama ducks unlimited, ameristep quality hunting, bass hunter, big game fishing journal, big game forever, big game hunter, big game hunting in idaho, big game sports, bird hunting, black bear hunting, boar hunting, bow hunting, bow hunting divas, bring back fox hunting, cabellas, dear hunter, deer hunter, deer hunting, delta waterfowl foundation, duck goose hunting, duck hunting, ducks unlimited, ducks unlimited memphis, gander mountain, global hunting network, hardcore hunting tv, hunter blog, hunter boots, hunter brothers, hunter love, hunter store, hunter x hunter, hunters, hunters club, hunters collectors, hunters gold, hunters helping kids inc, hunters hut, hunters run, hunters world, huntersclubcom, huntin, huntin fishin, hunting, hunting bears, hunting beast forum, hunting beastcom, hunting books, hunting books dvds, hunting buddies, hunting camping, hunting channel, hunting chronicles tv show, hunting club, hunting collecting, hunting country, hunting deer, hunting dogs, hunting fishin, hunting fishing camping, hunting fishing camping deals, hunting fitness magazine, hunting games, hunting golf, hunting hobby, hunting horn, hunting hotties, hunting in rut, hunting lodge, hunting magazines, hunting party, hunting photo, hunting photography by sarah farnsworth, hunting rifles shotguns, hunting season, hunting shooting, hunting show, hunting sports, hunting strangers, hunting talestipstactics, hunting trophy whitetails, hunting with dogs, hunting with my dad, hunting with my husband, huntingfield, huntingfishing, huntingfishing4x4com, huntinggpsmapscom, huntingleaguecom, huntinglifecom, huntingnet, huntrush hunting network, idahos greatest big game inc, keep hunting, mule deer hunting, north american deer hunting association, online hunting shows, pheasant hunting, pheasants forever, pine ridge hunting lodge, predator hunting talkcast, primos hunting calls, primos truth about hunting, real hunting magazine, save hunting right bear arms, shaping up for hunting, sniper hunting buggy, supreme deer hunting, thermacell hunting, town huntington huntington new york, turkey hunting, upland bird hunting, waterfowl hunting, wehmeyer elk hunting, whitetail deer hunting, world hunting

Winter Sports and Activities

Snowmobiles Estimated Reach: 273,280 people who live in the United States, are age 18 and older, and like:

arctic cat snowmobiles, i love snowmobiling, polaris snowmobiles, riding snowmobiles, skidoo snowmobiles, skidoo type snowmobile, snow mobiling, snowmobile calendar, snowmobile fanatics, snowmobile racing, snowmobile stunt, snowmobilecalendarscom, snowmobileing, snowmobilerscom, snowmobiles, snowmobilin, snowmobiling, worlds fastest snowmobiles, yamaha snowmobiles

Alpine Skiing Estimated Reach: 1,179,160 people who live in the United States and like:

aboutcom skiing, alpine skiing, arctic heli skiing, atomic skiing, backcountry skiing, beyond skiing 2015, biggest skiing in america, blizzard skiing, cmh heli skiing heli hiking, cxc skiing, down hill skiing, downhill cross country skiing, downhill skiing, extreme skiing, fis crosscountry skiing, fis freestyle skiing, freeride skiing, freestyle skiing, gmc world skiing, going skiing, golf skiing, i 3 skiing, i enjoy skiing, i love skiing, i skiing, id rather be skiing, love skiing, maine handicapped skiing, mike wiegele helicopter skiing, more skiing, mountain skiing, onelove skiing, skate skiing, skiing, skiing austria, skiing backcountry, skiing boarding, skiing downhill, skiing etc, skiing in winter, skiing is my life, skiing lyzovanie, skiing magazine, skiing new zealand nz, skiing snow, skinny skiing, slalom skiing, slopeforce skiing network, snow skiing, sports skiing, swimming skiing, tele skiing, walter wood skiing, water skiing, we love skiing seufdk, wetrope wakeboarding water skiing network, winter skiing

Snowboarding Estimated Reach: 2,535,920 people who live in the United States and like:

100one tonale snowboard shop, 3 snowboarding, academy snowboard co, all cal ski snowboard fest, angry snowboarder, antero snowboarding company, artec snowboards, ballistyx snowboard show, bardonecchia ski snowboard, bataleon snowboards, bataleon snowboards ch, bataleon snowboards italy, be snowboard, bergs ski snowboard shop, bonfire snowboarding, british snowboard association, bsa snowboarding, buck hill ski snowboard area, bump ski und snowboard shop, burton snowboard co, burton snowboarding, burton snowboards, burton snowboards france, burton snowboards norge, caked snowboards get wit it, capita snowboarding, carnival snowboard session, celsius snowboard footwear, comunidad del snowboard, contract snowboards, daily snowboarding videos, darkside snowboards, downhill snowboard 2, downhill snowboard pro team, downhill snowboarding, eastern snowboard league, ecs magazine east coast snowboarding, edge world snowboard shop, elan skis snowboards, elan snowboards, fis snowboard world cup, flow snowboarding, flow snowboarding europe, flow snowboards, forum snowboards, forum snowboards europe, forum snowboards slovakia, freeride snowboard, freestyle snowboard, freestyle snowboarding, frequency snowboarders journal, fyve snowboards skate, gnu snowboards, gravity snowboards, head snowboards, high cascade snowboard camp, hot ice snowboard, i 3 snowboarding, i love snowboard, i miss snowboarding, i snowboarding, imperium snowboards, istc freestyle snowboarding, jibswitch snowboarding network, jones snowboards, k2 snowboarding, k2 snowboarding spain, kayak ve snowboard sevenler, las vegas ski snowboard resort, launch snowboards, learning snowboard, marhar snowboards, mitch snowboard camps, nazca snowboard camp, niche snowboards, nidecker snowboards, nike snowboarding, nitro snowboards canada, nitro snowboards italy, nonstop ski snowboard, o2 snowboard tour, onboard snowboarding magazine, one snowboarding, palmer snowboards skis, pelican ski snowboard shops, play downhill snowboard 2 game, potter brothers ski snowboards, prior snowboards skis, prospect snowboards, r5 skateboarding snowboarding, raging buffalo snowboard ski park wakeboard school, reason snowboard magazine, ride snowboards, ride snowboards spain, ride snowboards uk team, rome snowboards, santa cruz snowboards, scotlands ski snowboard show, sentury snowboards, sequence snowboarding, shaun white snowboarding, showcase snowboard surf skate, sierra snowboard, signal snowboards, sigsagsug snowboard skateshop, skateboard bmx snowboard, skateboarding snowboarding, ski dazzle ski snowboard, ski snowboardschool cima, ski und snowboard fahren, snowboard, snowboard asylum, snowboard club uk, snowboard coach, snowboard cross, snowboard daily, snowboard fahren, snowboard film on rocks, snowboard instructor, snowboard jackets on sale, snowboard jib contest, snowboard journal, snowboard madness, snowboard magazine, snowboard neve fresca, snowboard patagonia, snowboard rulez 4board, snowboard shop, snowboard team austria, snowboard world, snowboard zezula, snowboard3, snowboard6punto9, snowboardaddictioncom, snowboardbg, snowboardcanadacom, snowboardclearance, snowboarde, snowboardel, snowboarden, snowboarden 3, snowboardende, snowboarder, snowboarder guide, snowboarder magazine, snowboardermbm, snowboarders over 30, snowboarders popova shapka, snowboarderscz, snowboardforbundet, snowboardforum, snowboardgreen, snowboarding, snowboarding 3, snowboarding dx, snowboarding etc, snowboarding finnish open, snowboarding game, snowboarding in winter, snowboarding more than skiing, snowboarding new zealand, snowboarding skateboarding, snowboarding surfing, snowboarding wakeboarding, snowboardit, snowboardn, snowboardonline, snowboardpl, snowboardquebeccom, snowboardro, snowboards, snowboardscom, snowboardscz, snowboardski, soka skateboards snowboards, solid snowboards, tahoe snowboarder magazine, taste snowboard magazine, team utah snowboarding inc, thespotgr skateboard snowboard wakeboard in greece, transfer snowboard magazine, transworld snowboarding, tyrol basin ski snowboard area, völkl snowboards, venture snowboards, we love snowboarding, world snowboard day, xtrem snowboarding, zebra snowboard, zoopark snowboard surf skate street shop

Sports

Golf Enthusiasts Estimated Reach: 2,409,460 people who live in the United States and like:

adam scott golf, adams golf, adidas golf, adidas golf official site, alfs golf shops, assistant golf professional, bridgestonegolf, callaway golf, callaway golf official page, callaway golf women one game, cleveland golf, cobra golf, dream golf job, eat sleep golf, enjoy golfing, fishing golf, fishing golfing, fit for golf, going golfing, golf, golf ace, golf basketball, golf bowling, golf breaks, golf channel, golf channel amateur tour, golf clearance outlet, golf deals, golf digest, golf digest magazine, golf drinking, golf essentials for women, golf etc, golf fishing, golf fix, golf fix with michael breed, golf football, golf for women magazine, golf galaxy, golf game, golf glove, golf golf, golf golf golf, golf golf more golf, golf gti, golf hockey, golf holidays, golf hunting, golf ii gti, golf is not game perfect, golf journal, golf just love be outside, golf league, golf magazine, golf magazines, golf more golf, golf nut, golf occasionally, golf pride, golf prime, golf pro game, golf professional, golf reading, golf skiing, golf soccer, golf sometimes, golf swimming, golf tennis, golf time, golf tips magazine, golf tips quips, golf travel, golf when i can, golf when i have time, golf work, golf world golfworldcom, golfcom pro challenge, golfing, golfing fishing, hockey golf, i enjoy golfing, i like play golf, i love golf, i love play golf, i love playing golf, improving your golf, jeff ritter golf, like play golf, love golf, love golfing, love play golf, love playing golf, mizuno golf, never compromise putters, nike golf, ogio golf, play best golf your life, playing golf, sassy golf, scratch golf tour department, sean cochran golf fitness, soccer golf, softball golf, solus golf, srixon, titleist, titleist ap2, titleist golf, totally driven golf, underground golf secrets, walthers golf fun, wilson staff, world golf hall fame, yo quiero jugar golf, zen golf

Football Estimated Reach: 8,361,120 people who live in the United States, are age 18 and older, and like:

american football, baseball football basketball, college football playoff, ea sports fantasy football, ea sports football world, epl fantasy football, epl fantasy football 2010, especially football, especially football basketball, espn rise football, everything about football, fantasy football, fantasy football 2009, fantasy football 2010, fifa football world cup worlds largest event, fly your football flag, football, football 4 ever, football américain, football american, football americano, football arena, football babes fc, football baseball basketball, football basketball baseball, football basketball track, football boxing, football coach, football coaching, football d, football dancing, football dream factory, football drinking, football factory, football fan, football fan challenge, football fanatics, football fans, football fans challenge, football first, football focus, football football, football football football, football gameplan, football games, football girls, football grounds, football gym, football hd, football hero, football highlights, football in general, football is better than soccer, football is life, football is my life, football its my life, football life, football manager, football manager 2009, football mom, football more football, football most other sports, football most sports, football movies, football nascar, football news, football nfl, football on sundays, football player, football players, football players are sexy, football players are soooo hot, football playing, football playing watching, football quarter, football quiz, football referee, football season, football season baby, football sunday, football sundays, football superstar, football superstar season two, football swimming, football tennis, football time tennessee, football trials, football video games, football volleyball, football watching, football watching playing, football weight lifting, football wrestling, girls that love football, hockey football, i love football season, i miss football season, i play football, joey doyles football sunday, monday night football, nfl football, play baseball football, play basketball football, play football basketball, playing american football, playing baseball football, playing football, post season fantasy football, premier league fantasy football, semi pro football, sun football, sunday afternoon football, sunday football, sunday night football on nbc, tackle football, thehuddlecom fantasy football, throwing football, watch football, watching basketball football, watching football, watching football hockey, watching football on sunday, watching my son play football, what football position are you, yahoo sports fantasy football, yahoo world football

Green Living

Conservation Estimated Reach: 269,140 people who live in the United States and like:

conservation, conservation fund, conservation international, conservation northwest, conservation safari visit wildearthtv, conserve, ecology, ecology center, ecology club, ecology commerce, human ecology, national parks conservation association, natural resources, nature conservation, nature conservation foundation, open source ecology, panama amphibian rescue conservation project, sea shepherd conservation society, urban ecology center, wildlife conservation

Sustainable Estimated Reach: 143,380 people who live in the United States and like:

ecobusiness sustainable development, foundation for sustainable development, organic islands festival sustainability expo 2009,sustainability, sustainable agriculture, sustainable cleveland 2019,sustainable coastlines, sustainable development, sustainable earth, sustainable food, sustainable groupies, sustainable industries magazine, sustainable jakarta convention, sustainable living or sustainable living roadshow

Environmental Activism Estimated Reach: 159,340 people who live in the United States and like:

2009 environmental priorities, ecological environmental movement, environmental activism, environmental awareness, environmental causes, environmental club, environmental conservation, environmental education, environmental issues, environmental justice, environmental protection, environmental rights actionfriends earth nigeria, environmental services, environmental stuff, environmentally friendly, environmentaltld, pick 5 for environment from us epa, save environment, saving environment, sleepbot environmental broadcastor us environmental protection agency

Alternative/Renewable Energies Estimated Reach: 313,580 people who live in the United States, are age 18 and older, and like:

alternative energetiche, alternative energy, alternative energy sources, american solar energy society, energy efficiency, festival energie alternative, green energy, green mountain energy company, green technology, midwest renewable energy association, renewable energy, renewable energy for arizona, renewableenergyworldcom, renewamerica, solar energy, solar energy international sei, solar power, southwest windpower, space solar energy by sig space island group inc, space solar power, wind energy, wind turbines

Anti-Oil Estimated Reach: 466,240 people who live in the United States, are age 18 and older, and like:

boycott bp oil, bp gulf oil spill 2010, bp oil news, end oil, floridians against big oil, gulf coast oil disaster, gulf oil spill truth, ocean without oil in it, oil spill, oil spill clean up, oiled wildlife care network, plug oil leak now, save louisiana coast oil spill, stop oil spill, stopping gulf coast oil spill, stopping oil speculation now

Wine

Wine Cellar/Clubs Estimated Reach: 1,264,780 people who live in the United States, are age 21 and older, and like:

19th hole wine club, arrowhead wine cellars, brydens trinidad wine club, cellar wine bar, city cellar wine bar grill, collecting wine, divas uncorked inc wine club, margaret river wine club, red newt cellars winery, retro wines wine club, rosehill wine cellars, santa barbara wine club, vigilant wine cellars, wine, wine academy, wine alchemy, wine appreciation, wine appreciation guild, wine artist, wine bars, wine by wine searcher, wine cellar, wine cellar sorbets, wine cellar vestavia hills, wine cellar wisconsin, wine club, wine club guide, wine club zagreb, wine collecting, wine collective, wine gums, wine hotels collection, wine library tv, wine making, wine marketing, wine spectator, wine tasting, wine tasting collecting, winecom, winery collective sf, wines world, zagat ratings review, zambrano wine cellar

Home/Garden

Home Design/Remodel/Renovate Estimated Reach: 182,580 people who live in the United States, are age 24 and older, and like:

fixing house, fixing my house, fixing things around house, fixing up house, fixing up my house, fixing up our house, flipping houses, hgtv home improvement shows, home building, home design, home design creation, home design ideas, home design magazine, home design network, home design remodeling show, home design shows, home designing, home improvement books, home improvement decorating, home improvement pages, home improvement repair, home improvement stuff, home improvements, home improvments, home renovating, home renovation, home renovations, home repair, home repairs, house flipping shows, house remodeling, house renovating, house renovation, house renovations, martins remodeling, novel home design, remodeling, remodeling homes, remodeling house, remodeling houses, remodeling my home, remodeling my house, remodeling our house, remodeling projects, remodelingcentercom, renovating, renovating house, renovating houses, renovating my house, renovating our house, renovation, renovation style, renovations, this old house, working on my house yard

Entertaining Estimated Reach: 493,200 people who live in the United States and like:

celebrations, cocktail parties, dinner parties with friends, entertaining, entertaining at home, entertaining family friends, entertaining friends, entertaining friends family, entertaining guests, entertaining people, event planning, having dinner parties, hostess, hostess with mostess, hostess with mostest, hosting dinner parties, hosting parties, metropolitan cooking entertaining show, planning events, planning parties, planning things, throwing dinner parties

Discount

Couponers Estimated Reach: 654,740 people who live in the United States, are age exactly 18 and older, and like:

alaska coupon diva, baby cheapskate, bargain divas, bargain hunt, bargain hunting, bargain shopping, bargains, bargin hunt, bargin shopping, become debt free, become thrifty, budget babe, budgeting, clipping coupons, coupon clippers, coupon codes, couponcabin, debtproof living, discount hunt, discounts vouchers, discountvouchers, feisty frugal fabulous, free stuff, free stuff cheap stuff, free stuff for college students, free stuff times, freebie blogger, freebie reporter, freebies, freebies 4 mom, frugal coupon living, frugal freebies, frugal girl, frugal girls, frugal sally, frugality, grocery coupons, hot coupon world, i discounts, i want student discounts, money saving methods, money saving mom, mrdealfindercom online coupons, my frugal adventures, promos discounts, redplum deals values coupons, retailmenot, save your money, saving money, savingsangel com, somehow save money

Garage Salers Estimated Reach: 186,380 people who live in the United States and like:

brooklyn flea markets, city wide garage sale, estate sales, estatesalesnet, flea market, flea market directory, flea marketing, flea markets, flea markets yard sales, fleamarkets, flee markets, garage sale, garage saleing, garage sales, garage saling, going flea markets, hells kitchen flea market, online garage sale, rummage sales, yard sale, yard sales, yard sales flea markets, yard saling, yardsales

Tough Times

Debt/Bad Credit Estimated Reach: 162,960 people who live in the United States, are age 18 and older, and like:

bailout our student loans, become debt free, couponing be debt free, debt loan consolidation talk, debtproof living, debtsorters debt advice, defeat debt, get out debt, getting out debt, hate having no credit, home loan hints, how stop foreclosure, i hate bank america, i hate chase bank, i hate having no credit, interestfree student loans, money as debt, mortgage advice, neighborhood loans, opportune home loans, payday loans, payday loans quick cash now, quicken loans, rapid debt settlement, savings loans credit union, savvy debt coach, sme rescue loans program, student loans

Job Hunters Estimated Reach: 275,220 people who live in the United States, are age 18 and older, and like:

careerbuilder, careerbuildercom, damn i need job, finding new job, hot jobs, i need job, job hunting, job hunting careers, job searching, job seeker, jobs indeed, looking for job need change, looking for new job, pray for new jobs, snagajobcom, super resume, we want job

Music

Dubstep Estimated Reach: 1,117,340 people who live in the United States and like:

16bit, atlanta dubstep, bar 9, bass drops you can feel, bassnectar, benga, borgore, boxcutter, caspa, caspa rusko, chase status, chasing shadows, circus records, coki, cotti stn dubstep, crissy criss, deckadance drum bass breaks dubstep, deepstep, detroit dubstep, digital mystikz, dj hatcha, dmz, doctor p, dub deep underground beats, dub dubstep tour, dub fx, dub police, dub step, dubplate drama, dubstep, dubstep cornwall, dubstep mix, dubstepforumcom, emalkay, evol intent, flux pavilion, flying lotus, funtcase, getdarker dubstep, glitch mob, hijak, hotflush recordings, hyperdub records, i love dub step, i love dubstep, itchy robot afterdark dubstep, jaime le dubstep, kode 9, kode9, kromestar, kryptic minds, loefah, mary anne hobbs on radio 1, mary anne hobbs on radio one, mistabishi, ntype, oneman, pantyraid, plastician, rusko, skepta, starkey, subscape, tes la rok, trolley snatcha, uk garage, ukf dubstep, vexd, werd2jahvoice southern dubstep

Classical Music Estimated Reach: 745,020 people who live in the United States, are age 18 and older, and like:

achilleclaude debussy, amadeus mozart, bach, bach cello suites, beethovan, beethoven, beethoven symphonies, beethovens 9th, beethowen, bethoveen, brahms, brahms johannes, clair de lune by debussy, classical mozart, classical music bach, classical music mozart, claude debussy, debussey, debussy, franz peter schubert, franz schubert, j s bach, johan sebastian bach, johann s bach, johannes brahms, js bach, ludvig van beethoven, ludwig v beethoven, ludwig van beethoven, ludwig van beethoven 17701827, ludwig von beethoven, lv beethoven, mozart, mozarts requiem, peter ilyich tchaikovsky, peter tchaikovsky, pyotr ilyich tchaikovsky, r strauss, requiem k 626 by mozart, richard strauss, schubert, strauss, strauss waltzes, tchaichovsky, tchaicovsky, tchaikovski, tchaikovsky, tchaikowsky, w mozart, wolfgang amadeus mozart, wolfgang mozart, wolfgang wolfer amadeus mozart

Hobbies

Collectors Estimated Reach: 180,400 people who live in the United States, are age 18 and older, and like:

antique collecting, art collecting, autograph collecting, book collecting, coin collecting, collecting, collecting action figures, collecting angels, collecting antiques, collecting art, collecting autographs, collecting barbie dolls, collecting baseball cards, collecting books, collecting cds, collecting coins, collecting comic books, collecting comics, collecting cookbooks, collecting dolls, collecting dvds, collecting football cards, collecting guitars, collecting guns, collecting hot wheels, collecting junk, collecting keychains, collecting knives, collecting movies, collecting old books, collecting old coins, collecting perfumes, collecting pictures, collecting postcards, collecting recipes, collecting records, collecting rocks, collecting shoes, collecting shot glasses, collecting sneakers, collecting sports cards, collecting sports memorabilia, collecting stamps, collecting stickers, collecting stuff, collecting teddy bears, collecting things, collecting toys, collecting vinyl, collecting vinyl records, collecting watches, collections, doll collecting, gun collecting, hoarding, i collecting, knife collecting, record collecting, rock collecting, stamp collecting, star wars collecting, toy collecting, watching collecting movies

Business

Money Management Gurus Estimated Reach: 939,620 people who live in the United States, are age 25 and older, and like:

dave ramsey, dave ramsey show, dave ramseys total money makeover, dylan ratigan, dylan ratigan show, financial peace by dave ramsey, jim cramer, jim cramers real money, mintcom, nightly business report, nightly business report nbr, peachtree by sage, quickbooks, quickbooks proadvisor program, quicken, quicken loans, quicken loans arena, quicken online, suze orman, suze orman show, total money makeover dave ramsey, women money by suze orman

Internet Marketing Publications Estimated Reach: 52,160 people who live in the United States and like:

blueglass, daily seo tip, danny sullivan, econsultancy, internet retailer, matt cutts, raven internet marketing tools, readwriteweb, reelseo, search engine journal, search engine roundtable, search engine watch, seomasters, seomoz, social media examiner, social media explorer

Chatting/RPG

MMO Estimated Reach: 1,063,660 people who live in the United States, are age 18 and older, and like:

9dragons, 9dragons gamersfirst, 9dragons official page, adventurequest, aion tower eternity, alliance world warcraft, anarchy online, archlord, asherons call, atlantica online, battlefield heroes, battlestar galactica online, cabal online, classic ragnarok online, dark age camelot, dc universe online, dead frontier, dead frontier mmo, dragon oath, dragonica online, eve online, everquest, everquest 2, everquest ii, everquest two, firefall, free realms, global agenda, guild wars, guild wars 2, guild wars 2 guru, guild wars factions, guild wars nightfall, happy farm, i play world warcraft, official free realms page, phantasy star online, play world warcraft, playing guild wars, playing runescape, priston tale, priston tale 2 sea, priston tale 2 second enigma, ragnarok online, ragnarok online 2, ragnarok online two, requiem bloodymare, rohan blood feud, rose online, runescape, runescape help, spacewar 2moons, star wars galaxies, starquest, torchlight, torchlight mmorpg, vanguard saga heroes, warhammer online, warhammer online age reckoning, world warcraft, world warcraft alliance, world warcraft burning crusade, world warcraft cataclysm, world warcraft horde side, world warcraft strategies, world warcraft warth lich king, world warcraft wrath lich king, world warcraftwarcraft, world world warcraft, wow, wow cataclysm, wow wrath lich king

Chatting Estimated Reach: 5,432,220 people who live in the United States, are age 18 and older, and like:

adult chat, adult conversations, aim, best chatroom, camfrog video chat, chat, chat emoticons, chat emoticons smileys symbols, chat emotions, chat globalchat, chat online, chat room, chat room for bored people, chat rooms, chat rooms youcams, chat roulette, chat smileys, chat symbols, chat with friends, chat with my friends, chating online, chating with friends, chating with my friends, chatroom, chats, chattin online, chatting, chatting etc, chatting friends, chatting on computer, chatting on facebook, chatting on internet, chatting on msn, chatting on net, chatting online, chatting w friends, chatting with friends, chatting with friends online, chatville, chit chat with friends, clobby group chat, conversation, conversations with other women, deep conversations, deep meaningful conversations, ebuddy, english conversations, facebook chat, facebook chat room, facebook chatroom, friendcam video chat, gay chat, gchat, good conversation, google talk, great conversation, great conversations, gripping conversations, having deep conversations, having good conversation, hearttoheart conversations 3, hearttoheart conversations3, hottest dating chat with girls, i love chatting, i love talking, icq, instant messaging, intellectual conversation, intellectual conversations, intelligent conversation, interesting conversation, interesting conversations, jabber, lets start talking, long conversations, lunch table conversations, meaningful conversations, meebo, messenger, obssessed with chatting, omegle, online chat, online chatting, online dating chatting, online people chat, philosophical conversations, pidgin, random conversations, social chat, social chat rooms, stimulating conversation, stimulating conversations, talking, talking about life, talking about music, talking about politics, talking about random things, talking alot, talking friends, talking in general, talking listening, talking lol, talking lot, talking most time, talking on computer, talking people, talking strangers, talking talking talking, talking til sunrise, talking too much, trillian, ungu chat room, video chatting, when did conversation end, windows live messenger, windows live messenger 2009, yahoo messenger, yahoo messenger faces, yahoo messenger pingbox, zoosk

Media with Cult Followings

Lord of the Rings Estimated Reach: 2,945,920 people who live in the United States, are age 16 and older, and like:

all lotr movies, anything by tolkein, aragorn, baggins, bilbo baggins, elrond, frodo, frodo baggins, gandalf you shall not pass, gimli, gollum, hobbit, hobbit lotr, hobbit, there back again, hobbit tolkien, hobbit trilogy, hobbiten, hobbiton, jr tolkein, jr tolkien, jrr tolken, jrr tolkien, jrr tolkien hobbit, jrr tolkiens, jrr tolkiens lord rings, jrr tolkienthe hobbit, jrr tolkienthe lord rings, jrrtolkien, lord ring one, lord rings, lord rings film, lord rings film trilogy, lord rings movie series, lord rings one, lord rings one two three, lord rings online, lord rings return king 2003, lord rings trilogy film, lord rings two towers 2002, lord rings1, lord ringsall, lord ringstrilogy, lordofthering elseñordelosanillos, lordoftherings, lotr, lotr 123, lotr all them, lotr books, lotr fellowship ring, lotr hobbit, lotr iiii, lotr movies, lotr one, lotr series, lotr soundtrack, lotr tolkien, lotr trillogy, lotr trilogy, lotr triology, lotr two towers, lotrs trilogy, mithrandir gandalf, peregrin pippin took, pippin mcgee, return king, samwise, samwise gamgee, samwise gamgee sam, silmarilion, silmarillion, silmarillon, simarillion, sméagol gollum, smeagol, tolken, tolkien, tolkien books, tolkien trilogy, tolkiens lord rings, trilogy lotr, two towers

True Blood Estimated Reach: 4,351,400 people who live in the United States and like:

addicted true blood, anything by charlaine harris, charlaine harris, charlaine harris books, charlaine harris sookie stackhouse series, charlaine harris southern vampire mysteries, deborah ann woll jessica from true blood, dexter true blood, hbo true blood latinoamérica, lafayette true blood, pam true blood, prime true blood, sookie stackhouse, sookie stackhouse books, sookie stackhouse novels by charlaine harris, sookie stackhouse novelspage, sookie stackhouse series, sookie stackhouse series by charlaine harris, sookie stackhouse true blood, true blood, true blood dexter, true blood hbo, true blood news at nest, true blood official fan page, true blood on hbo, true blood page officielle, true blood season 2, true blood series, watch true blood online, we all love true blood

Twilight Estimated Reach: 7,769,920 people who live in the United States, are age 18 and older, and like:

addicted twilight, alacakaranlık 2008 twilight, alacakaranlık twilight, all gossip from twilight saga, all things twilight, all twilight books, all twilight saga, all twilight series, all twilights, best film award twilight, currently reading twilight, currently reading twilight series, dazzled by twilight, defining twilight, edward cullen alacakaranlık twilight, edward cullen twilight, family twilight saga, fanfics twilight, fantasy twilight tour, forever twilight, get free twilight t shirt, gossip news twilight saga, harry potter twilight, harry potter twilight series, history twilight, how much do you know about twilight sega, i love twilight, i love twilight saga, i love twilight series, inspired by twilight, who loves twilightwe do, jacob twilight is sex, james twilight, just finished twilight series, love twilight saga 3, love twilight series, loved twilight series, official twilight saga, official twilight saga gifts, othe twilight sagao, reading twilight, reading twilight saga, reading twilight series, real life twilight love story, right now twilight, right now twilight series, roba da twilighters, robert pattinson twilight, scene it twilight, stephenie meyers twilight series, three twilight, twilight, twilight 2 new moon, twilight 2008 film, twilight 3, twilight 4 breaking dawn, twilight addicts, twilight alacakaranlık, twilight all, twilight all them, twilight all way, twilight battles, twilight beauty cosmetics, twilight book, twilight book movie, twilight book series, twilight books, twilight breaking dawn, twilight by stephanie meyer, twilight by stephenie meyer, twilight character which are you, twilight characters, twilight co, twilight collection, twilight continued from another point view, twilight duh, twilight e new moon, twilight eclipse, twilight eclipse countdown, twilight eclipse release early, twilight edward bella jacob, twilight etc, twilight examiner, twilight eyes, twilight fan channel, twilight fanpires, twilight fans, twilight film, twilight films, twilight forever, twilight forum saga, twilight game, twilight gift, twilight gifts, twilight guide, twilight harry potter, twilight harry potter series, twilight his collection, twilight i know, twilight idols, twilight inside, twilight is my life, twilight jaime jassume, twilight love, twilight lovers, twilight many more, twilight more, twilight movie, twilight movie poster, twilight movies, twilight n new moon, twilight new moon 3, twilight new moon eclipse, twilight new moon eclipse breaking dawn, twilight new moon eclipse breaking down, twilight new moon movie, twilight new moon serisi fan, twilight novel, twilight novels, twilight official page, twilight one, twilight others, twilight p, twilight page, twilight quiz, twilight quotes, twilight robert pattinson, twilight saga, twilight saga best forever, twilight saga books, twilight saga books movies, twilight saga breaking dawn, twilight saga by stephanie meyer, twilight saga by stephenie meyer, twilight saga collection, twilight saga eclipse 2010, twilight saga eclipse fanatics, twilight saga movies, twilight saga new moon, twilight saga official uk page, twilight saga quotes, twilight saga three, twilight saga twilight, twilight sequel new moon, twilight series, twilight series 3, twilight series by stephanie meyer, twilight series by stephanie meyers, twilight series by stephenie meyer, twilight series course, twilight series host, twilight series i know, twilight series right now, twilight series stephanie meyer, twilight series stephenie meyer, twilight series three, twilight series twilight, twilight series yes, twilight society world, twilight soundtrack, twilight stephanie meyer, twilight team, twilight tentation, twilight three, twilight tr, twilight trilogy, twilight tshirts, twilight twilight twilight twilight p, twilight two, twilight two new moon, twilight two tentation, twilight ultimate gifts, twilight vinculum, twilight watch, twilight weekly spotlight, twilight what obsession, twilight whole series, twilight world, twilight yes, twilightbella edward, twilighters around world, twilightfans website forum community, twilightnew mooneclipsebreaking dawn, twilightnorge, twilightt homepage, twimoms moms who love twilight, vampire twilight, watch twilight eclipse, watch twilight eclipse online, we love twilight saga, what twilight character are you, which female twilight character are you, who is your twilight guy, whole twilight series, whos your twilight soulmate, why i love twilight saga, win twilight box set, yo amo twilight, you read twilight now its your life

Zombies Estimated Reach: 2,987,500 people who live in the United States, are age 18 and older, and like:

28 day later, 28 days, 28 days 28 weeks later, 28 days later, 28 days later 28 weeks later, 28 days weeks later, 28 weeks later, 32 rules zombieland, anything by george romero, anything with zombies, anything with zombies in it, army darkness, being prepared for zombies, call duty zombies, chicago zombie pub crawl, class 3 outbreak zombie rts, dawn dead, day dead, days you will survive in zombie invasion, dead alive, downtown lansing zombie walk, evil dead, for love zombies official page, gangsta zombies, george romero, going school as zombie, h2 official page for new film by rob zombie, having zombie plan, how survive zombie apocalypse, humans vs zombies, i have zombie apocalypse plan, i love plants vs zombies, i love zombies, its beginning look lot like zombies, killing zombies, land dead, marvel zombies, max brooks, melbourne zombie shuffle, mpls zombie society, night living dead, not being eaten by zombies, not being killed by zombies, not being turned into zombie, not being zombie, planning for zombie apocalypse, plant vs zombies, plants versus zombies, plants vs zombie, plants vs zombie philippines, plants vs zombie war, plants vs zombies, plants vs zombies battle, plants vs zombies, play zombie farm, play zombie farm game, playing plants vs zombies, preparing for zombie invasion, pride prejudice zombies, real zombie survival odds, redneck zombies, return living dead, sas zombie assault 2, sas zombie assault ii, silent night zombie night, tattooed zombie accessories, tennessee zombie response unit, voodoo zombie, welcome zombieland, white zombie, world war z, world war z max brooks, wwz max brooks movie 2010, zmd zombies mass destruction, zombie

apocalypse, zombie apocalypse preparation, zombie books, zombie boutique, zombie command, zombie emergency defense, zombie emergency management agency, zombie farm, zombie films, zombie flesh eaters, zombie flicks, zombie girl, zombie girl movie, zombie hunters, zombie hunting, zombie kids, zombie kill week, zombie land, zombie movies, zombie movies in general, zombie nation, zombie powder, zombie prom, zombie research society, zombie slayer, zombie squad, zombie strippers, zombie survival guide, zombie walk, zombie walk san diego, zombie wars, zombie women satan, zombie zone news, zombieaid, zombiebooth, zombieland, zombieland singapore, zombieland uk page, zombieland zombify yourself, zombiemecom by adnan saleem, zombies are delicious, zombies ate my neighbors, zombies daylight, zombies fans, zombies toys, zombies video production

Fantasy Estimated Reach: 537,980 people who live in the United States, are age 18 and older, and like:

3 fantasy 3, 3 fantasy3, amy brown fantasy art inc, animated fantasy art, anything sci fi, fantasy, art fantasy, dark fantasy, eclectic fantasy, fantasy, fantasy adventure, fantasy art, fantasy art gallery, fantasy art molly harrison, fantasy art photography, fantasy books, fantasy castles, fantasy celebrations, fantasy clothing, fantasy costumes estonia, fantasy creatures, fantasy dream paradise, fantasy fest, fantasy film, fantasy filmfest, fantasy films, fantasy flight, fantasy games, fantasy horror, fantasy is love, fantasy kingdom, fantasy kingdoms, fantasy literature, fantasy love, fantasy magazine, fantasy movie, fantasy movies, fantasy novels, fantasy over reality, fantasy paranormal book group, fantasy photography, fantasy picturedesign, fantasy romance, fantasy sci fi, fantasy science fiction, fantasy scifi, fantasy stuff, fantasy tours, fantasy twilight tour, fantasy warrior dress, fantasy work art, gothic fantasy art, heroic fantasy, i like fantasy, i love fantasy, love fantasy novels, love romance fantasy, magical fantasy, medieval fantasy, monster fantasy, most fantasy, mostly fantasy, my fantasy, nicole west fantasy art, pegasus fantasy, reading fantasy, reading fantasy books, reading fantasy novels, reading fiction esp fantasy, realms fantasy, sci fi fantasy, science fantasy, science fiction fantasy writers america, scifi fantasy horor, tales fantasy, tamora pierce fantasy author, urban fantasy, world fantasy convention 2010

Index

Note to the Reader: Throughout this index **boldfaced** page numbers indicate primary discussions of a topic. *Italicized* page numbers indicate illustrations.

A

A/B testing, 132
Accel Partners, 3
account structure, **66–68**, *67–68*
accountants, **223–224**
Acquisio tool, 34, 190
ad fatigue, **193**
Ad ID metric, 199
Ad Name column in Campaign screen, 179
Ads Manager
　Advertiser Performance reports, **194–197**
　All Ads screen, **182–183**, *183*
　All Campaigns screen, **175–177**, *176*
　Campaign screen, **177–181**, *178, 181*
　Inline Ad Preview, Targeting, and Performance screen, **181–182**, *182*
　introduction, **174**
　navigating, **174–175**, *175*
　optimizing
　　for CPC, 188
　　for CPM, 189
　　for CTR, **185–187**
Ads: Targeting Options, **62–63**, *63*
Advanced Demographics settings, **56**, *57*
　birthday targeting, 57
　languages, **59**

relationship status and sexuality, **57–59**
　targeting attributes, 40
Advertiser Performance reports, **194–199**, *198*
aerobics segment targeting, **229**
affiliations, targeting, **90–93**, *91–92*
age
　in compound targeting, **112–115**, *113–114*
　in Demographics attributes, **48–49**
　in relationship status, 123
All Ads screen, 175
　ads in, **182–183**, *183*
　optimizing
　　for CPC, 188
　　for CPM, 189
　　for CTR, 186
All Campaigns screen, 75, **175–177**, *176*, 183
Allport, Floyd Henry, 7
Allport, Gordon Willard, 7
alpine skiing segment targeting, **235**
alternate ad variations, **74–75**, *74*
alternative/renewable energies segment, **238–239**
alumni, targeting, **121**
Alzheimer's disease, 112–113, *112, 114*
American Express ad, 151, *151*
and operator, **40–42**
Angooroo ad, 151, *151*

animal rights groups, 92–93
anti-oil segment targeting, **239**
applications users, **101–102**, *102*
ascending CTR order, 185, *185*
Ash, Tim, 130, 191
aspect ratio for images, 142
assertions in ads, 15
at-home mom segment, **229**
Atlantis Blue Capital, 13
"attention" in headlines, **138**
attributes
    stacking. *See* compound targeting
    targeting, **39–40**
Attribution CC BY licenses, 146
attribution in Facebook Ads, **33–34**
authors, targeting, **98–99**

B

B2B clients, 87
bad credit targeting, **240–241**
bar managers targeting, **224**
beauty product sites, 101, *101*
beliefs, targeting, **108–109**
benefits touting in headlines, **136–137**
bids
    in ad creation, 70
    on Campaign screen, 181
    setting, **160–163**, *162*
Billing Manager, 158
Bing
    for magazines, 94
    as stemming tool, 56
birthday targeting, 57
boating magazine readers targeting,
    96
body copy, **147**
    best practices, **147–152**, *148,*
    151–152

in brand clarity, 128
    length, **152–154**, *152–154*
bodybuilding magazines, 97, *97*
bodybuilding segment, **229**
books, targeting, **98–99**
borders of images, 143–144, *143–144*
brainstorming targeting options, **100**
brand clarity levels, **128–130**
branding KPIs, **22–23**, *23*
broad categories targeting, 54–56,
    55–56
Broad Category tool, 56
Broad Match age parameter, 48
budgets and budgeting, **156–157**
    All Campaigns screen, 176
    daily campaign, **158–160**
    lifetime, **157**
Bulk Import function, 66
business platforms, 87
business segment targeting, **242**
buying fans, **170–172**

C

call-of-duty guns, **225**
calls to action in body copy, **148–150**
Campaign ID metric, **199**
Campaign Reach metric, 179
Campaign screen, **177–181**, *178, 181,*
    183
campaigns, **63–64**, *64*
    All Campaigns screen, 176
    budgets, 158–160
    selecting, 71
Campaigns & Ads screen, **175–177**,
    176
camping segment targeting, **232–233**
canoeing and kayaking segment
    targeting, **231**

caps, spend, **158–159**, *158*

categories, targeting
    broad, **54–56**, *55–56*
    products, **102–104**, *102–103*

Chat, release of, *5*

chatting/RPG segment targeting, **243–244**

checklists, prelaunch, **172**, **206–207**

Childhood Online Protection Act (COPA), 49

Chrome browser, 66, *66*

City attribute, **47**, *47–48*

CityVille segment, **227**

classic headlines, **135–138**, *138*

classical music segment, **241**

clichés in headlines, **137**

click-through ratio (CTR)
    in brand clarity, 128
    in Campaign screen, **180–181**
    expectations, 20
    KPIs, 22
    optimizing for, **185–187**, *185*

ClickEquations tool, 34, 190

Clicks column in Campaign screen, **180**

clip art, **147**, *147*

club managers, **224**

CNN Live, *5*

coaches segment targeting, **222–223**, **230**

Cohen and Orland v. Facebook, 13

collectors segment targeting, **242**

college students targeting, **120–121**

color in images, **142–144**, *143–144*

community relations KPIs, **28–29**

competitive practices, 15

competitive targeting, **79–80**, *80*

competitors
    body copy by, 148, *148*
    legal considerations, **82–83**

negative sentiment toward, **80–83**, *80–82*

compound targeting, **111**
    age, interest, and gender, **112–115**, *113–114*
    country and language, **123–126**, *124–125*
    education and interest, **119–121**
    sexuality, relationship status, and interests, **121–123**
    workplace and Precise Interest, **115–118**, *115–118*

conflict targeting, **84–85**, *85*

Connections column in Campaign screen, 180

Connections metrics, 179, **191–192**

Connections on Facebook targeting, 39, **61–62**

conservation segment targeting, **238**

conversions
    optimizing for, **189–193**
    tracking, **167–169**, *168*

Conversions by Impression Time reports, **201**

Conversions metric, 192

COPA (Childhood Online Protection Act), 49

cosmetic product sites, 101, *101*

cost per action (CPA), 22, 188

cost per click (CPC), 22
    in bid setting, **160–163**, *162*
    vs. CPM, **63–64**
    optimizing for, **188**

cost per fan (CPF) acquired, 170

cost per thousand impressions (CPM)
    in bid setting, **160–163**, *162*
    in brand clarity, 129
    vs. CPC, **63–64**
    expectations, 20

KPIs, 22
  optimizing for, **189**
countries in compound targeting, **123–126**, *124–125*
Country attribute, **45–46**, *46*
couponers segment targeting, **240**
CPA (cost per action), 22, 188
CPC (cost per click), 22
  in bid setting, **160–163**, *162*
  vs. CPM, **63–64**
  optimizing for, **188**
CPF (cost per fan) acquired, 170
CPM. *See* cost per thousand impressions (CPM)
crazy things in targeting, 86
Create A Similar Ad button, 181
creation user interfaces, **35**
  ad design, **36–37**, *36*
  campaigns, pricing, and scheduling, **63–64**, *64*
  Power Editor, **36**
  targeting. *See* targeting
Creative Commons photos, 146
creepy ads, **16**
crisis management KPIs, 27–28
cropping images, **144–145**, *144–145*
CSV exports, 192, 195, **199**
CTR. *See* click-through ratio (CTR)
cult followings segment targeting, **244–247**
cultural activities, **105**
cultural sensitivity, **130**
currencies supported, 156
customer service KPIs, **26**
cyclists segment, **231–232**

D

daily campaign budgets, **158–160**
daily spend limits, **157**

damage control in crisis management, 27–28
Davis, Marvin, 112
debt/bad credit segment targeting, **240–241**
demographics and Demographics attributes, **48**
  age, **48–49**
  birthday targeting, 57
  broad categories targeting, **54–56**, *55–56*
  headlines for, **135–136**
  Interests bucket, **49–51**, *51*
  languages, **59**
  production workflow, **69**
  relationship status and sexuality, **57–59**
  social synonyms, **51–54**, *53*, *55*
  targeting, 39
deploying Facebook Ads, **155**
  finances, **156**
    bids, **160–163**, *162*
    budgeting and spend limits, **156–160**, *157–158*
    payment options, **156**
  landing pages. *See* landing pages
  prelaunch checklists, 172, **206–207**
descending CTR order, 185
Design Your Ad module, **36–37**, *36*
designated market areas (DMAs), 33
dieters segment targeting, **229–230**
Digital Sky Technologies, 5
direct response (DR) KPIs, **23–24**
discount segment targeting, **240**
Display Network, 20
distance runners segment targeting, **230**
DMAs (designated market areas), 33
DR (direct response) KPIs, **23–24**

draft ad copies, 70
drug lords, **226**
drugs, targeting, **85**
dubstep segment targeting, **241**
Durkheim, David Émile, 7
dynamic landing pages, **167–169**, *168*

E

eCPM (effective cost per thousand impressions), 184
Edit Facebook Ad screen, 181, *182*
Education & Work attributes, **59–61**, *60–61*
Education & Work targeting, 40, **89–90**, *89*
education in compound targeting, **119–121**
effective cost per thousand impressions (eCPM), 184
efficiency, 184
employees in internal relations, **29–30**
employment
    Interests Bucket, **87–89**, *88*
    job titles. *See* job titles segment targeting
    targeting, **86–90**, *88–89*, **116–118**, *116–118*
End Date column in All Campaigns screen, 176
entertaining segment targeting, **240**
entertainment activities, **105**
Estimated Reach, **38–42**, *38*
ethics, rules of engagement in, **14–17**
Everystockphoto.com site, 146
exact match age parameter, 48
expectations, setting, **20**
Experian Hitwise
    Internet traffic graph, *5*, *5–6*
    search term data, 2

external landing pages
    socializing, **169–170**
    tracking, **190–191**
external URLs, 36–37

F

f8 Event, 4
Facebook, growth of, **2–6**, *2*, *5–6*
Facebook Ads, **127**
    attribution, **33–34**
    body copy, **147**
        best practices, **147–152**, *148*, *151–152*
        in brand clarity, 128
        length, **152–154**, *152–154*
    brand clarity, **128–130**
    creation user interfaces, **35**
        ad design, **36–37**, *36*
        campaigns, pricing, and scheduling, **63–64**, *64*
        Power Editor, 36
        targeting. *See* targeting
    deploying. *See* deploying Facebook Ads
    development of, 4
    guidelines, **10–13**, 71
    headlines. *See* headlines
    images. *See* images
    KPIs. *See* Key Performance Indicators (KPIs)
    privacy, **10**
    production workflow. *See* production workflow for Facebook Ads
    rules of engagement, **14–17**
    social graphs, **8–9**, *8*
    terms of services, **10–13**
Facebook Mobile, 45
Facebook Places, 45

Facebook Platform, 4
Facebook Reports, **194**
    Advertiser Performance, **194–199,** *198*
    Conversions by Impression Time, **201**
    Responder Demographics, **199–200**
    Responder Profiles, **200–201,** *201*
Facebook v. Adam Guerbuez and Atlantis Blue Capital, 13
Facebook v. Sanford Wallace, 13
Facebook v. Spammers, 13
family roles targeting, **106–108,** *107,* **228–229**
fans, buying, **170–172**
fantasy segment targeting, **247**
figureheads, targeting, **106**
file types for images, **142**
filters for reports, 195
finances, **156**
    bids, **160–163,** *162*
    budgeting and spend limits, **156–160,** *157–158*
    payment options, **156**
fishing segment targeting, **233–234**
follow list, **209–217**
football segment targeting, **237–238**
forbidden activities in Facebook Ads, **10–13**
Ford, Harrison, 112
Fortune 500 companies, **220–222**
foursquare, 203, *203*
fraud, 14
Frequency metric, **179–180**
friending KPIs, **25–26**
friends
    acquisition packages, 171
    targeting users with, 62
Full Report option, 179
future outlook, **201–204,** *203*

G

game social segment, 84
gamers, **226**
garage salers segment targeting, **240**
gay people, targeting, **121–122**
gender in compound targeting, **112–115,** *113–114*
geotargeting, **44–45**
    City, **47,** *47–48*
    Country, **45–46,** *46*
    State and Province, **46–47**
GNU Image Manipulation Program (GIMP), 142
goals. *See* Key Performance Indicators (KPIs)
golf enthusiasts segment targeting, **236–237**
Google
    Advanced Image Search, 146
    Adwords Keywood Tool, *56*
    Analytics tool, **190–191**
    books and magazines, 94, 97, *97*
    Chrome browser, 66, *66*
    Content Network, 4
    CPM costs, 17
    Display Network costs, 20
    Insights for Search, 2, *2,* 23
    market share, *5*
    YouTube, 202
green living segment targeting, **238–239**
Greylock Partners, 3
grouping ads, 68
groups, targeting, **90–93,** *91–92*
Guerbuez, Adam, 13
guidelines
    Facebook Ads, **10–13,** 71
    headlines, **138–139,** *139*
guns, **225**

H

headline theory, 131–132

headlines, 37, **130–131**

  "attention" in, **138**

  benefits touting in, **136–137**

  body copy, **150–151**, *151*

  in brand clarity, 128–130

  classic, **135–138**, *138*

  clichés in, **137**

  controlling, **131**

  for demographic segments, **135–136**

  guidelines, **138–139**, *139*

  literal, **131–133**, *133*

  negative consequences in, **137**

  phonetics, **138**

  with questions, **136**

  sideways, **133–135**, *134–135*

  tips, **139–140**

health segments targeting, **229–230**

Help Center, **62–63**, *63*

help pages for Precise Interests, 8–9, *9*

heterosexuals, targeting, **121–122**

high impressions, 129

high school students, targeting, **119–120**

Hitwise

  Internet traffic graph, 5, *5–6*

  search term data, 2

hobbies segment targeting, **242**

home design/remodel/renovate segment targeting, **239–240**

home/garden segment targeting, **239–240**

homosexuals, targeting, **121–122**

hooks, 132

hotel managers, targeting, **224**

Hughes, Chris, 3

humor in images, 141

hunting segment targeting, **234**

husband segment targeting, **228**

hyperzoomed effects, 145

I

ideas and ideals, targeting, **108–109**

images, **140–141**, *140–141*

  in brand clarity, 129–131

  color, **142–144**, *143–144*

  guidelines, **142**

  size and file types, **142**

  sources, **145–147**, *146–147*

  zooming and cropping, **144–145**, *144–145*

impressions, CPM, 22, **63–64**

incredible things users reveal, **85–86**

infantry, **226**

inferred targeting, 83

inline ad preview, targeting, and performance screen, **181–182**, *182*

Insights for Search tool, 2, *2*, 23

intellectual property, 14

Interested In attribute, 58

Interests attributes, 39

Interests bucket

  and and *or* operators, 41–42

  authors, 98

  family roles, **228–229**

  magazines, 96

  occupations, 87–89, *88*

  overview, **49–51**, *51*

  Precise Interests bucket. *See* Precise Interests bucket and attributes

interface, creation UI, **35**

  ad design, **36–37**, *36*

  campaigns, pricing, and scheduling, **63–64**, *64*

  Power Editor, **36**

  targeting. *See* targeting

internal landing pages, **191–193**

internal relations KPIs, **29–30**
Internet marketing publications
    segment targeting, **242**
investor relations KPIs, **30–31**
Iron Man Magazine, 97, *97*

J

job hunters segment targeting, **241**
job titles segment targeting
    accountants, **223–224**
    coaches/personal trainers, **222–223**
    logistics, **224**
    multilevel marketers, **223**
    operations managers, **224**
    professors, **224**
    real estate agents, **225**
    restaurant/bar/club/hotel managers,
      224
    sales reps, **224–225**
    teachers, **223**

K

Kaushik, Avinash, 190
kayaking segment, **231**
Kern, Frank, 143
Key Performance Indicators (KPIs), **19**
    branding, **22–23**, *23*
    community relations, **28–29**
    crisis management, **27–28**
    customer service, **26**
    defining, **21–22**, *22*
    direct response, **23–24**
    expectations, **20**
    friending, **25–26**
    internal relations, **29–30**
    investor relations, **30–31**
    media relations, **31–32**
    realistic, 17

research and message-testing,
    32–33
KillerFBAds.com site, 194

L

*Landing Page Optimization: The
    Definitive Guide to Testing and
    Tuning for Conversions* (Ash), 191
landing pages, 36, **163–167**, *165–167*
    designating, **70**
    dynamic, **167–169**, *168*
    external, **169–170**, **190–191**
    internal, **191–193**
    social, **170–172**
language
    in compound targeting, **123–126**,
      124–125
    in demographics, **59**
large enough sampling for
    optimization, **185–186**
Lateral Stemming Thesaurus tool, *56*
lawsuits, **13–14**
lead-generation services, 171
legal drugs, targeting, **85**
legal issues, **14–17**
    negative sentiment toward
      competitors, **82–83**
    rules of engagement, **14–17**
legal-novel consumers, **98–99**
leisure activities, targeting, **104–105**
length of body copy, **152–154**, *152–
    154*
libel, 14
licenses, 15, 146
lifetime budgets, **157**
lifetime spend caps, **158–159**, *158*
"Like" element, addition of, *5*
Likes & Interests Targeting setting, 8
LinkedIn, 87, 202, *203*

literal headlines, **131–133**, *133*
literal targeting, **78–79**
Litwinka, Lauren, 141
Location attributes, **44–45**
   City, **47**, *47–48*
   Country, **45–46**, *46*
   State and Province, **46–47**
   targeting, 39
logistics jobs, targeting, **224**
logos in brand clarity, 128–129
Lord of the Rings segment targeting,
   244

M

Mafia Wars, 101, *102*
magazines, targeting, **94–98**, *94–98*
manipulation in ads, **16–17**
Marin Software tool, 34
Max Bounty, Inc., 13
mechanical solidarity, 7
media influencers, targeting, **115–116**
media relations KPIs, **31–32**
media with cult followings segment
   targeting, **244–247**
medical conditions, targeting, 85
memorable phonetics, **138**
Meritech Capital Partners, 3
message-testing KPIs, **32–33**
micro military, **226**
microsite landing pages, 191
Microsoft partnership, 4
MMO segment targeting, **243**
money management gurus segment
   targeting, **242**
Moskovitz, Dustin, 3
motorcycles, 103
mountain bikers/cyclists segment
   targeting, **231–232**

multilevel marketers, **223**
multivariate message-testing, 32
music segment targeting, **241**
musicians, targeting, **96–97**
My Family/Wife/Husband segments
   targeting, **228**

N

naming conventions, **75–76**, *76*
Nancy Walther Graf v. Facebook, 14
negative consequences in headlines,
   137
negative publicity in crisis
   management, **27–28**
negative sentiment toward
   competitors, **80–83**, *80–82*
newspapers, 32
Nine Facebookers v. Facebook, 13
Nintendo segment targeting, **227**
non-calls to action in body copy, 149
notorious drug lords, **226**

O

Occam's Razor blog, 190
occupations and employment
   Interests Bucket, **87–89**, *88*
   job titles. *See* job titles segment
      targeting
   targeting, **86–90**, *88–89*, **116–118**,
      116–118
off-Facebook sites, targeting, **99–102**,
   101–102
offers in body copy, **150**
Omniture tool, 34
online university degree programs, 83,
   83
operations managers, **224**
optimization, **184–185**

ad fatigue, rotation, and variants, **193**
for conversion, **189–193**
for CPC, **188**
for CPM, **189**
for CTR, **185–187**, *185*
Optimizing for Connections, 184
or operator, **41–42**, 46
Orland, Marcia J., 13
outdoor activities segment targeting, **231**
    camping, **232–233**
    canoeing and kayaking, **231**
    fishing, **233–234**
    hunting, **234**
    mountain bikers/cyclists, **231–232**
outside pages, sending users to, 171

P

parameters
    targeting, 38, *38*
    URL, 168–169
Pattison, Pat, 138
pay per click (PPC), 79
payment options, **156**
Pearle Vision ad, 151–152, *152*
Per Day campaign budgets, 158–159
Performance screen, 181, *182*
periodicals, targeting, **94–98**, *94–98*
personal platforms, 87
personal trainers, targeting, **222–223**
Personality Traits: Their Classification and Measurement (Allport and Allport), 7, *7*
phonetics, memorable, **138**
pictures. *See* images
Places application, 5
planning, demographic research as, 69

political orientation, targeting, **105–106**
politicians, targeting, **115**, *115*
Pottery Barn, 79, *80*
Power Builder, 66
Power Editor, 36, **66–67**, *66–68*. *See also* production workflow for Facebook Ads
power tools, 103, *103*
PPC (pay per click), 79
Precise Interests bucket and attributes, 8–9, *9*
    in compound targeting, **115–118**, *115–118*
    Interests bucket. *See* Interests bucket
    targeting, 25
    typing patterns in, 43
predatory targeting, 83, 85
prelaunch checklists, **172**, **206–207**
presidential debates, 5
Price column in Campaign screen, 181
pricing, **64**, *64*
privacy and Facebook Ads, **10**
product categories, targeting, **102–104**, *102–103*
production workflow for Facebook Ads, **65**
    account structure, **66–68**, *67–68*
    ad creation, **69–72**, *70*
    alternate ad variations, **74–75**, *74*
    naming conventions, **75–76**, *76*
    Power Editor, **66–67**, *66–68*
    structural best practices, **72–74**
    wireframe demographic research, **69**
professors, targeting, **224**
promises in ads, 16
public domain images, 146, *146*

public relations KPIs, **28–29**
publications, **93–94**
   books, **98–99**
   magazines, **94–98**, *94–98*
pundits, targeting, **105–106**

Q

quality score (qscore), 160–161
questions, headlines with, **136**
Questions application, 5

R

reach, estimated, **38–42**, *38*
real estate agents, targeting, **225**
real-life groups, targeting, **90–93**,
   91–92
real value marketing in ads, 16
real-world publications, **93–94**
   books, **98–99**
   magazines, **94–98**, *94–98*
realistic KPIs, 17
recipe sites, **100**
recording engineers, targeting, **96–97**
related segments, typing patterns for,
   42–44, *43–44*
relationship status attributes
   in compound targeting, **121–123**
   sexual interest, **57–59**
religious groups, targeting, 93
Remaining column in All Campaigns
   screen, 177
remodel segment targeting, **239–240**
renaming ads, 75
renewable energies segment targeting,
   238–239
renovate segment targeting, **239–240**
reports, 179, **194**

Advertiser Performance, **194–199**,
   198
Conversions by Impression Time,
   201
Responder Demographics, **199–200**
Responder Profiles, **200–201**, *201*
Reports link, 195, *198*
Reports screen, 195, *198*
reputation risk in crisis management,
   27–28
Require Exact Age Match option,
   48–49
research KPIs, **32–33**
Responder Demographics reports,
   191, 193, **199–200**
Responder Profiles reports, 191, 193,
   200–201, *201*
Response graph, 178
restaurant managers, targeting, **224**
retired segment, **229**
return on ad spend (ROAS), 188
return on investment (ROI), 167
Review Ad button, 75
Richter, Steven, 13
ROAS (return on ad spend), 188
ROI (return on investment), 167
romance-novel readers, 99
rotation in optimizing, **193**
rules of engagement, **14–17**
Run my campaign continuously
   starting today option, 63, 158
runners segment, **230**

S

sales reps, targeting, **224–225**
sampling for optimization, 185–187
Saverin, Eduardo, 3
scams, 14

scheduling, **63–64**, *64*

search engine results page (SERP), 90, *91*

segments
    related, **42–44**, *43–44*
    targeting. *See* targeting

Select Existing Creative feature, 37

Select Rows To Edit option, 177, 182

self-improvement books, **99**

semantic stemming tools, **56**

SERP (search engine results page), 90, *91*

Set a Different Bid (Advanced Mode) option, 163

sexuality, **57–59**
    in compound targeting, **121–123**
    in demographics, 48

Share functionality, 3

sideways headlines, **133–135**, *134–135*

sideways thinking, 51

Simple bid settings, 64

SIMS segment, **227**

size of images, **142**

skiing segment targeting, **235**

Skype segment targeting, **226–227**

slander, 14

smartphones, 203

snowboarding segment targeting, **235–236**

snowmobiles segment targeting, **234–235**

Social Clicks metric, 199

Social CTR metric, 199

social graphs, **7–10**, *7–9*

Social Impressions metric, 199

social landing pages, **170–172**

Social % metric, 199

Social Reach
    in Campaign screen, 180
    in conversions, 193

Social Reach metric, **178–180**

social synonyms, **51–54**, *53, 55*

socializing external landing pages, **169–170**

sock puppet avatars, 15

software, targeting, **104**

spectators, sports, **105**

spend limits, **156–157**
    daily, **157**
    lifetime, **158–159**, *158*

Spent column in All Campaigns screen, 177

sponsored stories, 37, 70

sports, **104–105**

sports mom role, targeting, **229**

sports segment targeting, **236–238**

stacking attributes. *See* compound targeting

stakeholders in internal relations, **29–30**

Start Date column in All Campaigns screen, 176

State and Province attribute, **46–47**

Status column
    All Campaigns screen, 176
    Campaign screen, 179

stemming tools, **56**

stories, sponsored, 37, 70

straight people, targeting, **121–122**

structural best practices, **72–74**

subjects, targeting, **98–99**

Suggest An Ad button, 37

sustainable segment targeting, **238**

Swan, Jason, 13

synonyms, social, **51–54**, *53, 55*

T

tagging, **167–169**, *168*

Target People On Their Birthdays option, 57

targeting, 37, *38*
  alumni, **121**
  and operator, **40–42**
  applications users, **101–102**, *102*
  attributes, **39–40**
  books, **98–99**
  brainstorming, **100**
  checklist, **77–78**, *78*
  college students, **120–121**
  competitive, **79–80**, *80*
  compound. *See* compound targeting
  conflict and violence, **84–85**, *85*
  connections in, **61–62**
  Demographics attributes.
      See demographics and
      Demographics attributes
  Education & Work attributes,
      59–61, *60–61*
  Estimated Reach, **38–39**, *38*
  in Facebook Ad creation, **70**
  family roles, **106–108**, *107*
  figureheads, **106**
  Help Center, **62–63**, *63*
  high school students, **119–120**
  ideas, ideals, and beliefs, **108–109**
  incredible things users reveal in,
      85–86
  inferred, **83**
  legal considerations, **82–83**
  legal drugs and medical conditions,
      85
  leisure activities, **104–105**
  literal, **78–79**
  Location attributes, **44–47**, *46–48*
  media influencers, **115–116**
  negative sentiment toward
      competitors, **80–83**, *80–82*
  occupations and employment, **86–90**,
      88–89, **116–118**, *116–118*

  off-Facebook sites, **99–102**,
      101–102
  or operator, **41–42**
  political orientation and pundits,
      105–106
  politicians, **115**, *115*
  product categories, **102–104**,
      102–103
  real-life groups and affiliations,
      90–93, *91–92*
  real-world publications, **93–99**,
      94–98
  segments, **219–220**
    business, **242**
    chatting/RPG, **243–244**
    discount, **240**
    Fortune 500 companies,
        220–222
    green living, **238–239**
    health, **229–230**
    hobbies, **242**
    home/garden, **239–240**
    Interests Bucket family roles,
        228–229
    job titles, **222–225**
    media with cult followings,
        244–247
    music, **241**
    outdoor activities, **231–234**
    sports, **236–238**
    tech and gaming, **226–227**
    tough times, **240–241**
    weapons, **225–226**
    wine, **239**
    winter sports and activities,
        234–236
  software, **104**
  things people dislike in, **83–84**, *83*
  typing patterns, **42–44**, *43–44*

Targeting screen, 181, *182*
teachers, targeting, **223**
tech and gaming targeting, **226–227**
terms of services (TOS)
    Facebook Ads, **10–13**
    rules of engagement, **15–16**
testing, A/B, 132
thesaurus, 51, 56
things people dislike in targeting,
    83–84, *83*
Torrent segment targeting, **226**
TOS (terms of services)
    Facebook Ads, **10–13**
    rules of engagement, **15–16**
tough times segment targeting,
    240–241
tracking conversions, **167–169**, *168*
trade groups, targeting, 92, *92*
traffic bleed, 191
travel books, **98**
travel sites, **100**
Trellian Keywood Discovery stemming
    tool, 56
trigger pages, conversion technology
    on, 190
True Blood segment targeting,
    244–245
truthfulness of ads, 14
Twilight segment targeting, **245–246**
typing patterns for related segments,
    42–44, *43–44*

U

unconnected users, targeting, **62**
unions, targeting, 92
Unique Clicks metric, 199
Unique CTR metric, 199
University of Phoenix, 83, *83*
UrbanDictionary.com, 51

URLs
    external, 36–37
    parameters, 168–169
    vanity, 5
Use Suggested Bid option, 64, 163
user benefits in body copy, **147–148**
user interface, creation, **35**
    ad design, **36–37**, *36*
    campaigns, pricing, and scheduling,
        63–64, *64*
    Power Editor, **36**
    targeting. *See* targeting
Usernames application, 5

V

vanity URLs, 5
variants in optimizing, **193**
vendors in internal relations, **29–30**
video chat segment targeting,
    226–227
video editing interests, **227**
video-game social segment, 84
View Advertising Report page, 179
violence, targeting, **84–85**, *85*
viral media, 9
voice-recognition software, 104

W

Wall, 3
Wallace, Sanford, 13
Walther Graf, Nancy, 14
weapons
    call-of-duty guns, **225**
    infantry, **226**
    notorious drug lords, **226**
Web Analytics 2.0 (Kaushik), 190
web UI. *See* creation user interfaces
wife segments targeting, **228**

Wikipedia
  for images, 146
  as stemming tool, 56
wine and wine tasting, **102**, *102*
wine segment, **239**
wine cellar/clubs segment, **239**
winter sports and activities segment,
  234–236
wireframe demographic research, **69**
Wooopra product, 190
Word
  clip art, 147, *147*
  thesaurus, 51
WordTracker stemming tools, 56
working out segment targeting, **230**

workplaces
  in compound targeting, **115–118,**
    115–118
  in Education & Work settings, 61
Writing Better Lyrics (Pattison), 138

Y

yoga segment targeting, **230**
youth coaches segment targeting, **230**
YouTube, 56, 202

Z

Zombies segment targeting, **246–267**
zooming images, **144–145,** *144–145*
Zuckerberg, Mark, 3, 6–7
Zynga, 14